J. Moray Brown

Shikar Sketches

With Notes on Indian Field-Sports

J. Moray Brown

Shikar Sketches
With Notes on Indian Field-Sports

ISBN/EAN: 9783337061104

Printed in Europe, USA, Canada, Australia, Japan

Cover: Foto ©ninafisch / pixelio.de

More available books at **www.hansebooks.com**

SHIKAR SKETCHES

WITH

NOTES ON INDIAN FIELD-SPORTS

BY

J. MORAY BROWN
LATE 79TH CAMERON HIGHLANDERS.

ILLUSTRATED.

LONDON:
HURST AND **BLACKETT, PUBLISHERS,**
13, GREAT MARLBOROUGH STREET.
1887.
All rights reserved.

TO

COLONEL HEBBERT, R.H.A.

TO WHOM I AM INDEBTED FOR MY INITIATION

IN THE NOBLE SPORT OF HOG-HUNTING,

AND

IN WHOSE COMPANY MANY OF THE INCIDENTS DESCRIBED

IN THESE PAGES OCCURRED,

THIS **VOLUME IS DEDICATED**

BY

HIS AFFECTIONATE FRIEND,

THE AUTHOR.

INTRODUCTION.

This work was originally begun in the form of articles for a sporting magazine. I was, however, through the persuasion of friends, induced to add to and enlarge them, and so present them to the public in the form of a volume. I have given merely plain records of some incidents of Indian sport that came under my own observation and within that of my friends. Where I have been in doubt on points connected with Natural History, I have not hesitated to consult and quote from authorities who can be relied on, viz., such writers as Forsyth, Kinloch, McMaster, etc. On the latter's writings, as a dear and valued friend, I have ventured to draw largely, knowing that at his hands, if haply he were alive, I should have had every encouragement in undertaking my present task.

I must disclaim any intention of writing for the veteran sportsman, though I daresay several occurrences may be found detailed in these pages that may interest and amuse him, and also corroborate his own experiences.

Most of the sporting incidents have been compiled from my own journal and rough notes taken at the time; for the rest, I am indebted to the experience of others. It has been my endeavour to describe the events naturally, and devoid of any artificial or dramatic element. The few observations connected with Natural History, it will at once be perceived, are those of a sportsman more than of a naturalist, to which latter title I can lay no claim.

To those whose names I have mentioned, and from whose writings I have quoted, I must tender my most humble apologies for the liberty I have taken in doing so, but I trust that the desire to foster in the rising generation a love of sport, and Indian sport in particular, will be accepted as my excuse.

I have confined myself strictly to the description of such animals and their pursuits as I was myself familiar with, and outside these bounds I have not ventured to travel. To Lieutenant-Colonel W. Brough (R.H.A., retired) and J. C. Dollman, Esq., R.I., as the artists of the illustrations, I must tender my warmest and most grateful thanks for the happy manner in which they have caught the spirit of the sport, and the faithful way in which the incidents described have been delineated; and in this opinion I think most Indian sportsmen who have participated in like scenes will agree.

Lieutenant-Colonel Brough's sketch illustrates a scene described in these pages in which he himself actually took part, and is true to the life; whilst Mr. Dollman's have been elaborated from my own rough sketches (done whilst the incidents were fresh in my memory), aided by my own personal explanations of technical details, position, scenery, etc., and so I can vouch for their accuracy.

Should, therefore, this volume meet with any slight approval from sportsmen, it will, I believe, be more due to the clever pencils of the artists than to the unskilled pen of the author, who is but a novice in the fields of literature, and whose hand has been more accustomed to the use of rifle, spear, and gun than of the pen.

If the perusal of these pages should prove the means of wiling away an idle hour, one of the writer's objects will have been attained; and if further it should induce younger men to devote their superfluous energies to excelling in the sports of the field, and acquiring some knowledge of Natural History, instead of wasting time, money, and health in vice and frivolity, these pages, if they do no other good, will not have been written quite in vain.

THE AUTHOR.

Greenham House,
  Beaminster.

CONTENTS.

CHAPTER I.

A MOONLIGHT SHOT 1

Night in the Jungle—Preparations—Bansolee—Animal and Bird Life—A Bear—Successful Shot—More Bears—Effects of a Shell—Bad Luck—Tracking—The Trail Lost—Return to Camp.

CHAPTER II.

A TOUGH CUSTOMER 14

An old Journal—Pig-sticking—The Sports of the East—Contrast between British and Indian Sports—Kamptee and the Nagpore Hunt—Hunting Arrangements—Karlee—'Warree'—Manajee, the Hunt shikari—The Beat—Gone Away!—A Plucky Boar—The Fight—Broken Spears—Horse Ripped—The Fight Resumed on Foot—Death of the Boar—Narrow Escape.

CHAPTER III.

A BONNIE BAG 31

Start for the Jungles—Disappointment—Bustard—Stalk and Bag Him—Move Camp—Cheetal—A Lucky Shot—A Forest Glade—Bison—Is it a Miss?—Follow Him Up—Hurrah! Muntjack and Peafowl—A Curious Right and Left—My Friend's Bag—Excitement in Camp—A Kill by a Tiger—Sit up for Him—Peter's Mistake—Indecision—Failure.

CHAPTER IV.

TACKLING A TUSKER 46

Roorkee—Ten Days' Leave—Hurdwar—Game of the Doon Valley—Ramiah—The Rogue Elephant—See Tigers—News of the Tusker—Dawn in the Doon—The Sewalik Hills—Find the Tusker's Tracks—His Depredations—A Weary Tramp—Ramiah Wants to Give Up—Perseverance Rewarded—A Long Crawl—He Winds Us—The Shot—Misery—We Find Blood—Hopes Revived—Pursuit—Is it Him?—Disappointment—Elephant Pits—The Fate of the Rogue.

CHAPTER V.

HOG-HUNTING 64

Antiquity of Hog-hunting—Celebrated Hog-hunters—The Charms of the Sport—Comparison of Hog-hunting with Fox-hunting—Qualifications to ensure Success—Some Rules and Axioms—Description of Ground—Spears—Modes of Using—Measurements of Hog—A Savage Boar—Camel Ripped—A Queer Mount—On the Pig's Back—Determined Courage of a Boar—Biting Sows—Boar's Lips Pinned by Spear—'Parachute'—Solitary Chase—A Kill on Foot—Horses used in Hog-hunting—'Parachute's' Love of the Sport—Concluding Remarks.

CHAPTER VI.

FAREWELL TO THE SPEAR 93

A Last Day—The Meet—Offer of a Mount—The 'Caster'—Not so Black as he's Painted—Exciting Bit of News—Efforts to Dislodge the Game—'Muzzle'—Change our Tactics—The Panther Breaks—Race for the Spear—'There's Many a Slip'—My Turn—Failure—Success—Danger of Beaters—The 'Caster' Declines—A Beater Mauled—On Foot in the Bajree—'Muzzle' Comes to the Rescue—Death of the Panther—A Plucky Youngster—The Colonel and the Cubs—Quotations from Major Shakespear—Advice.

CHAPTER VII.

BLACK-BUCK SHOOTING 106

Black-Buck Shooting—Spearing Wounded Antelopes—An Unsuccessful Gallop—A Plucky Buck—Stalking, and Other Methods of Pursuit—Ground Antelope are Found on—Snaring—My First Black Buck—Empty Pockets—A Novel *Coup-de-Grâce*—Circumventing a Wary Herd—Strategy—A Long Shot at Dusk—Curious Effect of a Bullet—Chikara, or Ravine-Deer—Their Habitat and Horns—Concluding Remarks.

CHAPTER VIII.

SMALL GAME SHOOTING 124

Small Game Shooting—Pea-fowl—A Creep through the Jungle—Probable Disappointment—Pea-fowl Sacred to Hindoos—A Shot at Night—Spearing a Peacock—Ability of Concealment—An Upset—Best Shot to Use—Jungle-fowl—Different Species—Their Pursuit—Large Bags never Made—A Beat—The Result—Amateur Doctoring—Spur-fowl—Their Habitat—A Clever Greyhound—Spur-fowl Shooting amongst the Coffee in Ceylon.

CHAPTER IX.

WILD FOWL, SNIPE, ETC. 139

Varieties of Wild-fowl—Hindoo Legends—Native Mode of Capturing Wild-fowl—Munchur Jheel—Solitary Snipe—Pintailed, Painted, and Jack Snipe—Black, Painted, and Grey Partridge—Quail—A 'Family' Shot—Mixed Bag—Variety of Game at Delhi.

CHAPTER X.

TIGER-SHOOTING 153

Tiger-shooting—Expenses of Camp Equipage—Preliminary Arrangements—'Hailas'—Ringing the Tiger—The Beat—Following up wounded Tigers—Precautions to be Taken—My first Tiger—

Death of a Villager—Successful Right and Left—Bag the Cubs—Tigers' Whiskers—Curious Anatomical Structure—An Impudent Kite—The Khandla Tiger—The Artful Dodger—Cannibalism of Tigers—Frogs as a Diet—Tigers' fondness of Bathing—Attacked by Red Ants—A Shot in the Water—Tigris Redivivus!

CHAPTER XI.

TIGER-SHOOTING (CONTINUED) 172

First Encounter on Foot with a Tiger—Apparent Failure of Beat—Sudden Appearance of the Tigress—Too Close to be Pleasant—What shall I do?—Close Quarters—In quest of Bears—A Blank—Unexpected Meeting with a Tigress—Wound Her—Follow Up—She charges—Her Death—Extraordinary vitality—Tiger's powers of Concealment—The Tandla Tiger—An awkward Predicament—He is very Sick—Precautions to be taken in Approaching dead Tigers—The Daba Tiger—'Independent Firing'—The Death-spring—Impotent rage of a wounded Tiger.

CHAPTER XII.

TIGER-SHOOTING (CONTINUED) 189

Noiseless Motion of Tigers—Death of a Man-eater—Scene on the Neilgherry Hills—The Stalker Stalked—The Pipulkulti Tigress—A Good View of her Stalk—Apparent momentary Fascination of Cow—The Charge—Unconcern of Remainder of the Herd—The Cow Avenged—Tigers' Mode of Killing their Prey—Curious Incident with Black Buck—An Invulnerable Jackal—Assam Man-eater—Sitting Up as a 'Bait'—The Plan Succeeds, though not quite in the Manner Intended—Wonderful Presence of Mind—A Narrow Shave.

CHAPTER XIII.

TIGER-SHOOTING (CONCLUDED) 211

Unlucky Days—Ningnur—I nearly make a Fatal Mistake—Folly of Changing One's Mind—Useless Pursuit—Blank Day—'If——'—Another Try for Bears—Gallop after a Boar—Lose Him—Sold by a Panther—Tigers' and Panthers' Mode of Devouring their Prey—Start for the other Kill—Mistakes—The Tiger Roused—My Folly—Bad Luck with a Boar—A Chapter of Accidents.

CHAPTER XIV.

ABOUT SOME DEER 225

The Poetry of Sport—Long Shots to be Avoided—Varieties of Deer—Sambur—Beating—Stalking—Amongst the Sewalik Hills—The Twelve-tined Deer—Spotted Deer—Their Habits—An Imaginary Stalk—A Wounded Stag shows Fight—Good Bag out of a Herd—Riding down Spotted Deer—Para, or Hog-deer—Shoot One in a Snipe Jheel—The Muntjak—Description—Their curious Bark—'Paloo'—A Shot in the Hills—Jungle Fare—The Four-horned Antelope—Description.

CHAPTER XV.

WILD DOGS AND HYÆNAS 259

Wild Dogs—Description—A Jungle Course—Native Belief in Wild Dogs killing Tigers—Their supposed Method of Doing so—Deserted Temples—Wild Dogs attacking Tiger—Curious Scene on the Neilgherries—The Madras Hounds run with a Panther—The Kill—Names of Hounds—'Evangeline'—'Hawk-eye's' Description of Sambur Hunted by Wild Dogs—The Striped Hyæna—Spearing Hyænas—A Startling Adventure—Relief!—Cowardice of Hyænas—A Hyæna 'Leaps before he Looks'—A Mixed Bag.

CHAPTER XVI.

ON RIFLES, GROUND AND OUTFIT . . . 277

India as a Field for Sport—Comparison with other Countries—Indian v. African Sport—Where to Go—Cost of a Shikar Trip—Rifles and Guns best Adapted for Indian Sport—Outfit—Arrangements for Supplies—Beaters to be Paid Personally—Conclusion.

INDIAN SPORTING SONGS 295

ILLUSTRATIONS.

"The pluckiest charge on record,"(p. 203)..............*Frontispiece*
    (By Lieut.-Colonel Brough.)

"I aim between her shoulders and pull,"...............*To face p.* 9

"Fell dead with a grunt of defiance,"..................... ,,   28

"I took the best aim my excited feelings would allow," ,,   57

"Scrambling up the boulder-strewn side of the hill," ,,   77

"She turned and seized the shaft between her teeth," ,,   103

"She was slouching sulkily along,"...................... ,,   163

"Came straight at us, the incarnation of fiendish rage," ,,   180

"The next moment the tiger was on the elephant's head," ,,   184

SHIKAR SKETCHES:

WITH

NOTES ON INDIAN FIELD SPORTS.

CHAPTER I.

A MOONLIGHT SHOT.

Night in the Jungle—Preparations—Bansolee—Animal and Bird Life—A Bear—Successful Shot—More Bears—Effects of a Shell—Bad Luck—Tracking—The Trail Lost—Return to Camp.

THERE are many men, very many, who have made bigger bags and seen more of shikar than your humble servant, kind reader. You are doubtless acquainted with General Mulligatawny, who has shot his three hundred tigers, and Sir John Spearshaft, late of the Bombay Civil Service, who can count his first spears by the hundred. Have we not all read Mr. Sanderson's delightful book, entitled, 'Thirteen Years amongst the Wild

B

Beasts of India'? and, if you are fond of Indian sports, your library will, I am sure, contain such volumes as, 'Hog-hunting in the East,' 'Wild Men and Wild Beasts,' 'Camp Life in the Satpura Hills,' etc., etc. In all these you will find accounts of many a wild and thrilling adventure—far more exciting than any I can offer for your amusement and delectation. Still I hope that, if you deign to peruse these pages—that, if you too, like me, have ever enjoyed a night in the glorious jungles of the Far East, they may bring to your mind happy halcyon days, and carry you back to the time when as yet your brow was unfurrowed by care, and your hair untinged with grey.

There are dozens of men, good and true sportsmen, who have slain numerous tigers and bears, etc., in fair and open fight—aided, at least, by a small army of beaters and elephants—who have gone through all the glorious excitement of standing a 'charge;' others who have, on lonely hillside and in dense virgin forest, stalked and shot the lordly elephant, the bison, and sambur; but probably, if you asked any of them if they had ever sat up at night by a lonely pool of water in some dense jungle, your interrogation would be received with scorn. You would be told it was a 'nasty, native-poaching dodge,' unworthy of an English sportsman; that 'le jeu ne vallait pas la chandelle;' that you would be forced to sit for hours in an awkward and cramped position, half numbed with cold and damp; that you would be eaten up by mosquitoes, sand-flies, etc., and so on, *ad infinitum*. Personally, however, I must confess that this mode of shooting the wild denizens of the jungle always had for me a certain charm and attraction, in spite of numerous disappointments. During the witching hours of night—that is, if you be a lover of nature, and take an interest in natural history—you will have opportunities afforded you of seeing and observing, unseen yourself, the habits of many animals and birds that are invisible during the hotter hours of day, when they retire to cool dark spots in the jungle, where they are protected from the fierce rays of the mid-day sun, and are unlikely to be intruded upon by man; whilst your excitement will be kept up by the chance of at any moment seeing the monarch of the jungles, the royal tiger himself, stalk forth to quench his thirst.

In sitting up for game at night, there are two methods employed, either of which may recommend itself to the choice of the sportsman; but, of course, he must to a certain extent be guided in his choice—first, by the species of game he expects to shoot, and secondly, by the nature and configuration of the ground. The first plan is to have a méchan, or platform of branches, made in a tree overlooking the water. This platform is then covered with armfuls of *green* grass, *not dry*, on which you can place a rug or blanket, and surrounded by a screen of branches, with their leaves on. It is generally made large enough to accommodate yourself and an attendant, and long enough to permit you to lie down and enjoy a nap, should the tedium of watching prove too much, and the drowsy god assert his sway. The second method is to have a pit dug about four feet deep and as many wide within easy shot of the water. The earth removed from the pit should not be thrown up *à la* 'shelter trench' outside its mouth, but should be carried off and deposited some distance in the jungle. A few low branches may be stuck round the mouth of the pit to resemble bushes and form a screen. In the pit the sportsman and his attendant crouch, and, being level with the ground, are less likely to attract the attention of any animal. One trial, however, of this latter plan was enough for me, for, in addition to the exceedingly cramped position it entailed for several hours, and the attacks of mosquitoes, which are generally more numerous the nearer you are to the level of the ground, the pungent, and anything but aromatic, odour of 'bouquet de nègre' exhaled from my native attendant's greasy body made the vigil anything but a pleasant one.

Good reader, if you are of the type of the gallant general or worthy civilian I have alluded to, this chapter, I honestly tell you, will interest you but little; so, if you read thus far, skip the rest, and save me the scornful remarks you would be sure to make anent it, for there is no thrilling element of excitement to be found in these pages, and they might only weary you. On the other hand, if you are one of those who can have the patience to read the description of a night's sport told as a 'plain unvarnished tale' by one who has had but scant experience in the fields of literature, and whose hand is more accustomed to the rifle and spear than the pen, fill another pipe, and as you read let your mind accompany me whilst I detail for your edification my first experience of a moonlight shot.

Imagine me therefore one night, towards the middle of March, after a good dinner, making my final arrangements before leaving camp, which was pitched at a place called Bansolee in the Berar jungles. My shikari, yclept Lutchman, had informed me, during the morning, of the existence of a pool of water in the dry bed of a river only some three-quarters of a mile from my camp which, by the numerous footprints of wild animals all round it, was well used, and he had urged the advisability of my going and sitting up over it during the night on the chance of getting a shot. Bears' footprints, he said, were particularly numerous, and he almost guaranteed my seeing and getting a shot at 'Ursus labiatus.' This was an extra inducement to me, and he, during the day, having made all arrangements, we started about nine p.m., and ere long reached the dry bed of the river; following this a short distance we soon reached the scene of action. The pool of water was a comparatively small one, and lay at the foot of a bank of reddish clay some ten feet high. On the top of this bank, and overlooking the pool, Lutchman had constructed a circular screen of branches (what would now be called a 'zareeba'), and had cut and laid a quantity of green grass on which a couple of 'cumblies,' or native blankets, being laid, we soon were comfortably ensconced and ready for any animal that might visit the water.

Soon the moon rose slowly over the dense, dark shadows of the primæval forest, and poured down a flood of chastened silver radiance on the scene around, lighting up the arches formed by the graceful, feathery bamboos,* illuminating the bed of the river, and making the minute, quartz-like

* Bambusa Arundinacea.

grains of sand, of which it was mainly composed, sparkle and shimmer like crystals. In the background the depths of the jungle lay in dense, dark shade, whilst the trunks and foliage of the trees on the opposite bank were mirrored life-like in the pool at our feet.

A hushed silence prevailed, only broken now and then by the loud bell of a sambur, the curious cry of the cheetal, or spotted deer, the fierce, short bark of the muntjâk, or barking deer (and what a terrifying sound it is to be produced from so small an animal), the loud 'Mi-a-u, mi-a-u, pā-oo, pā-oo,' of a peacock, or the irritating cry of 'Did-he-do-it, did-did-did-he-do-it,' of the Indian plover; the melancholy note of the wood-owl floated on the still, night air, as he flitted backwards and forwards, ghost-like, in the moonlight; occasionally, too, might be heard the loud 'whoop-whoop' of the 'lungoor' or 'Entellus monkey,' the crash in a distant tree-top denoting the spot where, doubtless, some monkey midnight revels were being carried on; whilst once our nerves were quickened and our pulses beat higher by hearing the distant 'Aa-ooungh' of a prowling tiger, a sound seldom heard, though once heard never to be forgotten. *He*, however, was a long way off, and, to our disappointment, did not favour us with a visit. These noises would at times be varied by a night-jar rising from the ground, and, as he floated by in his peculiar moth-like flight, giving vent to his curious, monotonous cry of ' Chukoo-chukoo,' repeated and answered by his fellows over and over again.

Some half-hour had passed, and, though the numerous sounds gave evidence of the presence of plenty of animal life in the jungle, as yet we had seen nothing. Presently there is a rustle among the dead leaves close by, and, looking over the screen, I see a porcupine scramble down the bank near me, trot up to the water, look suspiciously around, and then, giving his 'quills' a shake, drink, and slowly retire up the sandy river-bed. He is shortly followed by a mungoose, or ichneumon, and a hare; then we see a dainty, airy little form emerge from the jungle on the opposite bank, and, after standing for a moment, step lightly out in the bright light of the moon, which reveals the delicate form and limbs of the little four-horned antelope (A. quadricornis) more commonly known among Indian sportsmen as the 'jungle sheep'—though why he should have had this peculiar form of nomenclature devoted to him, goodness only knows. He is suspicious, however, and thinks it better to go and slake his thirst elsewhere. Shortly after his appearance a small herd of cheetal, or spotted deer, saunter slowly round a

"I AIM BETWEEN HER SHOULDERS AND PULL."

bend of the river; the oldest stag bringing up the rear, and occasionally butting a younger one, or bringing to order some recalcitrant member of his harem who seemed inclined to stray. On they come, and, keeping quite motionless and peering through the interstices of my screen, I see them all drink and then depart, ignorant that within a few feet of them lay their enemy, man, armed with the death-dealing tube they had such cause to dread.

Then came a long pause, and, being weary of watching, I had dozed off when I was awoke by Lutchman pressing my arm, and pointing down in the direction of the water. Silently cocking my rifle, I look and see, to my intense delight, a dark, shadowy form scrambling down the opposite bank, sending down in its passage quite a little avalanche of earth and pebbles. Is it? Yes, by Jove! it is a bear, coming straight on to me too. What luck! The breeze, such as there is, is *from* her, and so there is no chance of my being winded. On she comes, slowly, till at last she reaches the brink of the pool, and, looking up and down for a moment, begins to drink. Now is my time. Slowly rising, I aim between her shoulders and pull. As the smoke clears away, and the echoes of the report cease from reverberating through the jungle, I see her lying stone dead—dropped actually in her tracks—a little crimson stain trickling down the sand and dyeing the water of the pool. I want to go down and examine my prize at once, for it is my *first* bear, but Lutchman puts his veto on this proceeding, saying other bears will probably come ere long, so I acquiesce, and, again seating myself, am prepared to watch. How long I did so I know not, but it seemed an age, and I had again dropped off to sleep, only shortly to be awoke by Lutchman in the same silent fashion.

On looking out I saw two well-grown bear-cubs coming across to the water. Suddenly they pulled up and began to sniff about and look in my direction. Whether they had scented me or the dead bear, I know not (the wind had changed slightly), but anyhow they seemed to think there was something uncanny about the spot, and made up their minds to decamp. I had one of them covered with my rifle as they stood some forty yards off. The piece of white cotton wool I had pasted on my foresight stood out clear against the black shaggy hide, and as they turned to go I fired. Almost simultaneously with the flash of my rifle, I saw, as it were, a circle of fire on the cub's shoulder (I was using a percussion-shell, which I conclude burst on his shoulder-blade and ignited the long hair of his coat), something like a miniature 'Catherine wheel;' then he turned round savagely and began pitching into his brother. I fired my left barrel at the black, tumbling, squabbling mass, and then the most awful din arose,

> 'As if fiends fought in upper air,
> And *beasts* on earth below.'

The two cubs tumbled off into the jungle, howling, snarling, and fighting, and finally disappeared into the dark depths of the jungle; sambur bellowed and peafowl screamed, whilst every jackal, as it seemed, for a radius of miles gave vent to his unearthly wail of 'I smell a dead Hind-o-o-o, where? where? where? he-eah, heah, heah,' and every feathered as well as four-footed denizen of the forest seemed to consider themselves bound in honour to join in the infernal chorus. I do not think I ever heard such a discordant row in my life except in the parrot-house at the Zoo. Then like magic the noise ceased, and all again became still. The sweet charm of the moonlight could be felt as well as seen, and, as the breeze of approaching dawn gently stirred the tree-tops clothed in their chastened brilliance, I felt that, even if I had no more sport that night, my vigil would not be unrewarded.

As there was no chance of getting another shot,

I ventured to light the soothing pipe, and, whilst discussing it, Lutchman asked me why I had fired at the cubs instead of the big bear that was close to me? I said I did not understand him.

'I only saw two cubs.'

'Sahib,' he said, 'they were not what I saw; when I awoke you, there was another very big bear not fifteen yards from you on *this* side of the river.'

What infernal bad luck, I thought; for, in watching the cubs, I had not seen the other bear, and the cubs *had*, and were afraid to come on whilst *he* was present. However, it could not be helped; so, making the best of matters, we both composed ourselves for a snooze, and, as soon as day broke, a fact we soon were made aware of by the shrill crowing of numerous jungle-cocks, we got up and went down to inspect our prize, which proved to be a large female black bear with a fine shaggy hide. Covering up the carcase with branches to keep off the vultures, and tying my handkerchief to a stick to warn off any prowling jackal, we next inspected the spot where I had fired at the cubs. The sand was all kicked up by their scuffle, and there were a few drops of blood, by now dry. We followed the tracks for a short distance into the jungle, when the blood ceased, and then, getting upon stony ground, all traces vanished, and we had to give up, and make the best of our way home to camp, where a tub and breakfast were by no means unwelcome, and I must say I did not regret the hours spent in the solitude of the jungle waiting for a 'moonlight shot.'

CHAPTER II.

A TOUGH CUSTOMER.

An old Journal—Pig-sticking—The Sports of the East—Contrast between British and Indian Sports—Kamptee and the Nagpore Hunt—Hunting Arrangements—Karlee—' Warree '—Manjee, the Hunt shikari—The Beat—Gone Away!—A Plucky Boar—The Fight—Broken Spears—Horse Ripped—The Fight Resumed on Foot—Death of the Boar—Narrow Escape.

'Hæc olim meminisse juvabit!' Such is the legend inscribed on the cover of an old leather-backed 'company order-book' in my possession, in which are written records of many pleasant days' sport both at home and abroad, with rifle and spear, with rod and gun. And truly it *does* 'rejoice one' to read over these old notes roughly jotted down at the time, and they carry one back to many a tiger-haunted jungle, many a vast expanse of plain over which waves the yellow rumnah grass; to swirling, rock-bestrewn stream, to stretches of purple heather, to snipe and duck-frequented marsh, and to green fields of turnips and mangold, and brings back vividly to memory days when 'all the world was young,' and life had but few cares.

Ah, me! what would not one give to live some of those years over again, and participate once more in the darling sports of one's youth? Once more feel the quick bounding stride of the game Arab, and poise the glittering spear! Once more watch, with finger on the trigger of our trusty rifle, for the king of the jungle approaching with noiseless and stealthy footfall! Once more face the charge of a gallant old bull bison, or again wander through the trackless depths of the virgin forest in quest of the lordly sambur and elegant cheetal!

It is somewhat difficult to contrast British and Indian field sports further than by attempting to point out the extent to which they differ—to my mind in no slight degree. *British* field sports have the charm, and that no slight one, of being pursued with greater ease and less personal discomfort to their votary, whilst the Indian sportsman must prepare himself for both exposure to sun and storm, to discomforts of all kinds, to constant failures and disappointments, to trials of temper and health, and to wear and tear of constitution. But, on the other hand, his rewards are great, and his exertions are certain to win for him sooner or later some glorious trophies, and introduce him to scenes of jungle life the recollection of which will never be erased from his memory, and which, even when his eyes begin to grow dim, and time to silver his once dark locks, when he gets on a strange horse with less confidence than in former days—in short, to use the words of that grand old Indian hunting-song—'The Mighty Boar'—

> 'When age hath weakened manhood's powers
> And every nerve unbraced,'

the remembrance of such scenes *must* make the pulse beat faster, restore for the moment the worn-out nerve, brighten the eye, re-kindle the fire of youth, and prove, whilst memory lasts, a source of honest pride to him who has had the good fortune to witness and participate in them. But a truce to moralizing, for I now propose to relate a good 'scuffle' (as a dear old friend of mine used to term it) I once had with the 'grim grey boar,' in the hope that it may bring back memories of pleasant pig-sticking days to those who have participated in this, to my mind, *most* enjoyable of sports, and fire generous youth, who has not yet had the opportunity, to go and do likewise when it *does* occur.

It was my good fortune some years ago (a good many, alas!) to be quartered at Kamptee, in the

Central Provinces of India, where there was a very good hog-hunting club called the Nagpore Hunt. It was composed mostly of 'gunners' (three batteries of artillery being quartered at the station), and a rare lot of good sporting fellows they were, one or two of the brigade staff, a few of the native cavalry, and some three of my own regiment, Her Majesty's 79th Highlanders. The hunting season began about August, and lasted till March. We had a meet lasting from two to three days generally once a week, with a ten days' meet at Christmas, which was a sort of big picnic that some of the ladies of the station generally graced with their presence, and another ten days' meet in March to wind up the season. Each member on joining the Hunt paid an entrance fee of ten rupees, and a small monthly subscription besides. Out of these funds the Hunt provided tents, shikaris, beaters, crockery, butler, cook, and blacksmith; and a fixed daily charge was made for messing, which included breakfast, tiffin, and dinner. Each member took his own servants, liquor, and camp furniture. During the hunting season a book used to be sent round every Saturday giving the proposed meet for the following week. If three members put down their names as intending to hunt at that particular meet, the Hunt camp, kit, etc., was sent on, and all necessary arrangements made. If there were less than three names down, there was no meet.

A dear old friend, now, alas! gone to the 'happy hunting grounds,' had, in recognition of the hospitality shown him at the 'gunners'' mess, presented them with a very handsome cup, on the condition that at the end of each season the name of the member of the Hunt getting the most 'first spears' should be inscribed on it, and this gave rise to much emulation and generous rivalry, not to say hard riding among us, and some of the races for the coveted honour of 'first spear' were often worth going a long way to see.

The incident which I now propose relating occurred one 12th of August, a day when brother sportsmen were busy with the grouse on many a wide expanse of moorland and purple heather. The previous day the Hunt had met at a place called Karlee, only four of us being present. We had beaten a big hill all day in pouring rain (*such* rain, too, as one only sees during the monsoon in India's sunny clime) unsuccessfully, as the pig would *not* break, do what we would; so about four o'clock we gave it up as a bad job, and returned to camp to change our soaking garments, and while away the time till dinner. Two of our party had to return to cantonments that evening, being 'on duty' the next day, but the third of the party (Captain Thompson, Royal Horse Artillery) and myself determined to remain, and have another beat, and try to atone for our hitherto worse than bad luck.

The morning of the 12th broke fine, and promised well for sport. Every blade of grass and bush sparkled with raindrops that flashed and glittered in the sunlight, and there was that pleasant smell of damp earth so grateful to those who have frizzled and sweltered through a 'hot weather.' After breakfast we sallied out to beat a large conical hill called 'Warree,' that stood isolated in the midst of a wide 'maidan,' or plain. The hill itself was composed principally of boulders of rocks, interspersed amongst a mass of loose, rolling stones, and was clothed from base to summit with dense brushwood, some three to four feet high. The top was a table-land covered with coarse rumnah grass about a foot high, now waving green after the refreshing rains of the monsoon. To the south, east, and west the plain extended as far as the eye could reach in one level streak of black cotton soil, only broken here and there by some small rocky hillock with an occasional ravine or 'nullah,' whilst to the north and some two miles distant lay a long ridge of low hills covered with thick scrub jungle, and separated from the 'Warree' hill by a wide and boggy 'nullah.'

Thompson had two horses out, one a bay Waler mare, very fast, but as yet untried after pig, the second a grey Arab who was a clever and seasoned hog-hunter. I had only one, an iron-grey Persian gelding, seven years old, which I had lately purchased at one of the artillery 'carter' sales for the magnificent sum of sixty-five rupees, or some six pounds ten shillings. Though perfectly sound, he had been 'cast' for *vice*. He was a sour-looking, three-cornered sort of devil, rather slack in his loins, but with a good shoulder, fairish hocks and quarters, though somewhat goose-rumped, and with legs like iron; he pulled like a fiend, would strike, kick, and bite at anyone or anything on the very slightest provocation, but could gallop and stay, and jumped like a deer, and so was eminently suited to be the mount of an impecunious ensign, who in those days thought little of risking his precious neck on any sort of animal that could aspire to the dignity of being called a horse. I had never yet ridden him after pig, and felt rather doubtful as to how he would acquit himself in the hunting-field. However, I thought his infernal temper would make him face any pig, and so did not feel uneasy on that score. Fast enough I knew him to be, and if I could only hold him, and get him to turn when the pig 'jinked' or turned, I thought I should not have got a bad bargain.

On arriving at the foot of the hill, we were met by old Manajee, the Hunt shikari, with a very long face, as he said that lately the villagers, 'may dog defile their graves,' had been shooting the pig—a crime as heinous in a pig-sticking district as vulpecide would be in a hunting country at home (at least, from a hog-hunter's point of view, though perchance the poor 'ryot,' or peasant whose crops had been destroyed hardly viewed it in the same light), and, as this involved a loss to Manajee's pocket in the shape of fewer pig ergo, less 'inām,' or reward for pig *found*, the said villagers' female relations, mothers, sisters, cousins, and aunts, were favoured with a shower of abuse, whereby their own virtue, and that of all their relations, was called in question.

Interrogated further, however, Manajee admitted that 'there were a few pig on the hill, and one dantwallah (boar), but he was not a big one.' On the strength of this he had collected some eighty beaters, and waited the sahib's 'hookum,' or order. These beaters were armed with old matchlocks, horns, tom-toms (native drums), and 'all manner of music' calculated to make the most discordant din, and rouse any decent-minded boar to a sense of the necessity of seeking safety in flight. The beaters having been all seated in a circle, next followed the distribution of small circular pieces of tin, stamped with the letters 'N.H.,' (Nagpore Hunt), the initials of the Hunt, and known amongst the natives as 'tikul,' 'tickkut,' and every possible pronunciation of the word ticket that could suggest itself to the unenlightened nigger's mind. No beater was paid at the end of the day unless he produced and gave up his ticket. This was necessary to prevent fraud, as otherwise the number of men, and even children, who would vow they had been beating all day was innumerable.

The tickets being all duly distributed and counted, Manajee proceeded to marshal his forces, and with a 'Chulo baie,' or, 'Let us go on, brethren,' the little army got into motion preparatory to forming line, whilst Thompson and I rode on to post ourselves, accompanied by our horse-keepers, carrying spare spears. Thompson was riding his Arab, whilst I bestrode my three-cornered beauty, keeping my weather-eye open for any little ebullition of temper on his part. The spot we selected was in a gorge that ran up and half divided the hill, and from whence we could command a good view, whilst remaining concealed ourselves. Soon we heard the noise of the tom-toms, etc., and the shouts of the beaters as they advanced towards us along the hill-side, and presently we saw one of our look-out men posted on the top of the hill frantically waving his flag.

I ought to have mentioned that we always employed a few men provided with little red and white flags as 'look-out men,' and it was their duty on seeing the pig to wave their flags silently in the direction they were going. By their doing this we knew where to look for the pig (often difficult to see in thick cover), and all risk of their being headed by the noise of shouting was avoided. These look-out men were generally posted in trees, or on a rocky eminence from whence they could obtain a good view of the covert and the surrounding country.

Looking in the direction towards which the flag was pointing, we soon descried the dark backs of a couple of pig blobbing along through the brushwood, amidst which they every now and then disappeared. As soon as they got within some one hundred and fifty yards of our station, I shouted, 'Ride,'* and, selecting the biggest (a

* Rule viii.—A captain to be chosen by vote.   ix.—In the field the captain to have the entire management of the beat, etc.   x.—On the pig breaking, no one to give chase till the captain or acting cap-

boar), 'laid in,' but soon lost sight of him in the dense jungle of bushes. On viewing him again, I found he had stopped, doubled back, and gone up the side of the hill, up which I very foolishly followed him, for it was a desperate scramble, whilst Thompson rode round the base of the hill to catch him as he broke. He, however, somehow lost sight of the pig, and, on reaching the summit, I saw the boar going away over the open plain some half mile off, with his head set straight for the low range of hills I have already mentioned. Giving a yell to Thompson, and pointing with my spear, I set the 'three-cornered one' going, and scrambled down the stony side of the hill in the succession of short jerky strides a horse takes going down a declivity, propping himself at every step almost, and anon twisting and bounding to avoid some boulder of rock, or extra thick piece of shrub. I got to the bottom safely, however, and then saw Thompson coming along about two hundred yards to my right. The boar was trotting on ahead sulkily, not seeming much inclined to make the most of the good start he had obtained. He crossed the boggy nullah, and I could see the water in it was pretty deep by the splash he made as he soused in and scrambled out.

tain gives the word, 'Ride.'—*Extract from Rules of Nagpore Hunt Club*

Following the old hog-hunting axiom that 'where a pig can go, a horse can follow,' I carefully noted the *exact* spot, and catching hold of the 'three-cornered one' short by the head, crammed in the spurs, and sent him at it full tilt. He acquitted himself well, for it was a widish place, and we landed on the *right* side with a peck and a scramble, but *no fall!* When he recovered himself, and I had pulled him together again, I saw the boar standing in the open, evidently waiting for me, and the thought uppermost in the porcine mind was apparently, ' Won't I just give this young shaver a lesson for disturbing a fellow like this, at this time of day too!' I went at him full tilt, when he met me with a gallant charge, but the spear sped true, and I rolled him over. This was repeated twice, when he went and lay down under a small bush. Thompson now joined me, his Arab having declined the water, and so forced him to make a considerable détour in order to cross the nullah.

Whilst we were consulting as to what tactics to pursue, the boar trotted out into the open, with the evident intention of renewing the fight; but on second thoughts he retired under another bush. As he lay here we galloped past in turns, he meeting us in a half charge each time we went by. I speared him twice, but the second time unfortunately twisted my spear-head. Thompson, however, being very short-sighted, missed him each time. Thinking he *must* be dead, as he made no further movement, I was preparing to dismount, when up he got and charged out like a shot at Thompson, whose Arab he cut badly above the stifle before he had time to spear. I then had a shy at him, but, my spear being practically useless for offensive purposes, all I could do was to fend him off in his charge. Here was a fine predicament! A boar speared several times, myself with a useless spear, and Thompson's horse badly ripped. Tossing the foam from his jaws, and eyeing us contemptuously, the boar trotted off with a surly grunt towards a small bush-covered hillock only a short distance from the main hills. All that we could do was to follow, and keep him in sight until our horse-keepers should come up with the spare spears, and Thompson's second horse. Whilst watching the boar, whom we had marked down under a thick bush, he suddenly charged out at Thompson, who speared him, but the spear head getting caught between the boar's ribs, and the horse wheeling away from the charge, he was forced to relinquish his hold, and the spear remained sticking in the unfortunate animal, who again retired to his stronghold, with what to him must have been a decidedly novel appendage! I now found my horse so stiff and lame that he could hardly put one leg before the other, so dismounting to ascertain the cause of the damage, I found that the boar had ripped him twice, though, luckily, not very severely, and that in addition he had lost three shoes, two in front, and one behind, which must have been pulled off coming down the stony hill where we had 'found.'

Many were the anathemas we bestowed on our dilatory horsekeepers, but at last they hove in sight, accompanied by old Manajee and a few beaters. Upon their joining us, I got on Thompson's mare, and, arming myself with a fresh spear, I waited outside the covert whilst he rode in to protect the beaters in case the boar should charge them. As they approached the spot where he was lying, he charged out at them directly, and Thompson speared him. This seemed rather to sicken him, and, retiring to the thick bush where he had been lying, nothing could again induce him to move. Volleys of stones were flung in at him, and he was yelled and shouted at, but he only acknowledged these compliments by a surly grunt every now and then. We therefore decided to finish him off on foot, so, dismounting, we withdrew all the beaters, and sent them out of harm's way; we gave old Manajee a spear, and, placing him between us, we advanced shoulder to shoulder against the now infuriated boar. This last taunt was too much for him, and, staggering up, out he came in a blundering charge. I caught him fair on my spear, which snapped in two, and over I went on the broad of my back, with a horrible sensation that I should shortly be disembowelled. But it was the gallant boar's last effort, for the steel had gone home, and he fell dead, with a grunt of defiance, within three feet of me.

He was not a large boar (only thirty-two inches high at the shoulder, with tusks five inches long), though long, lean, and muscular; but what a gallant heart beat within that bristly body! What other animal except the wild hog of India would exhibit such indomitable pluck? Speared no less than nine times, many of the wounds being in almost vital spots, knocked over several times, with a spear sticking in him that, as it swayed about with his every movement, must have been the cause of intense agony, he yet disdained from the first to seek safety in the flight that would probably have saved his life, but preferred to stand and fight like a hero, and 'die as a boar should die,' before he yielded up his gallant life.

Every true sportsman, I think, feels at times a certain amount of regret at taking the life of an animal that has fought well to defend itself, and,

"FELL DEAD WITH A GRUNT OF DEFIANCE."

once the excitement and effervescence of the 'scuffle' is over, cannot help wishing that he could restore the life he has been but a moment before so keen to take. I am sure we both had this feeling (though we naturally kept it to ourselves) at the death of the 'Warree' boar. It was a close, oppressive day, such as one experiences towards the end of the rainy season in India, and we were both pretty well 'done' after our exertions, and seldom, I ween, did thirsty soul enjoy a drink more than we did the copious swig of claret and soda water that we indulged in on the spot. On our thirst being assuaged, we had our horses fed and watered, and saw them despatched to camp, whither we shortly after followed them on foot. After a tub, and a good 'tiffin,' we lighted our cheroots, and, mounting our 'tattoos,' cantered in the twelve miles to cantonments.

The horses were not much the worse for their cuts, which soon healed up. I was much pleased with my 'three-cornered one's' performances, and accordingly named him 'Warree,' after the covert from which this gallant boar broke. He subsequently ran in a hurdle-race for me at our 'sky meeting' (which he ought to have won had he been properly ridden), and credited me with many another 'first spear;' and though his temper never became angelic, I sold him for a very decent sum when I left India the following year. More than a decade and a half has now passed since then, but I look back with pleasure through the mists of years on those joyous hog-hunting days, which seem ever fresh and bright in one's memory, only darkened by the loss of old and tried friends, with whom it was a joy and a pleasure to talk of

> 'The chases we had shared,
> And the tushes we had won.'

CHAPTER III.

A BONNIE BAG.

Start for the Jungles—Disappointment—Bustard—Stalk and Bag Him—Move Camp—Cheetal—A Lucky Shot—A Forest Glade—Bison—Is it a Miss?—Follow Him Up—Hurrah! Muntjack and Peafowl—A Curious Right and Left—My Friend's Bag—Excitement in Camp—A Kill by a Tiger—Sit up for Him—Peter's Mistake—Indecision—Failure.

I SUPPOSE at no period of our life do we enjoy such real good fun as we do between the ages of twenty and twenty-five, and, if of a sporting turn of mind, see more sport to a certain extent; though, of course, with age comes experience and coolness, two very necessary qualities to ensure success. It was my lot a good many years ago, when I was a youngster, to be quartered at Kamptee, where my sporting proclivities had full scope for development, and the day's sport that I purpose narrating, though rather better than the average as far as numbers go, will serve as a good specimen, as showing the game that could be met with and bagged.

I well remember my first start from the above-mentioned quarter in search of big game, with Captain, now Lieutenant-Colonel Clay, who, although my senior in point of service, was, as far as 'shikar' experience goes, not much in advance of myself. With what feverish excitement all the camp kit was prepared, stores laid in, cartridges loaded, etc., and, when the day arrived for us to start, I felt all aglow with sporting fire and ardour for the chase, and pictured our triumphant return to cantonments, at the expiry of our leave, laden with trophies, skins, skulls, and horns.

We had sent on our camp some twenty-five miles the day previous, and rode out in time for dinner, shooting our way, picking up a couple of black buck and a ravine-deer *en route*. To our great disgust, on our arrival, we found a message had preceded us from the adjutant, saying my friend was required the next day as president of a regimental court-martial. It was perhaps a bit of retributive justice, as we had started the day before our leave actually began, hoping to snatch two extra days' sport. However, there was no help for it, and, with many anathemas on our adjutant and the exigencies of Her Majesty's service, we could only make the best of a bad job, which on my friend's part involved getting on a fresh horse after dinner, and riding back the twenty-five miles by the light of the moon, whilst I remained behind, to work my wicked will on the antelope and small game that abounded, until his return.

He came back on the second day, and then we resumed our march towards the tract of heavy jungle where we hoped to meet with nobler and bigger game. During his absence I shot a couple of antelope and a splendid old cock bustard*, who was confiding enough to flop up out of some long grass, and was promptly bowled over with a charge of No. 6 shot before he got thirty yards away. This bird exhibited a curious mixture of wariness and stupidity. I had viewed him stalking about on the plains some two hours previously, and had done my level best to get within shot of him; but no, he was too wary. Several times did he lure me into a long and weary stalk, only on each occasion, just when a few yards more were all that were needed, to dash my hopes to the ground by rising and taking a long flight ere he pitched again. Having marked him down, the operation would be repeated *da capo*. In vain I tried to appear to be only engaged in geological pursuits, and pick up stones, etc., in which I appeared to be most intensely interested; it was no go. Then meeting a native, driving a bullock-

* Eupodotis Edwardsii.

cart, I got him to drive towards the bird, but in a circle, and, having covered myself with a native blanket, walked on the far side of the cart as it advanced. It was all useless; let me get within three hundred yards of him, he would not, and at last, rising, he took a long flight, and disappeared over a low, sandy ridge beyond which lay a small rumnah, or grass cover.

Utterly disgusted at all my futile endeavours, I had exchanged my rifle for my shot-gun, and strolled on in the direction of his flight, thinking I might get a few painted partridge and quail amongst the grass. No sooner had I entered it than my sly friend rose with a tremendous fluster, and met his fate. A very dainty dish he afforded us, and his feathers gladdened the hearts of several fishing friends at home.

'Come, get on,' I hear some of my readers say; 'we don't want to hear so much about your old bustard, tell us about the big game you got.' All right, my friends, I will; but let me tell you it takes a lot of science to bag a bustard, and good shooting, too, unless you have the luck to get within gunshot of one as I did on this occasion.

During a month we had every reason to be satisfied with our sport, for during this time we had bagged five tigers, a bear, several sambur, cheetal, or spotted deer, and four-horned antelope, besides small game. We had, however, hitherto been disappointed at not finding any bison* (Bos gaurus). We had gone to this particular part of the district in hopes of coming across this grand animal which our shikari had assured us was an inhabitant of the surrounding jungles, in spite of the reiterated assertion of other fellow-sportsmen who vowed they did not come so far north of the Nerbudda river, and who laughed at the idea of our shooting any. However, we were destined to be rewarded, and have the laugh on our side, and, oddly enough, we *both* saw and bagged our first bison on the same day. As our bag was a very mixed one (that great charm of shooting, to my mind, and, I fancy, to that of most sportsmen), a detailed account of our share of it may prove of some interest.

One morning, when we had almost despaired of coming across bison, we went to a hill the crest of which was covered with over-hanging rocks, under whose shade bears were reported as wont to reside. Bruin and family, however, were not

---

* Known as Bos gaurus, and Gavæus gaurus. The young bulls are a dark, liver-coloured chestnut, which becomes much darker with age—an old bull being nearly black—on the back and flanks, shaded off to light chestnut on the belly, and inside the thighs, with white marks on the pasterns. The cows are of a lighter colour. They are gregarious, though old, and solitary bulls are occasionally found. They have a very high wither, which is prolonged into a dorsal ridge

at home, so we had our walk for nothing—no, *not for nothing*, for on our way back to camp we came across undoubted tracks of bison, though they were somewhat stale. This considerably revived our drooping spirits, and we determined to send on our camp that night to a spot some eight miles distant, situated in the heart of dense bamboo-jungle, where we should be more likely to come across bison; sleep out ourselves, and shoot our way over the next morning. At daybreak, we were awoke by our trusty 'boys,' who had some tea and toast ready for 'master.' Discussing this as we dressed, we soon were on our way, and shortly separated.

I had been walking about an hour-and-a-half, when I saw a large herd of cheetal browsing through a pretty open part of the jungle, the stags stopping occasionally to have a little 'mill,' then chasing some errant hind, and anon rubbing their antlers against the stems of the forest trees, whilst their female kind looked on admiringly.

---

along the back. The bison prefers high altitudes and dense jungle, where bamboo grows, and are found at ranges varying from two to six thousand feet above the level of the sea. They attain a height varying from five feet four to seven feet two inches, measuring from the point of the wither to the fetlock. They have small, compact, game-like hoofs and short legs, and for their bulk are wonderfully active. Bulls are often very savage when wounded, and numerous instances are recorded of their charging sportsmen.

It was a charming, sylvan scene, and as the sunlight glanced and flickered through the leaves, and played on their dappled hides, I was so entranced that it was some time before I could make up my mind to disturb them. The savage instinct of sport inherent in man predominated at last, and I began to spot the best stag, and look about to see how I could best circumvent him. By taking advantage of the large ant-hills, which here abounded, clumps of bamboo, and trunks of trees, I managed to get within about eighty yards of the herd unperceived, and selecting my victim—a grand stag carrying a splendid head—I aimed at his shoulder, fired, and had the satisfaction of seeing him roll over, whilst the rest of the herd started asunder, and, dashing away in all directions, soon disappeared in the depths of the forest. I was administering the *coup de grâce* to the fallen stag, and admiring his beautiful spotted hide and the graceful sweep of his antlers, when I heard a scuffling in an adjacent clump of bamboos, accompanied by a gurgling, choking sound. Rushing in, with my hunting-knife in my hand, I there found *another* magnificent stag in the last agonies of death! What luck! Two good stags for one shot! On examining them, I found my bullet had gone *through* the loins of the first stag, very high up, so paralyzing him; and hit the second (who must have been standing directly behind him) through the shoulder and into the lungs.

In my haste in brushing through the underwood, a twig had sprung back, and hit me in the eye, causing for the moment intense pain; and, as the Gónd* who was acting as my guide intimated that there was a spring of water close by, I determined to go and bathe the injured optic.

Covering up the dead stags with branches, to keep off the vultures, I proceeded on my way, and soon came to a lovely glade in the forest, carpetted with emerald-green grass (rather an unusual sight in the hot weather, for it was the middle of April), through which meandered a tiny rivulet, whose clear waters danced and sparkled in the sunlight. The jungle on each side, some thirty yards from the stream, was composed of bamboo and 'sál'† trees, with here and there a gigantic teak,‡ and interspersed among these were ebony‖ and bastard teak,§ or palas, of lesser growth. I had bathed my inflamed eye, and was walking along carelessly, when suddenly my

---

* For an interesting account of Gónds, see 'The Highlands of Central India,' by the late Captain J. Forsyth, B.S.C. Chapman & Hall.

† Shorea robusta. ‡ Tectona grandis. ‖ Diospyros melanoxylon.
§ Butea frondosa.

friend, the Gónd, caught me by the arm, whispering, 'Bun-Bhinsa, sahib!' (Anglice, 'Bison, sir.')

In a moment, I was all attention, and, looking in the direction in which he was pointing, I saw a sight that made my heart beat and my pulse quicken; for *at last* my dream of seeing, and, I hoped, slaying, the mighty wild bull of the forest seemed about to be realized. I have taken many a head of game since then, but never have I felt the indescribable, almost breathless excitement and keen tension of the nerves that I did at that moment; for the sight that met my eager gaze was one worthy of being pourtrayed by the pencil of a Landseer, viz., a magnificent bull bison, standing half-hidden amid some low and thin bamboos, that ineffectually screened his massive proportions, and rubbing his horns against a tree! He was not eighty yards from me, and seemed quite unconscious of my presence. Taking a careful aim at his shoulder, I fired, and the answering 'thud' of the bullet told me plainly that I had scored a hit. With an indignant snort, he wheeled round, and, as he crashed into the jungle, I let him have the second barrel, I am afraid *anywhere!* I could hear him pounding away, and the sounds of his progress became fainter and fainter, till suddenly they ceased entirely. I and the Gónd gazed blankly at each other, and I fancy it was more with a view to comfort me in my disappointment than for any other reason that he remarked,

'Golee kya,' ('He has eaten the bullet').

'Yes,' I thought, 'I know he is hit, but goodness only knows where.'

The only thing to do, however, was to go up to the spot where the bull had been standing and see if there were any traces of blood. This done—not a drop was to be seen—our faces grew longer and longer, and yet I felt certain I had hit, so, taking up the tracks, we followed them. These showed that he had blundered blindly on his course, smashing down saplings that impeded his progress, like so much grass, and at one place he appeared to have staggered up against a large tree, and been knocked on one side by the concussion. Here, too, our hopes rose, for a little blood was visible against the stem. He then, apparently, diverged from his straight course, and led round in a semicircle towards where he had been originally standing. Following on for some three hundred yards we suddenly came upon him, lying stone-dead with the tell-tale little round hole above the elbow, and a little behind the shoulder, and with a stream of frothy blood oozing from his lips that showed he must have died from internal hæmorrhage.

How delighted I was; I could almost have hugged that nearly-naked, most odoriferous, grinning little Gónd! Lighting a pipe, I sat down, and kept gazing at the fallen bull's mighty form; noting the grand sweep of his horns, and the richly-blended tints of black and brown of his hide. However, it was no time for meditation, for the sun was getting hot, and I was still a couple of miles from camp and breakfast, for which my inward man craved; so, with a parting look, I tore myself away, and gave my rifle to the Gónd to carry, taking from him in exchange my shot-gun, into which I slipped a couple of cartridges loaded with number six shot, on the chance of picking up a jungle-fowl or something for the pot on my way home.

I had got within half-a-mile or so of the camp, and was walking through some dry grass about a foot high, when a muntjâk, or barking deer, jumped up, almost under my feet, so close that I easily rolled him over with my right barrel; as I fired a pea-hen rose about thirty yards from me, and got the contents of my left. I was just about pleased. Five shots fired, and a bag of a bison, two spotted deer, a muntjâk, and a pea-hen was one, I flattered myself, that would be hard to beat. On arriving in camp I found my friend had also made a capital bag, and he had got two bison, *viz.*, a young bull and a cow. He had come across a herd of about twenty and had got a right and left with the above result, though he had wounded another which he lost. The head of this, however, a fairish young bull, was brought in a few days later by some Gónds who had come on him lying dead. He had also bagged a couple of spotted deer, a sambur, with but a poorish head, and a four-horned antelope.

Fired with our success, we had 'bison on the brain,' and determined to go and sit up that night on the chance of bagging some more. My friend was to watch a pool of water, where he had seen numerous footprints, whilst I was to guard another, at which I was told bison frequently came to drink. After an early dinner, about half-an-hour before sunset, we started in opposite directions. I had not left camp more than five minutes when I was overtaken by one of our servants, who came running after me, and said he had just seen a tiger strike down a cow close to our tents! I ran back as hard as I could, and found the unfortunate cow still alive, but unable to rise, with the cruel fang-marks fresh and bleeding on its neck. I was young and inexperienced in those days, and foolishly followed the tiger's tracks into a nullah densely overgrown with creepers and bamboos, where, in the now failing light (for in the East there is no twilight, and darkness comes almost with a bound after sunset) I could not see two yards in front of me. Fortunately for me, if 'Mr. Stripes' was near me—and I expect he was not far off—he did not make his presence known, for I could not see anything of him.

Sending for my friend, I hastily had a couple of charpoys, or native bedsteads, lashed into trees near the dead cow—for I found the poor brute had expired on my return—and awaited his advent with impatience. He soon returned, in a great state of excitement, and then we posted ourselves, having previously tossed for first shot, which he won. We waited for nearly an hour and a half, and the moon was well up, but there was no sign of the tiger's return. Feeling very unwell, I suppose from the combined excitement of the day and the exposure to a hot sun in the morning, and knowing I was only to play second fiddle, I gave up, and returned to camp and bed.

Next morning, on awakening, my first interrogation to my friend was as to his success. He did not meet my inquiry in the cheerful spirit I had hoped; in fact, he seemed decidedly crestfallen, and this was what he said,

'Confound that fellow Peter' (our shikari) 'It was all his fault. You had not been gone twenty minutes when the tiger came out of the jungle, and, stalking quietly along, stood under the very tree in which you had been sitting, not thirty yards from me. He stood for a few minutes clearly defined in the bright moonlight, gazed suspiciously up at your méchan, but would not come up to the kill, which, you know, was close to me. Peter whispered to me to let the tiger come up to the kill, and begin eating before I fired, and, like an ass, I followed his advice. The delay was fatal, for old "Stripes," who was evidently suspicious, either heard or winded us, and promptly decamped without my firing at him. I waited on some three hours, and then got sick of it, so followed your example and went to roost.'

After breakfast we strolled down to view the kill, when lo! and behold, it was gone! The marks were plainly visible where the tiger had dragged it into the jungle, and we were soon guided to the spot by the vultures sitting over it. Yes, there it was, half-eaten, and *we* had been made fools of. We tried several beats on speculation, but never came across this most leary tiger. However, we had had grand sport, and could not grumble, and I can still look back on these happy days spent in the Danda jungles with pride and pleasure, and say, in the words of the old Indian hunting-song,

> 'Oh! who hath been in such a scene
> That scene can e'er forget;
> In sorrow's mood, in solitude,
> Its dream will haunt him yet.'

Yes, the dream does haunt me yet, and would you too, kind-hearted reader, had you like me made such a 'bonnie bag.'

CHAPTER IV.

TACKLING A TUSKER.

Roorkee—Ten Days' Leave—Hurdwar—Game of the Doon Valley—Ramiah—The Rogue Elephant—See Tigers—News of the Tusker—Dawn in the Doon—The Sewalik Hills—Find the Tusker's Tracks—His Depredations—A Weary Tramp—Ramiah Wants to Give Up—Perseverance Rewarded—A Long Crawl—He Winds Us—The Shot—Misery—We Find Blood—Hopes Revived—Pursuit—Is it Him?—Disappointment—Elephant Pits—The Fate of the Rogue.

It was on a warm afternoon in November when a solitary horseman might have been seen wending his way—but no, I will not inflict this 'G. P. R. James' style of beginning on my reader, and only ask him, or her—if any fair lady should deign to cast a glance over these pages—to imagine me a youthful ensign, mad on sport, cantering along the banks of the Ganges Canal, that runs from Hurdwar past Roorkee (at which station my regiment was stationed), full of delight at my first ten days' leave in India. This leave I had at last obtained, after several months strict attention to my drill, and mastering or endeavouring to master all those intricate details of regimental interior economy, a knowledge of which is supposed to be necessary for every future budding general. I could tell the most exacting inspecting-general officer the price of a flannel shirt, button-brush, tunic, etc.—in fact, of all the articles of Tommy Atkins' kit—and had been certified by the adjutant as being able to manœuvre a company without hopelessly or otherwise clubbing it. But, during the time I spent in acquiring this vast and varied store of knowledge, I am afraid my heart was more in the jungle than on the parade ground, and I longed for the time and opportunity when I should fire my first shot at big game. I had always, I fancy, been thought rather a 'duffer' in the regiment, and, though my brother-officers were nearly without exception a set of thoroughly good fellows and honourable *gentlemen*, they were none of them imbued with that *passion* for field sports which dominated my mind; and consequently when one night at mess I announced my intention of starting next day for the valley of Dehra Doon, some fourteen miles distant, I was assailed with a volley of chaff, and got many good-natured hints that I should spend my leave with more enjoyment to myself and benefit my health more by going to the adjacent hill-station of Mussourie, where the regiment had a comfortable bungalow, and a detachment mess. I was deaf, however, to all these kind suggestions, and, though a perfect 'griffin' as far as regarded the pursuit of big game, I determined to go and see what I could do in that line.

With this end in view, I borrowed a ten-bore double-muzzle-loading rifle, and this, with my own twelve-bore double breech-loading 'Greener,' and ditto shot-gun, constituted my battery. I had dispatched my camp-kit to Hurdwar (a large native town on the banks of the far-famed and sacred Ganges) the previous day, with instructions to my head-servant to secure the services of the best local shikari he could find, and make with him such arrangements as would ensure my having sport. I had a pleasant ride out, and the little 'tattoo,' or pony, I was riding made short work of the distance, titupping along gaily, snorting and playing with his bit as if he was as delighted as his rider to be *en route* for the jungles. I arrived about an hour before sunset, and found my little camp pitched snugly under the shade of some giant mango-trees,* about a mile and a half beyond the town, and on the banks of one of the tributaries of the main river. After dinner

* Mangifera Indica.

Ramiah, the local shikari, presented himself with many profound salaams, and gave me a most flourishing account of the game to be found in the adjacent jungle. According to him, sambur, cheetal, hog-deer, swamp-deer, and muntják were in swarms, whilst pea-fowl, hares, jungle-fowl, and black partridge were, like the Irishman's snipe, 'simply jostling one another for room.' There were also tigers, bears, and panthers, *ad lib.*, and *some* elephants.

'And,' he added, 'if the sahib had only come a month sooner, I could have shown him an enormous 'dantwallah' (tusker), 'with tusks so long,' —extending both his arms to their full width— 'he is a great 'bobberywallah' (rogue), 'and has been doing much damage, pulling down houses on the outskirts of the town even, and destroying rice-fields right and left, and doubtless, if your highness had seen him, he would have eaten your lordship's bullets.'

I replied, with the self-satisfied air of a superior being, 'that doubtless he would,' and expressed a hope that I might have the opportunity of offering him such delectable food, which doubtless he would swallow with avidity!

Much desultory talk ensued, and I finally dismissed Mr. Ramiah with the promise of a good 'inām,' or reward, if *he* managed to show me the said 'tusker,' and I on my part bagged him. Eight days of my leave had elapsed, and as yet I had not bagged any big game—by this I mean the *feræ naturæ* proper. I had caught glimpses of four or five tigers, and, like a young ass, had run after them into the high grass, hoping they would be accommodating enough to stop and give me a good shot. Needless to say, they were not such fools, and, luckily perhaps for me, held different opinions on the propriety of such a course. Bears I had not come across, nor panthers either, though their 'pugs' in the bed of many a sandy 'nullah' went far towards proving that they existed in fair numbers. Elephants' *tracks* I had seen, and had been awakened one night by a herd coming to drink close to camp. I had, however, shot several deer, and, *faute de mieux*, had made a fair bag of pea-fowl, black partridge, jungle-fowl, etc.

Oh! ye gentlemen of England who sit at home at ease, what would not some of you give to be put down in that little paradise of game that I wot of on the banks of the far-distant Ganges? No bother there about rascally keepers, poachers, birds dying of 'gapes,' loss by vermin, etc., and all the hundred and one worries attendant on game-preserving in Merrie England. All you have to do is to get a few beaters who will willingly drive your game for you for a sum equivalent to about threepence per diem, and *no lunch;* fill your cartridge-bag, take your stand at the end of a strip of cover, and blaze away to your heart's content at rocketing jungle-fowl, or black partridge, with the excitement varied occasionally by a hog-deer or a muntják cantering past, or an old peacock skimming over you, his metallic-like bronze, green, and gold plumage flashing and gleaming in the eastern sun.

But, 'revenons à nos moutons,' or rather 'à nos elephans.' As I said before, eight days of my leave had elapsed, and I felt rather glum at the prospect of having to return to the dull routine of station life without some trophy worthy of my rifle, or at all events being able to say I had had a shot at some real big game. I was sitting outside my tent after dinner cogitating over a pipe and lamenting my bad luck, when I perceived Ramiah approaching by the dim light cast by the embers of the camp-fire, now gradually dying out. After due obeisance, he spoke thus, in a hushed whisper, as if afraid of being heard:

'Gurreepurwur' (protector of the poor), '*he* is here.'

'What!' I exclaimed, starting up. 'What do you mean?'

'Sahib, the *dantwallah is in the jungle.* Your slave has seen him this very morning not two miles from your lordship's tent, and his " nusseeb "' (destiny) ' has brought him here, that he may eat your lordship's bullets.'

This piece of news effectually roused me up, and revived my drooping spirits, and on further inquiry I discovered that Ramiah had really seen the redoubtable tusker, and had actually come across him while engaged in his old pursuits of gorging himself on some poor ' ryot's ' (peasant's) scanty patch of rice; and, moreover, that *en route* to his feast he had amused himself by destroying the huts of some charcoal-burners. This latter episode sufficiently established his identity.

Giving Ramiah a good ' tot ' of whisky, to which he was by no means averse, after assuring himself that none of his fellow-natives were looking on, I dismissed him, having previously arranged that we should start at daylight the following morning, and try to circumvent the ' dantwallah.'

The night seemed interminably long; but at last day broke, and I was soon up, and ready for a start after snatching a hasty meal as I dressed. As the sun rose over the distant snow-clad peaks of the Himalayas, we made a start. Our way lay for some little distance along the valley, now shrouded in a gradually rising mist; the low range of the Sewalik hills was on our left, whilst on our right, in the far distance, towered range upon range of billowy, forest-clad hills, which were surmounted finally by the regions of eternal snow, whose rugged outline ever and anon changed from a vivid rose-colour to pearly grey and dazzling white as the sun rose higher and higher. Oh, the glories of a sunrise in those jungles! No pen can adequately describe them, no eye but that of an artist or a sportsman (who, I think, is generally a lover of Nature in all her varied scenes and moods) can appreciate. Kind reader, I am only one of the latter class, so I will not attempt a task that from sheer inability I could do but scant justice to. I can only leave it to your imagination, and get along on the track of the tusker.

After about two miles of sharp walking, we reached a small patch of cultivation where the jungle had been 'cleared.' Here our friend's handiwork was very apparent. The crop had been torn up, and trampled down, as if some playful locomotive, at least, had been engaged in some mad gambol, whilst the great pit-like impressions of the elephant's feet, as yet unhardened by the sun, bore out the truth of Ramiah's over-night statement. The tracks led into some high grass towards the low Sewalik hills, and these we followed for some distance, not without great difficulty, however, for they crossed and re-crossed each other in the most labyrinthine manner, as the 'pachyderm' had stopped here and there to browse on some more than ordinarily tempting morsel, and poor Ramiah was not much of a 'tracker,' whatever other pretensions he had to being a shikari. Some time was spent in following up and unravelling all these ramifications before we got on a direct line again. Soon after doing so, however, our hearts were rejoiced by the sight of fresh 'droppings,' and we knew that the object of our search could not be very far off. The tracks led up the hills, which, on the plateau at their summit, were clothed at intervals with clumps of bamboo and large forest trees. Following up the now plainly discernible track, we were constantly startled by either a herd of sambur or cheetal, who, roused from their mid-day siesta, dashed down the stony side of the hill with a clatter resembling a charge of cavalry. Needless to say, they were unmolested, for were we not in pursuit of larger and far nobler game? On, on we toiled, hot and weary, for the sun was now at its full height, and Ramiah more than once betrayed signs of giving in, and suggested that the 'dantwallah' must be off on his travels again and going away from the jungles.

At about three o'clock we stopped and ate our frugal lunch. After half-an-hour's rest, we took up the tracks again, which, as we progressed, got fresher and fresher, though they still led on and on. At last we reached a belt of thin bamboos. Ramiah was leading about a couple of yards in front of me, and we were moving along noiselessly, carefully avoiding treading on any dead twigs, leaves, etc. As we reached the edge of the cover, he squatted suddenly, with his open hand turned back, and extended towards me in a warning gesture. Taking the hint, I crouched also, and, edging gradually towards him inch by inch, as he sat motionless, with his eyeballs nearly protruding out of his head, I cautiously peered through the leafy screen, and there, *at last*, not fifty yards from me, the object of our search met my delighted gaze! A magnificent tusker truly! His long tusks: not the ivory-white my excited imagination had depicted them, but a noble pair, and plainly discernible, nevertheless. Nor was his hide the blueish-grey colour seen on a well-groomed elephant in captivity, but a dull, reddish, almost brick-dust colour, the result, as I afterwards discovered, of a thick coating of reddish mud, something the colour of Devonshire soil with which he had plastered himself, to protect even his enormously thick hide from the insidious attacks of flies, and that curse of the tropics, mosquitoes. He was standing under the shade of a large tree, nearly motionless, except for the occasional flap of an enormous ear, whilst every now and then, collecting a handful, or, to speak correctly, a proboscisfull, of dust, he blew it over his back and sides. How my heart beat! I could almost hear it. Here at last my dream of days, nay, of years, was realized, and I was face to face with a real wild tusker! I was shaking so with excitement, that I dared not fire; besides, he was too far to risk a shot. So I sat still for, I suppose, some five minutes, which seemed hours; then, taking the ten-bore rifle from Ramiah, shaking some powder into the nipples, and putting on fresh caps, I again peered out to survey the ground, and form my plan of attack.

Between me and the elephant the ground was almost bare of cover, but some twenty yards from him was a small bush, and, between it and my place of concealment, lay a couple of small rocks. If I could only get up to the bush unnoticed, I might have a chance, and, should fortune favour me, I might manage to get some five yards nearer my quarry, by gaining the shelter of a friendly tree-trunk. The wind, such as there was, was in my favour, and was blowing from the elephant and towards me. Whispering to Ramiah to follow

"I TOOK THE BEST AIM MY EXCITED FEELINGS WOULD ALLOW."

me with the spare rifle, and to be *very* cautious, I crawled out on my stomach, and, inch by inch, wriggled along till I reached the first rock. Then, after a moment's pause, on to the second; and so on, till I gained the shelter of the bush.

There I lay panting, but striving to be quiet. Oh! if I could only get to that tree. The effort *must* be made; and, as I was preparing to do so, the elephant again gathered up some dust, and, as he propelled it, with a shrill 'ph-r-ew,' (I am afraid I cannot phonetically imitate the exact sound) I skipped nimbly across to the tree, beckoning to Ramiah to lie *perdu*. I had only time to conceal myself behind the massive and gnarled trunk, and silently cock my rifle, with finger on the trigger, when I saw the tip of the tusker's trunk curl slowly round in my direction, whilst the huge ears were cocked forward in an attitude of expectation. I intuitively felt he had winded me, and I knew I had no time to lose; so, as his gigantic head was slowly turned full towards me, I took the best aim my excited feelings and trembling limbs would allow, and, covering the depression in his forehead above the trunk, pulled! 'Bang' went the old rifle, with a roar that re-echoed through the hills, nearly knocking me over, from the combined effects of six drams of powder and a ten to the pound bullet; and, as I stooped down and peered under the smoke, expecting to see my foe prostrate on the ground, there was a shrill trumpet, a scream of rage; and all I saw was a huge red stern bolting off as fast as it could!

In my rage and vexation at what I thought was a miss, I did a thing which only a tyro would have done under the circumstances, viz., I blazed away my left barrel into the said retreating stern. Needless to say, with no perceptible result, except to accelerate the elephant's flight. Stepping from behind the tree, I met Ramiah's reproachful look, and, as we both gazed mournfully in the direction in which our game had vanished, he observed, more by way of pleasing me, I fancy, than with a due regard for truth,

'Golee kya, sahib.' ('He has eaten the bullet, sir.')

'He might have eaten a cart-load like it, and be none the worse,' I mentally ejaculated, though, of course, I did not give expression to my thoughts, and merely remarked that 'I thought I had hit him,' though I had serious doubts in my own mind as to the veracity of this statement. However, on going up to the spot where the 'dantwallah' had been standing, my spirits were revived by the sight of a drop or two of blood, further on more, then a great splash on a stone, and so on. 'Come,' I thought, 'he *must* be badly wounded to bleed so!' I therefore determined to follow him up, on the chance of getting another shot. To this course Ramiah objected, saying it was useless; that he would go forty miles without stopping; that we were fourteen miles from camp; that it was getting late, and we might meet tigers on our return home; that it was not safe to stay out any longer—in fact, he adduced every argument his fertile brain could imagine in order to persuade me from continuing the pursuit. All in vain. My blood was up, and I resolved to go on.

The fact was Mr. Ramiah was in a mortal funk at the bare idea of encountering the wounded elephant, whilst I was proportionately keen to do so. After reloading, we took up the tracks, and I carried the big rifle myself, in case of a sudden charge. The jungle showed unmistakeable signs of the tusker's passage through it, and the bent and broken saplings, and bamboos crushed and trodden down like so much grass, and plentifully besprinkled with blood, indicated that he was hard hit, and half-mad with pain and fright. After following the track for some distance along the level of the plateau it turned off abruptly at right angles, and led down the steep side of a hill, clothed with high grass and thick vegetation. We passed through this, the 'sign' being only too visible; in fact, the veriest novice in jungle lore could have followed the trail without difficulty. Where this extra-thick bit of cover terminated, there was an open space, and, just beyond it, a very thick patch of bamboos. Here the ground dropped, or rather sloped abruptly downwards.

As we approached this patch of cover, we saw it in a most violent state of commotion. Ramiah stopped suddenly, and begged and implored me not to go on, saying the elephant was tearing the trees down in his rage, and was now very dangerous; and he further assured me it was certain death for me to face him in such a mood, in such thick cover, and on such unfavourable ground. I paid little attention to his entreaties, however. My nerves were strung to a tension of nervous excitement. I had now a chance of retrieving my previous shameful, bungling shot; and, besides, I knew that, if the elephant did charge, he would have to do so uphill, and over stony, rocky ground, which would give me a very decided advantage, and that, if I did not drop him, at all events, my shot would very probably turn him. So I crept forward. I got, I suppose, to within five or six yards of where all the row was going on, where there was a great shaking of trees, followed by successive crashes, as if some heavy animal was tumbling about. Parting the branches, I peered through. All I could see was a troop of 'lungoors' (monkeys!). At first I thought the elephant must be down in his agonies, and close at hand. But, no; no prone tusker was visible. Then the real state of the case flashed across my mind, viz., that he had *nearly* fallen into an old elephant pit, but had gone on. On approaching close, this surmise proved correct. There was the huge beast's footprints on the very edge of the pit, small particles of the earth still tumbling into it, and testifying to the narrow escape he had had!

Oh! the bitter disappointment, as I thought of how even a few more inches of ground might have put my foe within my reach. How I cursed my bad luck! though the result of my shot was more attributable to my own want of skill, and the excitement I was labouring under. But it was no good crying over spilt milk; and so, all we could do was to take up the tracks, and follow the elephant, on the chance of eventually coming up with him. This we did; and, to make a long story short, we went on and on, till the setting sun warned us that we must discontinue further pursuit; and so, at last, reluctantly, I had to tear myself away, and face a long, weary trudge of some ten miles back to camp, where I arrived, long after dusk, tired out, disgusted and miserable.

Many years previous to my adventure, elephants used to be caught in these jungles by means of driving a herd towards a line of pits, when some were nearly sure to fall victims; the ground was then dug away all round, and tame elephants employed to extricate and subdue the captured ones. There were several other pits on a line with the one that had nearly done me such good service, but time and decay had caused the coverings by which the others had been concealed to fall in, and so they were plainly visible, whilst this one above had remained tolerably intact.

Poor Ramiah was nearly as crestfallen as myself, but, with true Indian philosophy, bore the disappointment better than I did, merely remarking, 'Kismet hi, sahib' ('It is fate, sir'). I think, though, in his heart of hearts, he was glad we did *not* again come up with the tusker.

And so ended my first trip to the lovely Doon Valley, and, though I was certainly disappointed at not getting any of the nobler species of big game, still I had very much enjoyed myself, far more than if I had spent my leave at Mussorie.

This elephant was shot a few months later some fifty or sixty miles from where I came across him, and the fortunate sportsman obtained the five hundred rupees government reward that had been offered for him. In a future chapter I purpose giving some account of game that I did bag on this trip and on subsequent expeditions.

CHAPTER V.

HOG-HUNTING.

Antiquity of Hog-hunting—Celebrated Hog-hunters—The Charms of the Sport—Comparison of Hog-hunting with Fox-hunting—Qualifications to ensure Success—Some Rules and Axioms—Description of Ground—Spears—Modes of Using—Measurements of Hog—A Savage Boar—Camel Ripped—A Queer Mount—On the Pig's Back—Determined Courage of a Boar—Biting Sows—Boar's Lips Pinned by Spear—' Parachute '—Solitary Chase—A Kill on Foot—Horses used in Hog-hunting—' Parachute's ' Love of the Sport—Concluding Remarks.

> 'Oh! let not sage or moralist our well-loved sport decry,
> We'll claim a warrant for the game from all antiquity;
> 'Twas thus Meleager's prowess in the chase was tried,
> 'Twas thus Ascanius' youth was fired,
> 'Twas thus Adonis died.'

YES, every schoolboy knows that it was out hog-hunting that Adonis, the mythological type of manly beauty, met his death, and all those who have heard the magic word ' Ride !' as the sounder of hog breaks, will feel that he met his death at the hands of no unworthy foe. Was not Meleager too the ' captain ' of the Calydonian Hunt, the earliest tent club of which we have record, and has not the sport flourished even until now? In Meleager's hunt, too, the earliest 'first spear' we read of was taken by one of the fair sex, the lovely Atalanta, of whom we know that she was a most sporting damsel, and did as much mischief with her eyes as with the sterner weapons of the chase. She deserves undoubtedly great credit for having introduced a fashion that has never changed for some thousands of years (let us say), viz., that of giving the tusks of the boar to the gainer of the 'first spear,' and then can we have a doubt that hog-hunting, less euphoniously termed 'pig-sticking,' is an ancient as well as a noble sport? Think how often fashions have altered, say, in the last twenty years, and then imagine one far older than the nineteenth century.

Almost all great Eastern soldiers were hog-hunters. Alexander the Great was one, so was Wellington, so was William Havelock (*not* Sir Henry); so, and keener than most, was the renowned Sir Walter Gilbert, one of the few men who ever fairly rode and speared a tiger; so was Sutherland, one of the founders of the Irregular Horse; so was Shakespeare, Jacob, Malcom, *cum multis aliis*; so, last and best sportsman of all, was the world-renowned 'Bayard' of Bombay, the glorious James Outram, the truest type of chivalry in every way that modern times or trustworthy records wot of.

The great fascination, if I may use such a term, of the sport consists in the generous rivalry that it calls forth between man and man, between the closest of friends in a heart-stirring game that cannot be won without nerve and manhood, as well as science, being called into play, for the *honour* consists in drawing 'first blood' (although it may be only the tiniest drop) from the hog, and for this men risk their lives and limbs, their money and horses, much more cheerfully than in any other sport we wot of. Now, kind reader, if you are a keen fox-hunter (as I, too, am) do not snap me up, and say, 'Oh! nonsense, there's nothing like fox-hunting.'

You cannot compare the two sports together. To begin with, in fox-hunting you are dependent on *scent*, and the capability of your hounds being able to 'speak' to that scent. Granted the excitement of a fast burst over a grass country, and that you are well carried by your horse, and have perhaps 'cut down' or pounded most of the field, the end, what is it? a poor little fox, worried by at least forty times its number (twenty couple of hounds)! Has he a chance, bar his cunning, in baffling his pursuers? No, a thousand times, no! Now how different is the chase of the wild boar of

India! there you must depend on *yourself* in every way, and at the end your foe, or quarry, meets you on nearly fair and equal terms, and, though certain chances are in your favour, the odds are not forty to one against your killing him, as is the case in fox-hunting. Please do not think I am decrying fox-hunting, for I am not. I *love* it; I adore with a sort of venatic worship both a fox and a hound; but, if I were given my choice of the two sports, I should choose hog-hunting, just as you, dear reader, would prefer a gallop with the Quorn or Cottesmore to a day's 'jelly-dogging!' The first time I ever saw a pack of fox-hounds throw off, I thought nothing in the world could cause such a breathless, anxious state of excitement as I noticed first one hound feather, then another, and another, then a whimper deepening into a regular chorus, announcing that a fox was afoot, and finally the certainty that he had broken covert, conveyed by the shrill 'Gone—away—forrard away,' from the whip posted at the low end of the covert.

I have seen the royal tiger, the monarch of the jungle, approach with noiseless footfall, the incarnation of agile and sinewy strength in animal life; I have heard his terror-striking roar of mingled rage and pain as he charged home on receiving the leaden missile, and felt that my life, and perhaps that of others depended on my coolness, and the steadiness of my aim; I have shot bison, and *at* elephant, and stalked the lordly sambur, (the red-deer of India); I have felt the keen excitement generated in riding one's own horse in a race, when one was doing one's best to get the last ounce out of him at the finish—sometimes winning, and as often, and oftener, being beaten on the post; but all these were nothing compared with what I felt when I got my first view of a sounder of wild hog as they broke, and heard the word to 'Ride!'

In fox-hunting all a man has to do, once hounds have got away with their fox, is to sit down, and ride as straight to them as he can, and do his best to keep his place. No individual exertion, bar that of the huntsman, can tend much to ensure the death of the fox. I do not mean to say that a sportsman cannot make himself of use, during checks and emergencies that may occur, but in hog-hunting the case is widely different. When once away everything depends on the exertions of *all* the pursuers—eyes, seat, nerve, and judgment must all play their part, and, if not made good use of, there is but small chance of your meeting with success. Nerve is undoubtedly required in both sports; in hog-hunting it is indispensable; whereas in fox-hunting a man who knows the **country can** generally be near the pack, and see **a** lot of **sport** and hound work, often as much as those who consider it **a** point of honour to go **into every** field **with them.**

In hog-hunting, however, **many a good rider** makes but a ' poor tew of it' at the end with a fine fighting boar! Something more is required than being able **to** get **well and quickly** over a country. A man may **if well** mounted get up to a pig quickly enough, **but when he has done this** he must know how **to** tackle him and **have the requisite coolness and nerve to do it and do it** efficiently; for remember, a savage boar, determined to sell his life dearly, and utterly reckless of that life, is no mean antagonist. A wild hog,* heavy and lumbering as he looks, **can go a most** astonishing **pace for a** short distance, **and** must be rattled along and blown from the beginning. As long as the ground is good and favourable, most **men can do this, but when it is** beset with nullahs, stones, **stubs, and holes, all** concealed by long grass, then **the man with nerve and** judgment scores! Say a dozen men **start in** pursuit of a hog. After a short distance over rough ground the field becomes select, **and is** probably limited to three or four riders, **and with** them virtually rests **the** race for the honour of

* Sus Indica.

first spear. The fact is a hog goes so fast that any craning or stopping to 'choose a better place,' throws you out hopelessly, and the old hog-hunters axiom of 'where a hog can go a horse can follow,' is nine times out of ten not only a true one, but a safe one to follow.

The great thing is to endeavour at all hazards to keep the hog in sight; for, once out of sight, he is generally lost; unless of course he can be marked into a patch of cover from whence he cannot escape unseen, and even then it is astonishing how a boar will sneak away, though several sharp pairs of eyes may be watching him. We will suppose a cover is beaten—a solitary boar breaks; the word 'Ride' is given in low tones, but audible to all, by the captain of the hunt, and away we all go and devil take the hindmost!

The boar, hearing the rattle of the horses' hoofs as they approach him, pauses for an instant to listen, as if calculating if it is possible for him to regain the cover he has just quitted. This being decided in the negative in the porcine mind, he lays himself out at his best speed to reach the shelter of the next cover, which may be only a quarter-of-a-mile or two miles distant, or perhaps even more. If he has had a good start, the horses have to do their best to get up to him, and if the ground is rough and bad, of course the boar has a decided advantage. From the time the boar starts till he is speared it is nothing but a hardly-contested race, and the best man on the best horse has, of course, the advantage; but it is not all over yet, for it is one thing to come up first with the boar and another thing to take first spear, a feat requiring a deal of management which, to a novice, is not at all clear. If alone, a man can choose his own time to deliver his spear and make sure, but with several other competitors straining every nerve to pass you, and ready to take advantage of any turn, or mistake on your part, it is a different thing, and not quite so easy as it may seem. On the leading man coming within a few yards, the pig makes a sudden turn, or 'jink,' and with such lightning-like rapidity is it done that, unless the foremost horseman is mounted on a veteran hog-hunter that will turn with the pig, he is thrown out to an extent that it will take a good hundred yards to make up, for it is astonishing how much ground a pig will gain in these 'jinks.' Now is the time for the second rider to make his push, and, according as he displays more or less skill, the hog is either speared or missed. Perhaps four or five men come up in succession, each thrown out in turn, until at last the boar is blown, and succumbs. Occasionally, however, a hog is speared without a turn, meeting his foremost antagonist in a savage and sidelong charge. Of course the honour of touching the boar with the spear *first* is what all contend for. The slightest prick that draws blood is sufficient, though the hog may be quite uninjured by it, and the animal, by whomever actually despatched, is nevertheless said to be killed by the man who gets first spear (to whom the tusks belong) and is always alluded to as *his* hog.

Pig are generally found in the worst part of a bad country, and seem to feel bound in honour when once started to lead their pursuers over the roughest ground they possibly can; so, if you intend mischief, *go straight you must!* It is no good looking—the more you do so, probably, the less you will like it! Remember, the worse the ground is for you, the better it is for the pig; and, if not rattled and blown from the beginning, he may go on for miles, and eventually beat you. The stony and rocky nature of some of the ground you may possibly ride over, will perhaps at first alarm you—not for your own safety, perhaps, so much as for your horse's legs and feet. Often you cannot gallop safely for thirty or forty yards together, where holes or cracks in the sun-baked ground, probably covered with long grass, abound, and the best advice I can give you is to forget your horse has any legs, and go as straight as you can! I once had a description given me, by an old friend, of the best man in his opinion to get safely over a particularly nasty bit of ground we were talking about one day. Quoth he:

'Well, I should say the only man who had a chance, a *chance only*, mind, of crossing that ground after hog without coming to utter grief, would be a drunken sailor on a blind horse!'

Do not attempt to guide your horse over such ground. If he can see the holes and rocks, he will, depend upon it, avoid them for his own sake. If he cannot see them, ten to one you will not be able to, at least, in time to be of any good to you; so there is nothing for it but to sit tight, give your horse his head, and trust to Providence, and try and assume, even if you do not feel it, an utter indifference to any possible danger.

Now a word about using your spear. In Bengal the spear used is generally shorter than that used in either the Bombay or Madras Presidencies, and is weighted with a lump of lead at the butt end. I have had no experience, or next to none, of hog-hunting in Bengal, but when there I noticed the spear was short, some six and a half feet, and was always carried point downwards, the butt end being weighted with lead, and was used differently to what it is further south. The hog being 'jobbed' at as represented below.

Whilst in Bombay and Madras the spear was not only longer (some nine feet in length), but was carried, when riding after hog, with the point uppermost. On reaching the pig, within spearing distance, the spear is brought nearly parallel with the knee, and is allowed a free play from the wrist. The natural impetus derived from a horse going at full speed, carries it *into* the boar; and it generally goes in, when well directed, 'like a knife into a pat of butter,' as I once heard it described, as the horse gallops past. It is then easily withdrawn. On no account should the spear shaft be carried tucked under the arm, as shown in pictures of knights engaged in a tournament, in other words, 'in rest.' If a man does this, and spears his pig, ten to one he will be knocked out of his saddle, or get an ugly crack on his head from the shaft as he goes past; and the same thing would probably happen, even in the event of his missing his 'spear,' and striking the ground. The subjoined illustration will show more clearly than I can describe the method in which the spear is held in the Southern Presidencies.

The height of boars and the length of their tusks vary considerably. I believe that, in heavy forest jungle, enormous boars are occasionally met with, but in the plains they do not, as a rule, run so big. The biggest I ever speared myself measured thirty-four inches from the point of the wither to the heel—our method of measurement in the Nagpore Hunt. The average was, however, about thirty-one inches. The largest boar on record in the 'Hunt Book' was thirty-seven inches, and he must have been a monster. In 1870-71, the records of the Nagpore Hunt showed twenty-one boars measuring thirty-one inches or over: of these, one was thirty-seven inches, one thirty-six inches, one thirty-five and a half inches, three thirty-four and a half inches, five thirty-four inches, and five thirty-three and thirty-three and a half inches. The largest boars have not always the best tusks, and the thirty-four incher I have above alluded to—and which I killed with a single spear—had tusks nine and a quarter inches in length, and were the second-best pair on record in the annals of the Hunt, the best pair measuring nine and a half inches; whereas the thirty-seven incher had tusks only six and a quarter inches. Perhaps an account of how I got this boar may not be here out of place.

It was on the 18th of August, 1870, the week following the good scuffle related at page 28, and close to the same place. We had, late in the afternoon, roused this large boar out of a

"SCRAMBLING UP THE BOULDER-STREWN SIDE OF THE HILL."

thin bit of outlying cover, which extended some distance out into the plain from a large, steep, isolated hill, covered with rocks and boulders, and clothed with dense brushwood. H—— (the friend and sportsman to whom these pages are dedicated) and I got a start of the rest of the field, and had a good race for the spear. The boar ran the line of thin and detached bushes towards the hill. One of us was riding each side of the cover, and the boar kept jinking from one side to the other without affording either of us a chance of spearing. As we neared the hill, old 'Parachute' blundered into a large bush-covered sort of pit, which threw me considerably behind, and, when I emerged, I saw the boar had almost reached the base of the hill, with H—— close behind him, and evidently, and with good reason, pretty sure of the spear. The fates were, however, to him adverse; for his horse, a new purchase, could not be induced to face the pig. This gave me a chance; and, cramming in the spurs and scrambling up over the boulder-strewn side of the hill, I just managed to spear the boar (though somewhat far back) as he disappeared into the thick brushwood. Riding him further was impossible, for the cover was too thick; so, on the rest of the party coming up, we awaited the arrival of the beaters, who, on forming line, and beating round the hill, found the boar stone dead on the further side. The spear had entered his lungs, and he had died from internal hemorrhage. His tusks were most symmetrical, and, mounted, form nearly a perfect circle.

The following are the dimensions of a very handsome boar I assisted in killing at a place called Seroor, near Nagpore: Height, thirty-four and a half inches; length, taken from snout, along the back, to root of tail, eight feet two inches; length of tail, not including bristles at the end, eleven and a half inches; girth at shoulder, four feet six inches; tusks, seven and three-quarter inches. Sows—for, owing to a scarcity of boars, and owing to the depredations of the porcine tribe, we were sometimes obliged to ride them—as a rule, measured about twenty-nine to thirty inches, though I have speared one myself measuring thirty-two inches; and there were in the 'Hunt Book' above referred to instances of some measuring thirty-three inches. I have heard of boars measuring forty inches, and even forty-two inches, and of tusks twelve and thirteen inches long; but those must have been obtained in a more favoured part of the country, and the accounts flavoured *cum grano* as far as the tusks were concerned; for, as far as my little experience goes, even a thirty-four incher is a monster.

If any of my readers will take the trouble to mark out the measurements of the Seroor boar I have mentioned on a blank wall, and roughly fill in the outline with a bit of charcoal-stick, it will give him some idea of what a good-sized boar is, viz., an animal nearly three feet high, and over nine feet in length; and, when it is taken into consideration that these large-sized animals are speared often off a horse only about fourteen hands in height, or some four feet ten inches, it will be seen that hog-hunting is no mere child's play, but requires nerve, firmness, decision, and coolness—all qualities most necesssary for him who would succeed in the pursuit of the big game of India; but in none, I dare venture to state, are these qualities more indispensable than in the noble sport of hog-hunting.

And now, having given these few hints, let me conclude by relating a few pig-sticking anecdotes, and I think when you have read them, if you honour me so far by perusing these pages, you will allow that, for fierce, impetuous courage, dogged pluck, cunning, and rapidity both of movement and action, the wild boar of India has few, if any, equals amongst the beasts of the chase, and that, in the words of *the* hog-hunter's song, 'The Boar,'

> ' Youth's daring spirit, manhood's fire,
>   Firm hand, and eagle eye
>   Must he acquire who doth aspire
>   To see the grey boar die.'

As a proof of the boar's savage courage, combined with cunning, I will relate the following instance which occurred with the Nagpore Hunt (of which I was a member, though not present at the time). It happened on Christmas Day, 1869, and was thus graphically described by one of the party in a letter to the *Pioneer*. The writer signed himself ' Sport,' but was a well-known member of the Hunt, and a hard rider. He says :

'Last Christmas Day we beat a "sind-bund" (date-grove) that branched in two directions, and posted ourselves at the head of one branch under some mango-trees. A boar was signalled as having broken back, and riding about half-a-mile —the chase commencing with a pretty water-jump that brought two of our party to grief—we came on the boar just as he was breaking out, and, of course, in again he went. For about an hour he led us a life, making feints of breaking at various points, obliging us to cross and re-cross the difficult and boggy nullah along which the cover winds, at last coming out with us in close pursuit near our original post, and he just succeeded in getting into some thick bushes in time. We put "Stumps" (a terrier) in to turn him out, which the plucky little dog did so effectually that the boar broke out with a rush, straight at one of our party, who found his horse badly ripped behind, before he had time to put down his spear, the boar again retiring into some bush-cover close by. "Stumps" not being successful in dislodging him from this second retreat, another of our party with a shot-gun mounted on a camel (we had no elephants) came up. The camel advanced bravely; "where ignorance is bliss," etc., but the boar, charging straight at its legs, completely routed the whole arrangement, knocked over and ripped the camel (in what in a horse would be termed the stifle-joint), which broke its leg in falling, and had to be destroyed, and then made away across some dhál-fields, getting some quarter-of-a-mile start unperceived, whilst we were wofully contemplating the success of his last attack. On our coming up, he charged at once, and was speared twice, the second time carrying the spear with him into another piece of bush-cover. Making sure he could not escape, we dismounted, and beat through the cover, but he had slipped away through some long grass down a nullah, and was never seen again.'

On another occasion a curious incident occurred which I am afraid some of my readers will read *cum grano*. I can only say that, though I was not an eye-witness of the affair, it was related to me shortly after by a brother-officer and several others who were present, and who vouched for the truth of the statement. I see no reason to doubt their word, for fact is indeed often stranger than fiction. This incident occurred in 1871, at a place near Nagpore called Warree,—in August, if I remember rightly. A large boar was started, and managed to reach a patch of 'sindee' (a sort of low-growing prickly palm), whether wounded or not, I forget. However, here the sportsmen surrounded him, waiting for the beaters to come up. This they soon did, headed by old Manajee, the Hunt shikari. He forthwith waxed valiant, and, picking up some clods of earth, advanced into an opening in the bushes, and began his bombardment of the pig's retreat. A few discharges were sufficient to bring his porcine majesty out, and he charged straight at Manajee, whom he promptly upset, cutting him on his hand. That old gentleman began to forthwith yell 'blue murder,' only in Hindustani.

On hearing his cries, one of the party named Going (I give his name to vouch for the truth of this statement, and, should he cast eyes on these pages, I trust he will forgive me for the liberty I have taken in making use of his name), a very light weight, jumped off his horse, and ran in on foot, spear in hand, to Manajee's rescue. That old gentleman promptly scrambled out of the way, and the boar charged Mr. Going, knocked him over, and began digging away at his prostrate form. Luckily he had on a pair of stout English cords, and, though the boar cut him several times on his thighs, the wounds were not serious.

As an Englishman, the fallen sportsman made use of his fists as his only weapons of defence, his spear having been knocked out of his hands, but, these being of slight avail against the boar's hard head, he had the presence of mind to seize the animal by the ears, and, scrambling up, *jumped on his back!* The boar, astonished at this novel burden, tried to retreat backwards into the bushes, but a good dig from his rider's spurs dissuaded him, and, in less time than it takes me to write it, the rest of the party dismounted, and, rushing in, soon put the boar *hors de combat*, one energetic sportsman in his excitement running his spear right through the boar, and actually pricking Mr. Going's leg on the off side! To further corroborate the truth of this story, I will venture, with many apologies to them for doing so, to name two other gentlemen who took part in the scuffle, viz., Lieutenant (now Major) West R.H.A., and Ensign (now Major) Chalmers of the 79th Highlanders. I regret that I forget the names of others present on the occasion.

During this same trip I also heard of another instance of a boar's courage. Lieutenant (now Major) West, R.H.A., speared a very large boar (a thirty-seven incher, I think), his spear stuck for a moment, and the boar, with the spear in him, charged at his antagonist, and actually *stood up* on his hind legs with his fore-feet on the sportsman's horse's withers in his endeavour to reach his foe.

A dear old friend and keen hog-hunter once told me the following anecdote, which I give as nearly as possible in his own words. 'We were riding a very fine boar that had every chance of saving his life, for he was unwounded, on bad ground, and within sixty yards at most of thick cover. He suddenly turned on the foremost rider, whose horse, swerving, caused him to miss his spear. The boar then charged his second foeman, who was my servant, carrying a spare spear, mounted on a very valuable Arab. To my horror I saw the pig get right under the horse, who jumped over him, and kicked him hard in the ribs, my servant, a Mussulman, swearing freely, but not using his weapon. The distance to the boar's haven was now so diminished that he had only to cross a narrow cart track, up which I was coming at best speed to reach it. Seeing me he turned, and charged home in a most determined manner, as only a hog can charge, springing almost off the ground and cutting my mare on the stifle in his rush on the spear.'

What other *unwounded* animal would have gone out of his way to meet and charge in succession three armed and mounted horsemen?

I once saw a lanky barren sow bite a man very severely. She had afforded us a good run, and had been repeatedly speared and was sinking back on her haunches in the act of expiring. One of the party who had been thrown out in consequence of a fall, at this moment came cantering up, and as he passed the pig, ran his spear through her to finish her off; upon which she seized him by the right foot, making her teeth meet, and dragging him off his horse; and she actually died with her foe's foot in her mouth! The wounded sportsman, a good and keen man, was some months laid up in consequence. On two other occasions I have seen sows act in precisely the same manner, though in these other cases the wounds were not of such a serious nature.

One of the first boars I ever rode, I saw during the run, and whilst unspeared, go out of his way to charge and knock over in succession two bullocks out of a herd that were feeding in a patch of rumnah grass! He then got into a patch of very thick 'sindee' bushes, where I could just catch the twinkle of his wicked brown eye. I rode in as far as I could, but could not reach him by some six feet, and though I did all I could to provoke him to charge, he declined, knowing the strength of his position. I happened to take my eyes off him only for an instant, and in that instant, though several of us were watching the nullah where the cover grew, he vanished like magic, and it was only by the merest chance that we ever saw him again! How such a large beast, for he was a thirty-four and a half incher, could have stolen away without disturbing a leaf or making the slightest noise is a wonder. Here was an instance not only of courage, but courage tempered with cunning and judgment!

I remember once assisting at the death of a boar who had been several times speared, besides having three spears broken *in* him before he succumbed, and then it was found that for some time he had been fighting with his jaws and lips completely useless, they having been pinned together, as it were by the first spear broken in him. I once had a capital scuffle with a boar by myself. I was the only member of the Hunt who turned up at a place called Sonegaon, some eighteen miles from Kamptee. However, as beaters were ready, and a sounder of hog was marked down, I determined to see what I could do. The ground was fearful, nothing but a mass of hills covered with rocks and stones, a maze of nullahs of all sizes, and a quantity of stunted brushwood. Added to this, it was a fearfully hot day, and there was not a particle of shade nearer than the camp, some two miles distant.

Well, the hog were soon started, and I 'laid in' to the biggest, a nice young boar. I rode him about half-a-mile, when he got into a fearfully rough bit of ground, covered with scrub, and, having to do all I could to keep my horse on his legs, I lost sight of the animal. However, catching sight of a small pool of water some distance ahead, I rode on, thinking the boar might have gone there for a drink and a wallow. My surmise proved correct, for, on getting up to it, there was my friend, who promptly decamped on seeing me. I soon got up to and closed with him on the side of a steep hill. Here I speared him, but the spear-head sticking between his ribs, I was unable to withdraw it, and it got round behind my back. —the boar all the time digging away at and trying to cut my horse, a dear old favourite called 'Parachute,' who, getting sick of this game, suddenly let fly both heels at the boar, knocking him over, and sending him rolling down the hill, and nearly upsetting me. The boar trotted off with the spear in him, but it soon fell out, and, dismounting, I picked it up and again went at him, when the same sort of scene was enacted, old 'Parachute,' however, this time 'milling' with both fore and hind feet. My stirrup-leather breaking, I had to let go the spear to save tumbling off on to the top of the now infuriated boar, who, however, trotted off with the spear, and, retiring into some thick bushes on the slope of the hill, lay down.

The beaters soon after came up and I dismounted, getting a fresh spear, and, accompanied by old Manjaree (the Hunt shikari) carrying a spare spear, I crawled in under the bushes on my hands and knees. As I approached the boar he charged straight on to the spear, nearly knocking me over. I managed, however, to hold him off for a moment, and as we reached, during the *mêlée*, a spot which was slightly more open, I jumped up on to my feet, and Manajee opportunely handing me the spare spear, I drove it with all my might into the boar, who was now getting weak from loss of blood, and had the satisfaction of seeing my gallant foe roll slowly over and expire with a surly grunt of defiance.

I think these few anecdotes, which I could considerably multiply were I not afraid of wearying my readers, will tend to show that hog-hunting is essentially a manly sport, and that to partake in it successfully both horse and rider must have pluck, nerve, and judgment, for all these qualities will be called into play. In conclusion let me devote a few lines with regard to the horses used for hog-hunting. They are of all sorts—Arabs, Walers (as Australian horses are called), Persians, country-breds, and even occasionally a good 'tattoo,' or pony, is pressed into the service. Of course, if you can afford the long price that a good Arab generally commands, there is nothing like him. He is very sure-footed over bad ground, can stand heat, hard work, and knocking about, has an excellent constitution, and, though generally very gentle, is exceedingly high-couraged, a very necessary quality for a hog-hunter. Walers are also good, though in many instances they do not stand heat and the rains so well as Arabs, and as a rule their tempers are more uncertain. Certainly they have greater speed, but I think most old pig-stickers will bear me out in the assertion that they will not stand the knocking about an Arab will. Persian horses are occasionally very good and hardy, but are blessed with vile tempers. Of country-breds I have not a good word to say. To my mind they combine all the bad qualities of all breeds, with none of the good ones, and I have seen very few that, in my opinion, were worth their keep as hunters.

I have ridden, and taken first spears off all three of the former, viz., Arabs, Walers, and Persians, and also off a good pony; but for choice give me the Arab. Few men, however, can afford to give a long price for a valuable Arab, and run the risk of laming or screwing him after a hog; but there is no doubt that, if you can afford the money, he will carry you better than any other breed. Good horses are often picked up cheaply, or used to be in my day, at the sale of cast-horses from the Artillery and Cavalry. They may be real good, sound horses, and only cast for some little fault that makes them unsuitable for military work. One of the best animals I ever knew was a Waler mare, cast from the artillery for restiveness. She turned out a grand hunter, and only cost her owner one hundred and fifty rupees, or about fifteen pounds. This mare afterwards won steeple-chases at Secunderabad, Bangalore, and Madras, against some of the best horses in Southern India. A horse is, however, as a rule, what his rider makes him, and the saying that 'there is no bond of union so close as that between a horse and his rider,' is a very true one. Horses learn to love hog-hunting, and take their part in it, and an old hog-hunter will turn with and follow a boar like a dog—often even if riderless. My old horse that I have alluded to used to do this in a most ludicrous manner. On one occasion we had come down a 'buster' at a nullah, and he got away from me; following the pig with ears laid back and making grabs at it with his teeth whenever he got a chance. The other riders could not spear until they had actually beaten him off with their spear-shafts.

There are scores and scores of men more fitted by far than your humble servant, kind reader, to describe the noble sport of hog-hunting, but few, I venture to hope, who loved it more, and pursued it with more zeal and delight in spite of many difficulties and a very, very shallow purse. I do not offer these lines for the perusal of experienced sportsmen, but in the hope that any young man beginning his career in the 'glorious East' may be induced thereby to take to hog-hunting. Depend upon it, if he does, it will benefit him both mentally and bodily, and keep him out of much mischief, and perhaps subsequent sorrow.

CHAPTER VI.

FAREWELL TO THE SPEAR.

A Last Day—The Meet—Offer of a Mount—The 'Caster'—Not so Black as he's Painted—Exciting Bit of News—Efforts to Dislodge the Game—'Muzzle'—Change our Tactics—The Panther Breaks—Race for the Spear—'There's Many a Slip'—My Turn—Failure—Success—Danger of Beaters—The 'Caster' Declines—A Beater Mauled—On Foot in the Bajree—'Muzzle' Comes to the Rescue—Death of the Panther—A Plucky Youngster—The Colonel and the Cubs—Quotations from Major Shakespear—Advice.

'The Rifle knows my hand no more,
 Adieu to Spur and Spear.'

I LITTLE thought some decade and a half ago when I heard the above lines quoted, how applicable they would be in my own case. I well remember the day—a jolly party at the artillery mess at Kamptee—on the eve of my last day's hog-hunting, and one which turned out about the most exciting day's sport I ever experienced. My regiment was to start for home in a few days, and the Nagpore Hunt, of which I was a member, had organized a farewell meet in honour of my brother-officers and myself who had been members of the Hunt. Personally, though delighted at the prospect of again being once more in Old England, my delight was tinged with a shade of regret at leaving the land where I had made good friends, such friends as are only made by the brotherhood of sport, and where I had spent some happy years, and seen for a youngster a varied and good amount of sport, and the tamer sports of the West, in prospect, contrasted somewhat unfavourably in my mind with the grander and wilder ones of the East I was leaving behind. However, a truce to moralizing. Let us come to the point, and I will endeavour with the best abilities of an unskilled penman to describe the events of a day, which in my sporting calendar and in my memory must ever be marked with a very red stone, for on that day I had the good fortune to participate in—nay, obtain ' honours ' in—a form of sport that does not very often fall to the share of many votaries of the chase.

It was on the 21st of September, 1871, that the Nagpore Hunt met at a place called Ghonee, and two friends had kindly sent on horses for me. Behold us then a merry party of some ten or twelve assembled round the breakfast-table in a large tent pitched under a giant banyan-tree. At the conclusion of the meal, an old colonel in the Madras staff-corps, a keen sportsman, but more noted for his good shooting than for the quality of his horse-flesh, called me aside and asked me if I would mind riding a horse of his that day. Knowing the dear old gentleman's character, I was not particularly keen to accede to his request; but eventually consented. He then informed me that my mount was an awful savage; that he had bought him as a cast-horse from the artillery (from which I found he had been cast for debility) for the sum of two rupees! and that he could not do anything with him; that when he attempted to mount, the brute bit at him, and before he got fairly seated in the saddle, there was such an amount of bucking, kicking, rearing, and every form of equine gymnastics, that it invariably ended by the old gentleman being deposited on the ground.

'Well,' I thought, 'this is a pleasant prospect. It would be just like my luck to get my neck broken by the brute just as I'm going home.'

However, I had not much choice after having given my promise, and so said I would do my best not to let the 'caster' get rid of me. Soon after the redoubtable animal was brought up. I said I would ride him first, thinking that I would only do so on the way to our first beat, and then could easily change him for a more tractable mount when the real business of the day began.

Now a word to describe my mount. He was a black or very dark-brown Waler, or Australian gelding, standing about fifteen hands three inches, with clean flat legs, muscular quarters, and thighs well let down, a lean, game head, and well set on neck with good sloping shoulders, a trifle slack in his loins, perhaps, but still an animal showing a deal of breeding and power. He was in wretched condition; every rib showed out clear and distinct, and one might almost have hung one's hat on his great ragged hips. He had on a regular buck-jumping saddle with knee and thigh rolls and surcingle, a great heavy double bit, and a running martingale. Going up to him, I patted and spoke to him, and after a snort or two on his part with ears pricked forward (not laid back as a really vicious horse would), he let me pick up his feet, feel his girths, and handle him all over. This I thought was a step gained, so I had the martingale removed, and the heavy, severe bit replaced by a plain, double-rimmed, smooth snaffle. Of course I was on the look-out for any tricks on his part, and getting a friend to give me a leg up, was soon in the saddle, and, pressing him with my legs, the 'caster' walked off in the most steady and sedate manner.

The walk soon became a trot, and, feeling delighted with the horse's springy action, I touched him with the spur, and gave him a spin of some half-a-mile. The further I went, the more I was pleased with my mount. He answered his bit, and turned and twisted like a pony; and such charming action I had seldom felt. As I pulled him up to return to the rest of the party, I met a 'ryot' running along in a great state of perturbation.

'Sahib,' he said, 'in yonder patch of sindee-bushes* there is a tigress and three cubs, who has terrified your slave; for, as long as she stays there, I dare not cultivate my fields.'

On further interrogation, the man seemed so positive as to the truth of his statement that I cantered back, and told the captain of the Hunt, who determined to beat the cover indicated, which lay in our way to the place we had originally intended beginning at. It was only a small patch of sindee-bushes, with two or three giant mango-trees growing out of its centre. The ground on all sides was level and open, and consisted of 'dhall' and grain fields, with here and there a field of 'bajree,' a sort of millet that

* Phœnix farinifera.

attains a height of some seven or eight feet, and in growth much resembles sugar-cane. Some two miles away lay a ridge of low, rocky hills, clothed with thick scrub jungle. So, taking all surroundings into consideration, no more favourable ground could be found for riding and spearing a tiger, if tiger there was.

This feat—rarely attempted, and still more rarely effected, by Indian sportsmen—we determined to attempt. The beat was accordingly formed, but hardly had the beaters commenced when they all rushed out, vowing the tigress was there, and that she was in a very bad temper. I must confess I myself, and one or two others who had seen some tiger-shooting, were rather sceptical about its being a tiger at all. However, the beaters' positive assurance, coupled with their firmly but politely declining to enter the cover again, rather staggered us. We determined, therefore, to go in on foot ourselves, some of us taking our spears, whilst others covered our advance with shot-guns and rifles. The gallant army therefore advanced, the 'spearmen' shouting, and throwing stones into the thickest parts of the cover, whilst every now and then a charge of shot was fired into any extra thick place. Nothing, however, appeared, and, on arriving at the far end, it was voted unanimously that our informant was a lying rascal, and deserved a good licking! One of the party, however, mentioned as the 'hero of the hog's-back' in a previous chapter, had a wonderful old dog, half Polygar, half bulldog, warranted to tackle *anything*, and rejoicing in the name of 'Muzzle.' It was suggested that Muzzle should be asked to decide the vexed question; and, accordingly, he was sent for. He soon arrived, and, on reaching the edge of the cover, began straining and tugging at his leash in a manner that augured well for our hopes. Giving orders to the dog-boy to loose him when he heard a shout, we proceeded to post ourselves.

The party was divided into two, one half being under the orders of the captain of the Hunt, whilst the remainder were placed under my command; and my party took up their position at the low end of the cover, some hundred yards away, at the edge of an awkward, boggy nullah. All being in readiness, the signal was given, and Muzzle being released he dashed into cover, with a low whimper. Presently, I saw something, which turned out to be a fine panther* (not a tiger), sneak out, and advance towards us down the nullah. Catching sight of us, however, she sprang out, and dashed away across the open, making for a field of dhall that lay some quarter-

* Felis **Pardus**.

of-a-mile ahead. Letting her get well away, I gave the word to 'ride,' and, having previously selected an easy place to cross the nullah, got a good start. I had got within some ten yards of the panther—who was now close to the dhall-field—when the owner of Muzzle, a very light weight, and excellent horseman, mounted on a very fast Arab, came past me with a rush, and all my hopes of obtaining the coveted first spear vanished! As he leaned forward to spear, his stirrup-leather broke! This caused him to miss, and he nearly came off. The panther dashed into the dhall with me close behind it, and almost immediately crouched between the rows of dhall. As I galloped up, and was preparing to deliver my spear, my large sun-hat, or 'solah-topee,' as they are called, caught by a gust of wind from behind, came over my eyes; and the consequent result was I missed. As I went past, I felt a decided creepy sensation, knowing that, ten to one, the panther would spring on me, or on my horse's back, from behind, when I should, in my blinded condition, be practically defenceless.

Luck, however, once more came to my rescue, for she (it proved a female panther) did nothing of the kind; and the 'caster' answering his bit, and allowing me to turn him round almost instantly, I dashed off the offending hat, and again got up to her before any of my opponents. The caster's superior speed had at the outset enabled him to keep the good start I had obtained, and my only dangerous rival, the owner of Muzzle, was practically *hors-de-combat*. Again the panther crouched, but this time I could choose my time; and, galloping past, I speared her through the loins. On receiving the spear, she at once scuttled off, and gained the shelter of a sort of blind lane that led in the direction of the cover where we had found her. Here she took refuge on the top of one of the banks, under a thick mass of thorns. The beaters, who had followed us *en masse*, now came running up towards her, though on the field side of the lane, shouting and yelling. They, of course, were unaware of their danger, and, though I shouted myself hoarse in trying to warn them, the din they were making made my voice inaudible. I felt sure mischief would ensue, so, though the panther lay on my bridle-hand, and so would oblige me to spear over-hand, always a risky proceeding, I determined to do so, and, squeezing the 'caster' through a thorny gap, I dropped into the lane. The panther was plainly visible to me in the lane, though the approaching beaters could not see her.

As soon as I tried starting the 'caster,' he declined, and a nice game of romps we had in the narrow confines of the lane. He kicked, bucked, reared, turned round and round every way but the one I wanted him; and whilst all this was going on, in less time than it takes to write it, some of the rest of the party found their way into the lane, and came riding down shouting to me to point out the whereabouts of the animal. This, of course, I was unable to do in the excited state my steed was in, and I could only yell out vague directions. The beaters were now close up, and making an awful din, when, with a crash of the bushes and an angry, 'wough-wough!' the panther charged straight out at them. There was a shout of fear and warning as they all scattered, and then above all rose a terrified scream, followed for one instant by a muffled, worrying sound. This was too much for me, so, jumping off the 'caster,' and leaving him to his own sweet devices, I scrambled over the fence into the field. There was the crowd some distance off, massed together and shouting, but, nigger-like, doing nothing to assist the prostrate form of a stricken man whom the panther was standing over, and shaking by the shoulder savagely, as a terrier would a rat.

As I ran up, she let go, and retreated into a high field of 'bajree,' which was adjacent. Like a young ass that I was, I promptly followed her,

"SHE TURNED AND SEIZED THE SHAFT BETWEEN HER TEETH."

and, after forcing my way in a few yards, came right on her, crouching and snarling, looking like a great big angry cat. Fortunately for me, the place where I found myself was to a certain extent open, the long stalks of the 'bajree' having been trodden down, probably by a 'sounder' of hog, whilst engaged in a midnight foray. This allowed me free play for my spear, and, rushing in, I drove the blade clean through her, pinning her to the ground. She turned at once and seized the shaft between her teeth, and it would probably have been soon all up with me, but at that moment up came old Muzzle, and without an instant's hesitation went straight at my foe, seizing her by the throat, and getting his own hindquarters fastened on to by the panther.

This scuffle had lasted, I suppose, about half-a-minute, which seemed an age to me, when two or three more of the party came up, and soon finished her off. Pulling the brute out of the the thick 'bajree,' Muzzle still holding on, and refusing to let go until ordered by his master, we then proceeded to look at the wounded man, whom we found in a mortal funk, thinking he was going to die. He had been badly bitten through the shoulder and a good deal clawed; so, presenting him with a handsome douceur, we sent him off to the hospital at Nagpore, some four miles distant, to have his wounds dressed. We found another among the list of wounded—a small boy about ten, who had got an ugly scratch down his posterior from the panther during her first rush out; but he was a plucky little chap, pooh-poohed his hurt, said he 'was going to be a shikari some day, and mustn't mind a scratch like that;' and he did not, and went on beating all day. Needless to say, he was not forgotten at pay-time.

The 'caster' was soon caught, and, with his reputation made, was led back to camp, though I did not say anything of how the brute 'cut it' at a critical moment. We then went on and had a beat for hog, and accounted for three, and I managed to get one first spear. The 'caster's' owner went back to look for the panther's cubs. He came across one lying under some thorns over a bank, and, as he was on foot, tried to catch it by taking off his coat and throwing it over it; but, the dear old gentleman's specs coming off at the critical moment, he made a bad shot, missed getting the cub, and only instead got his face, hands, and knees full of thorns. Such was my last bit of shikar in the 'gorgeous East'—a good termination, I think you will allow, reader, to some few years of varied sport, good fellowship, and happy youth.

I cannot, I think, conclude these lines more

appropriately than with a quotation from the pen of that well-known and gallant shikari, the *late*, I am afraid, Major Henry Shakespear—one of the best men on horse or foot, with spear or rifle, among the many good men that the Indian army is associated with. He says, 'The training that makes a sportsman makes a soldier; it gives him endurance, and ability to stand exposure to the sun and climate; it gives him an eye for country and familiarity with danger . . . . and I could mention names of men who have been well-known for their courage and skill in all noble wood-craft, who have from their early days followed the pursuits recommended in this book,* with advantage to their own health, and, what is of more consequence, to the benefit of mankind in general.' Never were truer words written. Do you, oh, young man, if ever you condescend to read these poor literary attempts of mine, follow the advice given above, and when, like me, you are incapacitated, either through circumstances or health, from again sharing in the darling sports of your youth, you will, on recalling them, be able to think with pleasure on 'the days that are no more.'

* 'The Wild Sports of India,' by Major H. Shakespear.

CHAPTER VII.

BLACK-BUCK SHOOTING.

Black-Buck Shooting—Spearing Wounded Antelopes—An Unsuccessful Gallop—A Plucky Buck—Stalking, and Other Methods of Pursuit—Ground Antelope are Found on—Snaring—My First Black Buck—Empty Pockets—A Novel *Coup-de-Grâce*—Circumventing a Wary Herd—Strategy—A Long Shot at Dusk—Curious Effect of a Bullet—Chikara, or Ravine-Deer—Their Habitat and Horns—Concluding Remarks.

WITHIN a ride of most Indian stations, the Indian antelope (antelope bezoartica) is found in more or less abundance, and affords capital sport both with rifle and spear; in fact, they may sometimes be bowled over with a charge of shot, and I have frequently bagged them in this manner when beating sugar-cane fields for black partridges and hares in the vicinity of Delhi.*

* This graceful antelope is too well known to need a detailed description, beyond mentioning that the female differs from the buck in being of a fawn colour, and hornless. The horns varying in length from nineteen to twenty-six inches, and the largest are ob-

The real and most sportsman-like manner however of pursuing them is to stalk, and shoot them with a rifle, having a horse and spear handy, when, if wounded, you can ride them down. Instances are recorded of unwounded antelopes being ridden down—but I never saw an instance of this, and, though I frequently tried to accomplish the feat, it invariably ended in failure and disappointment. I believe that in the recorded instances where unwounded antelopes have been speared, it has been during the rains, when the black cotton soil is heavy, and saturated with moisture. Into such ground the narrow foot of the antelope sinks more readily than a horse's, and so causes him to fall a comparatively easy prey to his pursuers.

Some of the best runs I have ever had with a spear have been after wounded antelopes, and I know of no termination to a successful shot more satisfactory than a gallop of this description. I was once most ignominiously beaten by a young wounded buck when trying to ride him down. I had the day previously fired at and hit him; but having no horse with me, and the light failing,

tained in Northern India and Goozerat. I never shot one myself with horns exceeding twenty-one inches, but I have seen a pair that measured twenty-five inches, and heard on very good authority of a pair measuring twenty-six and a half inches. These were shot in Goozerat.

for it was late on in the evening, I had to give up the pursuit. The following morning I thought I would go out and ride him down. I soon found my friend, who got out of a cotton-field not far from where I had lost sight of him the previous evening, and being mounted on an old Arab hog-hunter, famous for his staying powers, I 'laid in.' One of the buck's fore legs was broken, and I could see it swinging as he went dotting along on three legs. I did not press him much at first, thinking my task would be an easy one, and that when we got on better ground I should soon run up to and spear him. This better ground, consisting of a stretch of plain between the patches of cultivation, was soon reached, and then I woke up the old horse. The buck, however, still kept ahead of me, and, do what I would, I could not succeed in diminishing the distance between us. However, the wounded muscles must have relaxed as he warmed with exercise, and, after going some three miles, he got on broken ground, and amongst a network of nullahs, amid which I lost sight of him, and had to confess myself beaten.

I remember another occasion, where the riding down of a wounded buck might have been attended with fatal consequences to my horse. I had wounded a very fine old black buck, and had had a good gallop after him till I ran him to a shallow pond into which he rushed, and stood at bay. I rode in after him, the water reaching nearly to my girths, and on getting within some three or four yards of him down went his head, and he came at me most viciously. Luckily for me, however, as he got his long spiral horns almost under my horse's belly, his feet stuck in some bit of extra tenacious mud, and caused him to halt for a moment, and I seized the opportunity to spear him, and then, jumping off quickly, seized him by the horns and plunged my shikar knife into his throat.

It must have been a curious scene to any onlooker: the wounded buck and myself, struggling and floundering about in the muddy water, and my horse calmly quenching his thirst close by, whilst the setting sun in the background was sinking to rest in a flood of rosy light!

The stalking of antelope on the arid and burning plains of India is to my mind a greater test of a sportsman's capabilities in the art of 'venerie' than stalking the noble red-deer among the heathery braes and rocky corries of bonnie Scotland. In the latter you have the advantage of numerous inequalities of ground, besides another very important assistance in the shape of a less delusive atmosphere, for in the quivering haze caused by the fierce rays of the Indian sun reflected by the parched ground, objects appear much closer than they really are. This causes you to misjudge the distance between you and your quarry, and, ergo! the result is often a miss. I am speaking of some years ago, when Express rifles were not so much used as they are now. Of course, with the low trajectory of an Express this latter disadvantage is considerably reduced.

If the suspicions of the antelope are not roused, and there is any cover to be taken advantage of in the shape of nullahs, patches of grass, or detached bushes, they may be generally approached without very much difficulty; but given a bare, open plain, without a scrap of cover to hide even a hare, it is quite another thing, and on these occasions man must match the intelligence and inventive genius of the human brain against the cunning of the animal.

A good plan is to pretend to wish to pass on, and on no account look at them, as they are feeding in a certain direction, when they will of their own accord often cross the sportsman. If once they imagine a man wants to conceal himself, or if they lose sight of him for a moment, it is most difficult to obtain a shot. The does, as with most other animals, are the most suspicious and inquisitive, and if a herd is on the move it may be stopped for a moment or two by a low whistle.

They stop, stare, then there is an impatient stamping of feet, and presently the whole herd is off, taking those graceful stotting bounds so well known to the Indian sportsman.

There are numerous dodges of approaching a herd which perhaps from having often been shot at show signs of alarm, such as arraying oneself in a native blanket, and walking in a circle round the herd, stopping every now and then and pretending to be gathering grass, like a native grass-cutter.

Another good method of getting within shot is to walk on the far side of a native cart which is driven past the herd in a circle that is gradually lessened; but none of these methods will recommend themselves to the true sportsman, who will prefer to kill his game fair and square, if possible.

If, however, a man wishes to obtain a particularly good pair of horns, and cannot spare the time to devote a long day to the sport, a very good plan is to take up a position before dawn in their usual route to their feeding grounds; the grunting of the bucks will warn the sportsman of their approach, and he will be able to select one bearing a good head.

The best plan, however, to my mind, is always to go out on a steady horse with your syce, or groom, carrying a spear. On sighting the herd, and getting, say, within a quarter-of-a-mile of them, slip off your horse, and walk on his far side in such a direction as will take you past the herd within shot, and, if possible, with the wind blowing from the herd towards you. Let your groom lead your horse, and when any convenient cover offers itself, drop behind it, and let the horse be led on. The antelope will probably be so intent on watching the horse and man that they will possibly not notice you, and you will be enabled to creep up within one hundred or one hundred and fifty yards.

One great advantage of employing a horse in stalking is, that it will enable you to follow up and spear your quarry should you only wound it.

The black buck is never found in thick, uncleared jungle, and seems to follow the march of civilization, for where jungle has been cleared and planted with crops to any extent, there it will be found. In all the corn districts of Central India it is found in great abundance, and in the North-west Provinces, in Goojerat, and in Bhurtpore in Northern India vast herds will be met with. In most cultivated districts there are large tracts of grazing ground, and these are generally the favourite resorts of black buck, from whence at night time they sally forth and commit sad havoc by grazing on the young wheat and grain, returning to their coign of vantage in the covertless ground with the first grey streak of dawn. Some, however, remain in the fields all day sleeping and grazing at intervals, and the whereabouts of a lordly buck may often be ascertained by keeping a sharp look-out, when his horns may be seen projecting above the cotton plants amidst which he is taking his mid-day siesta. They often lie up, too, during the day in fields of sugar-cane and bajree, a high grain that attains a height of six or seven feet. In such places the cultivators usually erect platforms, whereon a watcher sits all night, keeping up a continual shouting to keep the antelope off the crops. It is doubtful, however, if they do much good, as in course of time the wily animal comes to disregard these shouts, and merely keeps moving about, taking a bite here and there, and in reality doing more damage than if allowed to remain quiet and blow himself out.

Natives often snare antelopes, and they are also caught by means of a tame and trained buck, who, having nooses fastened on his horns, sallies forth. He soon engages a wild buck in single combat, and so manages as to interlace the nooses that are attached to his own horns round those of his wild brother, until his owner comes up, and administers the *coup-de-grâce*. These methods, however, I have never personally seen practised, and so am unable to give any detailed description of them.

The first black buck I ever killed was finished off in such a novel manner, that it may not be out of place to narrate the incident.

I had but a short time previously landed in India, after a weary five months voyage round the Cape, and was on my way up country, with a draft, to join my regiment, then stationed at Roorkee.

Between Meerut and Roorkee there is a large tract of flat, sandy country, in which antelopes abound.

I had no rifle, only a sixteen-bore muzzle-loading shot-gun, and my youthful sporting ardour was fired by the sight of countless herds of these graceful antelopes. I had had many a futile shot with the old gun, loaded with ball, but the distance always proved too great to result in success. On this particular day, I had blazed away all my bullets except one, which was in my left barrel, and was returning to camp in moody silence, wishing, oh! so much, that my means would permit of my indulging myself by buying a good rifle, when, as I topped the brow of a low sandhill, a fine black buck jumped up almost under my feet.

Of course I let drive, and, to my delight, over he rolled. But, alas! my delight was only turned to bitter disappointment, as he picked himself up, and went off apparently uninjured. I was inexperienced in shikar in those days; and, knowing he was hit, I ran after him.

Needless to say, the further I went, the further I was left behind, and at last my quarry disappeared over a low ridge of sandhills some half-mile ahead, leaving me pumped, very hot, tired, and done to a turn!

Do you not know, reader, the feeling of bitter disappointment, when, in sport, the prize that is to reward you for your toil seems almost within your grasp? and yet there comes that one little slip between the cup and the lip which makes all the difference between sending you home happy and contented, and at peace with all the world, or disgusted, uncharitable, and disposed to eschew sport in general, and that individual one in particular in which you have been unsuccessful! If so, you can imagine my feelings.

Well, I strolled on, after a rest and a pipe, the consumption of which, I suppose, took perhaps a quarter-of-an-hour; and, under the circumstances, this got me my buck. For, once out of sight, he lay down, and his getting stiff from his wounds and exertions caused him eventually to fall a prey to me.

To resume, however. I sauntered on in the

direction he had gone, with no hopes of seeing him again, till, on gaining the summit of the ridge where he had disappeared, I saw, some three hundred yards below me on the plain, a dark object, apparently motionless.

Could this be my buck? My hopes revived. But, alas! they were soon dashed to the ground: for, even if it was, I had nothing wherewith to administer the *coup-de-grâce*. Knife I had not with me; my bullets were all expended. There was not even a stone that I could load my gun with, as a substitute for a bullet! Vainly I felt in all my pockets for a missile of some sort. Vain and bloodthirsty visions of strangling my victim, if I could only get hold of him, arose in my mind! Again I turned out my pockets. 'Hurrah! Eureka!' I mentally ejaculated.

Now, at the depôt it had been instilled into my mind, by means of the adjutant and a study of the 'Red Book,' that, in cases of emergency, 'numerous expedients will suggest themselves to the intelligent officer.' Here was a chance to prove, if even only for my own personal satisfaction, that I was 'intelligent' from a sporting, even were I not so from a military point of view.

My search was rewarded by finding, in the lining of my waistcoat-pocket, a four-anna bit (a small silver coin about the size of an English sixpence, only not quite as big, and worth about that sum.) Biting and bending it with my teeth, I reduced it sufficiently to enable me to hammer it down my right barrel, on top of a charge of powder; and, the wad being duly placed on top, I advanced to do battle.

The buck lay motionless till I got within some five yards of him, with his head and neck extended flat on the ground. Then, seeing he was discovered, he jumped up, floundered about, and lay down again. This went on for a few minutes, till at last the poor brute seemed quite exhausted.

Luckily for my prospects of success, I kept cool, and 'reserved my fire,' determined not to risk a shot till I could make sure.

At last the opportunity offered itself, and, walking up to the poor buck as he lay quite still, with his large, beautiful eyes fixed in a dazed, stony stare, I placed the muzzle of my gun close behind his ear, fired, and—had bagged my first buck.

In after years I had learnt more of the habits of the animal, and how he may often be bagged by the use of stratagem. Almost one of the last bucks I ever shot was obtained in this manner— when out on a hog-hunting expedition in Berar.

After the day's hunt, which had been fairly successful, we were marching on to our fresh camp, and, as custom was, had separated, shooting our way over different lines of country to the common rendezvous. Just before sunset I saw, with the aid of my binoculars, a large herd of antelope, amongst whom a fine buck seemed to hold command, and I could see him butt, and drive off every now and then, any of the younger bucks who seemed inclined to form a too intimate acquaintance with the ladies of his harem. The temptation was too great to resist, and though I had several miles to go ere I reached my destination, and daylight was failing, the shot-gun was exchanged for the rifle, and, ordering my syce to follow with my horse and spear, I set out to try and circumvent the herd. Stalking, in the ordinary sense of the word, was out of the question, for the ground at that season of the year was bare and black, and without a vestige of cover, and the only chance of approaching the game was to stroll towards them in a careless manner in the hope that they might mistake me, wrapped in my horse rug, for an itinerant native, and my horse for his baggage pony, or a bullock. The antelope were feeding quietly amongst a few scattered babool* bushes, and did not appear to notice me till I got within four hundred yards; then one by one the does began to move off in a nervous, suspicious manner. The herd was a

* Acacia Arabica.

large one, and, as is their custom, the oldest buck brought up the rear; so, showing myself as much as possible, as if either ignorant or careless of their presence, and marking the spot where they seemed likely to leave the scant cover afforded by the bushes, I walked along parallel with their course, keeping a keen watch on the buck, who seemed much disgusted at being disturbed at the commencement of his evening meal, and followed his consorts with sulky reluctance. I tried all the old dodges, but could not take *them* in, even by pretending to be a grass-cutter or an old woman gathering sticks, etc., etc. They had evidently been shot at before, and were up to all such tricks.

Suddenly a happy thought struck me. I turned away from them, and, walking back towards my horse, shouted some directions to the horse-keeper.

The ruse had a magical effect, for the leaders of the herd stopped on hearing the shouting, and, seeing only a noisy man walking apparently away from them, took it for granted he was not animated with any evil intent towards them. The head of the column having halted, the rest of the herd followed their example, the master buck taking advantage of this stoppage to administer punishment to some of the younger bucks, who, to his mind, had been guilty of some breach of antelopean discipline or etiquette. The commotion caused by this scuffle caused the herd to retrace their steps, and back they all came, some of the does passing within easy shot of me, but the buck still kept out of the way on the far side of the herd, going along at a sulky trot. It was a long shot and the light was bad, but it must be now or never; so, covering him with my rifle, I gave a shrill, sharp whistle which brought the herd up suddenly, and for an instant they stood staring at me, quite motionless, as if carved out of stone. The buck's shoulder is covered, the trigger pressed, and the rifle sends forth the leaden messenger of death.

As the smoke clears away the herd are in full flight, and soon disappear in the coming gloom—but one remains behind, kicking convulsively in the last agonies of death—and again—I have bagged my buck.

A dear old friend, a good naturalist and thorough sportsman, once told me of the curious effect of a bullet he had fired at a buck.

Whilst travelling in a palankeen on one occasion, for some reason or other he was obliged to halt for an hour or so just at dawn; so, taking his gun, a fourteen-bore smooth bore, he strolled out. The morning was misty, and he had not gone far when he found himself in the midst of a herd of antelope. Several does sprang up from the short, sweet grass on which they had been resting, and looking weird and ghost-like as they gazed on the intruder.

Presently a fine black buck followed their example, lazily stretching himself as he rose, and stood facing him about sixty yards off. My friend fired at his chest, missing that but breaking a foreleg just below it with the ball, which then passed through the hinder leg on the same side, smashing it close to the hock; the bullet then glanced into and broke the *other* hind leg, which must have been lazily stretched back as the buck, roused from his sleep, stood staring at the sportsman.

The chikara, or Indian gazelle (gazella bennettii), is another antelope common on the plains of India, though it prefers low scrub jungle to the more open plain. It is commonly known by the name of 'ravine deer,' from its habit of frequenting the banks of ravines or nullahs that so plentifully intersect the country. It is much smaller than the black buck. The male and female are both of a brown-fawn colour. The horns of the male vary from ten to thirteen inches in length, and are deeply annulated, curving slightly backwards, with the points bending forward. The female also carries horns; but they rarely exceed six inches in length, are slender, smooth, and slightly wrinkled at the base, inclining backwards with the tops bent inwards. From their peculiar colour, which harmonizes wonderfully with the ground they frequent, they often escape observation, though they sometimes attract the attention of the sportsman who would otherwise have passed them by, owing to their habit of giving a sharp hiss and stamp of the foot when alarmed. In the heat of the day they frequently lie up under bushes, or in the long grass, and as they get up very close a charge of shot will often bowl them over.

Though called 'ravine deer,' they are true antelope, and, unlike the black buck, when disturbed or shot at they never go very far, but dodge about any ravines that may be near, pursuing much the same tactics that a hare does when hunted by a pack of harriers. It is, therefore, advisable when pursuing them to note the spot where they may have disappeared into a ravine, observe the configuration of the ground, and keep a sharp lookout, when the graceful little animal will generally reappear at no great distance. The best pair of horns I ever got were those mentioned at page 219, and measured ten inches and a half; but I have seen a pair that were shot near Kamptee that measured thirteen inches. A shot can generally be obtained at a range varying from sixty to one hundred and fifty yards.

I am aware that amongst many Indian sportsmen antelope-shooting is looked down on ; but to my mind it had always a great charm, and I fancied that there was always a certain amount of patience and science which it was necessary to display if you wished to succeed.

In addition to this, it was a sport obtainable by all, and within reach of the most impecunious subaltern, for it involved no great preparation, and no expense, and, to reward you for time and labour expended, you obtained handsome trophies of the chase in the shape of horns and skins—for no real sportsman would shoot a doe (which are hornless), except when required for meat—and the exercise was beneficial to health.

On all these points, therefore, let me recommend the sport to anyone who may have the opportunity to indulge in it. Depend upon it, it is a far better manner in every way of passing the hours that often hang heavy in India, than by imbibing 'pegs,' and playing cards, as so many do.

CHAPTER VIII.

SMALL GAME SHOOTING.

Small Game Shooting—Pea-fowl—A Creep through the Jungle—Probable Disappointment—Pea-fowl Sacred to Hindoos—A Shot at Night—Spearing a Peacock—Ability of Concealment—An Upset—Best Shot to Use—Jungle-fowl—Different Species—Their Pursuit—Large Bags never Made—A Beat—The Result—Amateur Doctoring—Spur-fowl—Their Habitat—A Clever Greyhound—Spur-fowl Shooting amongst the Coffee in Ceylon.

I AM not writing for naturalists, for I have no pretensions of belonging to that scientific order. I merely offer these few notes from one sportsman to others of the same genus who may honour me by glancing over these pages.

To those mighty hunters who have bagged hecatombs of small game in the sunny clime of the East, they will prove but of little interest; but to those for whom happy shikar days are yet in store, a few hints as to the habitats, and the best mode of making a bag, may not be unacceptable. Let me begin my list, therefore, with the peacock,* firstly because he is the most gorgeous of all game, and secondly because each fresh sportsman, when first landing, longs for the time and opportunity to kill one, and obtain one of those magnificent green trains more than four feet long, which, overshadowing the true tail, makes such a handsome trophy.

If there be satisfaction—and all we shooters know that there is—in dropping a brace of partridges neatly right and left, still more in bowling over an old cock grouse in a 'drive,' as he comes past you like a bullet, and greatest of all in making a pretty shot at a woodcock as he turns and twists among the trunks and trees of a thick cover, how intense must be the glory and delight of killing a peacock!

Alas! the reality of peacock-shooting will surely disenchant anyone holding these views.

Imagine yourself, kind reader, some morning, when just at daylight close to your line of march, you hear from forest and hill all round you that wild call of 'Mee-aw, mee-aw, tok-tok,' so well known to all who have trod the paths of the jungles, and so musical to their ears; for, hear it when or how they may, it will recall many a happy day spent on mountain, or in forest, many a

* Pavo cristatus.

pleasant comrade, many a beat for large game, both successful and the reverse, passed amongst the wild scenery in which the peafowl delights.

You are forthwith fired with sporting ardour, and sally forth to obtain the coveted prize which you fondly imagine, with such numbers of the game calling all round you, will be a comparatively easy task.

How wofully disappointed, and how bitterly disgusted you will be, when, having seen from some eminence a magnificent bird feeding in a cleared patch of the jungle, you expend much time and patience in keeping up to your game through tangled thickets of thorn that not only try your temper, but damage your clothes, you at last arrive at the scene of action, only perhaps to catch a hasty glimpse of a peahen's head as she darts into the thick undergrowth!

Surely, you think, there must be a little bit of open ahead of you, and the birds are so large you are bound to get a shot as they rise, or run across the open space, and if a shot, you cannot miss.

Vain delusion. Suddenly all round, in front and rear, right and left, there arises such a flapping of wings as fairly bewilders you, and though each bird as he rises utters his loud cry of alarm, not a feather is visible.

Or perhaps you do see them as they rise. You cannot miss a thing as big as a haystack! you *must* bag a couple. You'll knock over the old cock, and get a hen with your left barrel!

'What, not down! Very odd, I heard the shot strike,' you say to yourself.

Bang! goes your left barrel without any further acknowledgment from the cock than an increased flapping of wings as the magnificent bird steadies himself in his flight, then skims over the tree-tops in that valley at your feet, and perhaps, as if to convince you that you have not damaged him much, ends up by running some fifty yards, and finally disappears from your gaze.

This sort of thing perhaps goes on for years, and each time you vow you will not trouble yourself about the brutes any more; and yet when the chance again offers itself you repeat the attempt, though probably, as in most other things by this time, you will have learnt experience, and something of the habits of the bird, and will therefore be more likely to have your latter efforts crowned with success.

There is no doubt about it that in thick jungle a peacock is a most difficult bird to circumvent, and in stalking him in such ground you must proceed with the utmost caution, and *not be in a hurry*. The quieter and more steadily you advance the greater will be the chance of your succeeding.

In the grain districts round Delhi, and in the north-west provinces, however, their pursuit is another thing. They are there so tame and so abundant that one is almost ashamed to shoot them. The Hindoos consider them sacred, and often disregard of the villagers' wishes on this subject may get one into hot water. In fact before the Mutiny peafowl shooting was forbidden by Government in many of the Hindoo states.

I remember once, coming back from a day amongst the snipe with another brother officer, we bagged seven peafowl walking along the road to our camp, the last one I ruthlessly potted actually in a large banyan-tree,* under which our tents were pitched. It was then so dark that I first thought he was a vulture, and only saw it was a peacock by seeing his tail against the fading light. His sudden descent, crashing and tumbling through the branches, caused quite a commotion amongst our horses and cart-bullocks.

In the same locality too on another occasion I fired at a splendid peacock, but he flew away apparently unharmed right out on to an open plain, and I could just see him alight, and run

* Ficus Indica.

into a small bush, a number of which were scattered about. There were no trees within a couple of miles, so I determined to see if he could keep up his flight for any distance, and with this object mounted my pony, and taking a spear cantered off. On approaching him, he ran out, and flew some three hundred yards before he again pitched, and ran into another small bush. On reaching the spot, I looked for him in vain; he seemed to have vanished into the air, or sunk into the ground, for there was not an atom of cover into which he could have run, and he could not have flown without my seeing him. Sorely puzzled, I was on the point of giving him up when I caught the glitter of a bright eye almost under my stirrup, and there was the beautiful bird, stretched beside me, his body partly concealed by a few sparse blades of dry grass that grew under the thorny bush, his long snakelike neck laid flat on the ground and stretched to its full extent, and his grand tail, closed, and pressed tight to the ground.

Here, I thought, was an opportunity of spearing a peacock, a feat I had never heard of! I accordingly leant over and ran my spear through his back, but alas, I was soon on my own! for the poor bird jumped up in a great fluster with a tremendous fluttering, and my usually sedate pony, being unaccustomed to having a great bird flapping about under his nose, whipped round, sending me into the middle of the bush, from which I extricated myself, not without some difficulty, to see my pony disappearing in a cloud of dust, and the poor transfixed bird tumbling about some thirty yards off.

However, he was quickly dispatched, and my pony soon caught and restored to me.

It is a common mistake to think large shot should always be used for pea-fowl—by doing so, you are often tempted to blaze away into the 'brown' of the bird; by this I mean his body. Of course you hit him, but generally fail to stop him. An Ely wire cartridge, No. 3, will of course, if the gun be held straight, kill most things, but I always found that if you have only number five, or six, shot in your gun, and will fire at the head and neck, you will generally stop your bird.

I have shot them also with a pea-rifle, but this has the same objection to it as the use of large shot—and though you may get a fair sitting shot at such a large bird as a peacock, he often goes off with the bullet through him, and is lost in the thick cover. Pea-chicks are uncommonly good eating, but the adult bird is dry and tough, and only fit to be made into soups, such as cock-a-leekie or mulligatawny.

Now a few words about jungle-fowl and spur-fowl.

As far as I am aware there are only two species of jungle-fowl found in India. The small, red jungle-fowl (Gallus Ferrugineus) and the grey jungle-fowl (Gallus Sonneratii). The former is pretty commonly distributed all over the continent of India, though it, as well as the other species, adheres to the jungles, and seldom, if ever, ventures far away from their outskirts.

The red jungle-fowl much resembles a game bantam, though slightly bigger. I have always found this species much easier to put up than its congeners, and it will rise freely before beaters. They are, too, much easier to approach than the grey kind. This latter species is very different, is far handsomer, and a more game-looking bird. He is much larger, and his peculiar hackles, the end of each feather tipped with a metallic-like, shiny yellow spot, are much prized by the fair sex as ornaments for hats, and also by fishermen for fly-dressing. This bird, I believe, is not found south of the Nerbudda, and in the Pachmari Hills, the Neilgherries, the Satpura Range, and all along the Western Ghauts it is fairly abundant.

Their pursuit is often as unsatisfactory and difficult as that of the pea-fowl, for no birds are more wide-awake, or more quick in hearing the approach of an enemy.

Handsome as a trophy, worthy as a gift, and dainty as a dish though he be, yet the pursuit of jungle-cock, as a rule, affords but little pleasure. It is too often a sneaking, ignominious sort of crawl through thick and thorny jungle, so thick that you probably cannot see three yards ahead of you, whilst all the while, perhaps, you hear the object of your search quite close to you, crowing defiantly, and flapping his wings. Another yard, you think, will reveal him to your anxious gaze, and your only dread is that he will probably be so close that you must either blow him to bits, or forego the shot. Slowly and noiselessly you creep forward, when 'snap' goes some abominable twig under your foot. The noise, faint though it be, is answered by a low, warning cackle, and when you hear this you may as well relinquish the pursuit of that particular cock or hen, for not a feather will you see.

When jungle-fowl are heard crowing and flapping their wings they may often be decoyed within shot by the sportsman remaining quite still, and at intervals clapping his hand sharply against his thigh. This produces a very fair imitation of flapping of wings, and will often bring a pugnacious and inquisitive cock up to the spot to see what rival has dared to invade the sanctity of his domain. This plan, however, no real sportsman would employ except he was anxious to obtain the game for some particular purpose, and could not afford the leisure to pursue it in the more orthodox manner. The most satisfactory way, to my mind, is to beat for them much as a covert is beaten at home for pheasants. They then rise well, and an old jungle-cock, as he comes rocketting over the trees, his long tail streaming behind him, affords as pretty and sportsmanlike a shot as any man need wish for.

I have never heard of any large bags of jungle-fowl being made, and the best that I ever made, individually, was three in one morning, but this was in the sneaking, crawling manner above referred to.

On one occasion, when out with a friend in the jungles in the Chanda district in Berar, at a place called Kussaboree, we got five grey jungle-fowl (three of them cocks) and a spur-fowl.

We had been disappointed in finding any large game, by which I mean tigers, bears, &c., at this place, and, hearing a good many jungle-cocks crowing in the morning, we organised a beat for them in the afternoon. The ground we beat consisted of two nullahs, that, after describing a somewhat tortuous course down the side of a hill, united at its base. The ground on each side was bare, and covered with 'mhowa' trees,* the sweet, luscious flower of which was now dropping, and a favourite food of jungle-fowl. We stationed ourselves at the bottom of the hill, and had the two nullahs beaten simultaneously towards the point of junction.

The fowl, as they came skimming down the hill, afforded us pretty shots, but the powder was not very straight, and many birds flew back.

Whilst encamped at this place, I remember making the only attempt in my life at amateur doctoring which might have been attended with fatal results, but which fortunately for my patient, as well as for myself, turned out a success. My grass-cutter, when out gathering grass for my

---

* The 'mhowa' (Bassia Latifolia) is one of the most useful trees in the forests of India. The flower has a fleshy corolla which is deciduous, and has a sweet, but somewhat sickly taste and perfume. These luscious flowers are greedily eaten by deer, bears, jungle-fowl, &c. The natives also prize them highly, and distil from them a highly-intoxicating liquor. After the flower has dropped, a large nut, somewhat resembling a horse-chestnut, is formed. It grows in bunches, and from these nuts a thick oil is produced, which is used for burning and also in the manufacture of soap. During the flowering season the ground beneath the trees is kept swept scrupulously clean, and free from dead leaves. It is computed that each tree will yield three rupees worth of flowers alone, besides the worth of the nuts for oil.

horse, was stung by a snake in the foot, and on our return to camp from the beat alluded to above, we found him in great pain, and the injured limb much swollen.

I therefore put a strap round his leg just below his knee, pulling it as tight as I could, made a slight incision where he had been stung, and rubbed some gunpowder into it. I then gave him a pint bottle of arrack (a strong native spirit, and the curse of the British soldier in the East who is wont to indulge too freely in it).

The man swallowed it after a little demur, and dropped off into a sound sleep, from which he did not awake for six and twenty hours; but by then the swelling had gone down, and he was free from pain.

It was certainly a case of kill, or cure, and several times I thought the man was dead, and was only reassured by feeling his heart beating, and seeing his breath on a small looking-glass held to his mouth. However, the tension of my feelings was such that I gave up being an amateur physician for the future.*

---

* Since writing the above I have come across a curious corroboration of my treatment. It is an old book, published in 1822, and written by a Dr. Daniel Johnson in the H.E.I.C.S. He describes being once bitten himself by a black snake, when, seizing a bottle of madeira, he drank the whole of it straight off, and then ran up and

After jungle-fowl our recollections naturally tend towards spur-fowl.

The scientific name of this bird (Gallo perdix) fully describes it, for it is half jungle-fowl, half partridge, and is generally armed with two spurs on each leg. Jerdon thus describes them: 'They are only about the size of partridges; have no comb or wattles, but they have nude orbits, quite the port of jungle-fowl, and the sexes differ nearly as much, in which point they do not agree with the partridge group. They, moreover, frequent woods and dense cover, never coming into the open.'

The male bird is generally armed with two spurs on each leg, though they sometimes have three, and sometimes two on one leg, and one on the other; whilst the hen has usually one on each, sometimes absent on one leg, and occasionally two on one, and one on the other. There are, I believe, two species, the red * and the painted † spur-fowl. Both varieties I have personally met with, but have shot most of the latter in the jungles of Berar, and also among the coffee-plantations of Ceylon.

---

down till exhausted. The pain gradually subsided, and then he fell into a sound sleep, from which he awoke perfectly well. The book is a most quaint one, and some of the descriptions of manners and customs in the East very amusing. It was published by Longman, Hurst, Rees, Orme, and Browne, and Thomas Fowler; Great Torrington, Devon.

  * Gallo perdix spadiceus.   † Gallo perdix lumlusus.

The spur-fowl does not readily get on the wing, and prefers running and creeping in the thick undergrowth, and amongst rocks and stones, at the edge of ravines or nullahs, into which, when flushed, it drops like a stone, but, when forced to rise, affords a pretty and by no means easy shot, for it flies with great rapidity amongst the stems of the forest-trees, and generally *descends* from the sportsman's post.

They generally lie close, and even when seen they cannot be shot without blowing them to pieces, as they run jauntily over the stones and rocks with their tails cocked up. They do not remain long in sight, however, and though they be seen again they remain so short a time in view that at best they only afford a snap shot.

They readily take to trees when pursued by a dog, and from their elevated position cackle and scold him with all the force of 'galline'* bad language that they are capable of. They here afford an easy pot-shot, which, as they are excellent eating, is often taken advantage of.

I once had an English greyhound that took very kindly to this sport, in the absence of her own particular one, viz., the coursing of jackals, foxes, and hares. 'Fanny,' for such was her name, would

* *Query*—Is this the derivation of the Hindustani word for 'abuse,' viz., 'gáli'?

often accompany me in my morning strolls in the jungle, and presently I would miss her, only to be guided, by her impatient whining, to a spot where she had successfully 'treed' a spur-fowl.

Whilst staying in Ceylon with my brother, he had a large Scotch deer-hound and an Australian kangaroo-hound that he was taking care of for a friend. These dogs were often my companions when out with my gun, and seemed to take a keen delight in hunting for and finding spur-fowl and the red jungle-fowl; and it was a pretty sight to see these huge and powerful dogs bounding up on all fours above the coffee-bushes on the edge of the jungle, with ears cocked and quivering with excitement, as some little spur-fowl dodged and sneaked about almost under their feet.

Like jungle-fowl, large bags of spur-fowl are never made, as they do not exist in sufficient numbers to allow of this, and their retiring and dodgy habits often cause them to be passed by. I do not think I ever bagged more than three in a day.

CHAPTER IX.

WILD-FOWL, SNIPE, ETC.

Varieties of Wild-fowl—Hindoo Legends—Native Mode of Capturing Wild-fowl—Munchur Jheel—Solitary Snipe—Pintailed, Painted, and Jack Snipe—Black, Painted, and Grey Partridge—Quail— A 'Family' Shot—Mixed Bag—Variety of Game at Delhi.

I THINK all sportsmen will allow that there is great satisfaction in making a bag of either duck or snipe, or a mixed one of both; and certainly in India one may enjoy the sport to one's heart's content.

With what a delightful 'thud' an old mallard comes down—and how very pleasing it is to bowl over the wily and twisting snipe!

These birds are found in much the same sort of localities all over the world, and their pursuit is conducted on much the same principles; so I shall not offer any remarks on these points. I will only endeavour to enumerate the different species of duck and snipe that a sportsman may expect to find in the East in the ordinary course of events.

Let us begin with wild-fowl. The following species are pretty generally distributed, and all except the first and second named are excellent for the table: Grey geese,* Brahmini duck,† mallard,‡ widgeon,‖ blue-winged teal,§ red-headed pochard,¶ pin-tail,** gadwal,†† common teal,‡‡ whistling teal,‖‖ and cotton-teal.§§

All these are found in greater or less quantities amongst the large tanks or reservoirs, and jheels with which the country abounds. Here too may be seen the handsome demoiselle crane,¶¶ a bird most wary and difficult of approach. Also the giant sarùs crane,*** a bird worshipped by the Hindoos as a type of conjugal affection. These latter are always seen in pairs, and should one be shot (no easy task) its mate will return, and hover over the body again and again.

The grey goose is in many places found in large numbers, and are exceedingly wary. They hardly, however, repay the trouble of shooting, as their flesh is coarse and rank. The cotton-teal is

---

* Anser cinereus. † Casarca rubilia. ‡ Anas boschas.
‖ Mareca penelope. § Querquedula circia. ¶ Anthia firina.
** Dafila acuta. †† Chandlelasmus streperus.
‡‡ Querquedula crecca. ‖‖ Dendrocygna awsuree.
§§ Nettapus coromandelianus.
¶¶ Anthropoides virgo. *** Grus antigone.

a real goose, however, a little fellow the size of a very small teal, and excellent eating. They do not go in large flocks like their grey brethren.

The Brahmini duck, a very handsome bird, has also a place in Hindoo mythology, as they are always seen in pairs during the day, but at night occupy opposite banks of the river, giving forth their melancholy wailing cry of 'chukwah—chukwi!' the name by which they are known in the vernacular. They are supposed to be the incarnation of the souls of lovers condemned by a cruel fate to pass their nights apart. Though a bird of rare and handsome plumage, they are worthless for the table, and only the tyro in Eastern sport wastes a charge of shot on them.

The native method of getting wild-fowl is very ingenious, but would not of course recommend itself to any British sportsman. On a tank frequented by wild-fowl a number of earthenware 'chatties,' or pots, are put to float on the water for a few days, till the fowl become accustomed to, and take no notice of them. The wily native then one day quietly enters the water with only a leathern belt round his waist, and placing on his head a 'chatty,' in which a couple of holes have been bored for him to see out of, very quietly paddles and floats towards the unsuspecting fowl. He is soon amongst them, when with a sharp twitch he pulls one after another under water by its legs, and runs their heads and necks through his belt, when they are drowned. It is all done so quietly, and with so little motion, that the poor fowl, until their numbers are sadly diminished, take no notice of the treacherous ' chatty.'

The perfection of duck-shooting, though, to my mind is to get into a native dug-out canoe, and, taking your seat at the prow, be gently poled along amongst the openings in the reeds of a large jheel; you then get very pretty shots, as the disturbed birds rise on each side of you, and keep circling round. As these native craft are, however, decidedly crank, one has to sit pretty steady. My first day's duck-shooting was pursued in this manner on the Munchur jheel, a large shallow lake lying some ten miles inland from the town of Séwhan on the Indus. A brother subaltern and myself were on our way up to join our regiment, and, having heard rosy reports of the sport to be obtained at this jheel, determined to ride out, and rejoin our steamer the next morning some miles further up the river. I remember we shot in about an hour sixteen couple of duck and teal, and several couple of snipe, nor shall I ever forget the ride we had, some eighty miles on bare-backed ponies, before we caught up our steamer again.

Of snipe there are five varieties found in India,

viz., the solitary, or **wood** snipe,* the common snipe,† the pin-tailed snipe, the painted snipe,‡ and the Jack snipe.‖ The first is exceedingly rare, and, as its name implies, is always found alone and in thick cover. I only ever saw one myself, and that I shot in the hot weather.

It was during a hot-weather trip in the Chanda jungles. We were encamped at a place called Marouda, and on the 25th of April, 1870, I went out to look at the 'hailas' (young buffaloes) that had been tied up for tigers. I had reached a charming little swampy glade in the forest, called the Kotal Zirun, surrounded by trees covered with the giant-leaved elephant-creeper,§ and, hastily satisfied myself that the 'haila' tied up at the spot had not been visited by a tiger during the night, I was turning away when a bird marvellously like a wood-cock rose almost at my feet. Having a rifle in my hand at the moment, I of course could not fire. I watched the bird, however, and after flying round once or twice he pitched under a bush some thirty yards off. Quickly taking my gun from the Gónd who was carrying it, I walked towards the spot, when the bird rose only to be bowled over. It was in

---

* Scolopax major solitaria. † Scolopax gallinago.
‡ Rynchœa bengalensis. ‖ Scolopax gallinula.
§ Bauhinia scandens.

grand condition, and in size between a wood-cock and a snipe.

The only other solitary snipe I ever saw was on Cove Common, near Aldershot. Strolling across this one December day in 1874, I rose and killed five snipe out of as many shots. One was a solitary snipe, two full, or common snipe, and two Jack snipe. As these pages are, however, only records of Indian sport, the reader must kindly pardon this digression.

The common Indian snipe is much the same as any other snipe, except that I do not think he has the rapid, twisty flight of his European congener. Paddy or rice fields are a very favourite resort of snipe, and I have even seen them amongst 'jow'[*] bushes, where there was no water, in considerable numbers.

With regard to the pin-tailed snipe, I shall take the liberty of quoting a letter from 'Smoothbore,' which appeared in the *Field* in 1866, and until reading his letter I had no idea of this variety—but subsequent examination proved his statement correct.

He says, 'The common and pin-tailed snipe are found in the same fields, and look the same colour when killed: yet there is a great difference

---

* Jow is a species of low bush cypress that grows on the banks of rivers. It is also a favourite cover for wild hog.

between them, if you examine them closely. The common snipe is white under the wing, with a few indistinct and irregular brown marks, and the feathers of the tail are soft. The pin-tailed snipe has the under-wing coverts richly and regularly barred, and the lateral tail feathers sharp, stiff, and pointed.' I believe the pin-tailed snipe is more common in Southern India; from my own experience I do not remember ever shooting one north of Kamptee, in the Central Provinces, where I got several in a day's shooting. The painted snipe is to a certain extent found in the same ground as the common snipe, but is generally looked down upon—both as an object for sport and as food. In flavour he is decidedly inferior to any other species, and his flight is so slow and owl-like that he can hardly be missed. His wings are beautifully marked with circular spots, or eyes, and the feathers on his back have a more uniform tinge of olive green than the common snipe's. His bill, too, differs from the rest of the snipe family by being slightly arched at the tip.

Last of all we come to the game little Jack-snipe, last in point of size, but not least certainly as far as his edible qualities are concerned, for I think few birds rank higher than he does as a *bonne bouche*. Like his European cousin, he lies very close and is difficult to flush.

Jack snipe are pretty evenly distributed all over India, but they select denser cover than other snipe do, with the exception of the wood, or solitary snipe. They are seldom found in great numbers, and three or four in a day's snipe-shooting are the most that have ever fallen to my gun.

A friend of mine, however, a general officer and keen sportsman, told me that he had in about twenty minutes bagged nine couple in a bit of ground only some fifty yards square, covered with reeds and flags.* Such a bag of Jack snipe is, however, I think, exceptional.

It may be fancy on my part, but to me the shooting of a Jack snipe always affords a certain amount of pleasure. The shot is always a satisfactory one; for, though his floating, butterfly-like sort of flight makes the shot an apparently easy one, sportsmen will, I think, in general bear me out in saying that is not so; and perhaps from this reason I think more Jack snipe are missed than any other bird. In addition to the gratification of shooting him, he is such a game, neat, glossy-looking little fellow, that handling him is alone to a certain extent a pleasure.

Partridges must come next in our list, and of these, three varieties are met with on the plains of

* Major-General W. C. Anderson, C.S.I.

India, viz., the francolin, or black partridge,* the painted partridge,† and the grey partridge.‡

The black partridge frequents high grass rumnahs or 'bheers,' and is also found amongst cultivation. They afford very pretty shooting, rising like rockets, with a loud 'whirr,' for some twenty feet, when they sail away for the next bit of cover, generally taking a longish flight. They are fair eating, but rather dry, like so much Indian game.

The painted partridge much resembles him, only that the cock bird has not got the handsome black breast of the black partridge, and more resembles the hen of that species. They are found in much the same sort of cover, and never very far away from jungle of some sort. It is very common in the Central and Southern Provinces, where it takes the place of the black partridge, which latter variety I have not seen south of Jubbulpore.

The grey partridge is very common, and much resembles our English partridge, only smaller, and has not the horseshoe on the breast. It is found in the vicinity of villages, and is a very foul feeder, not objecting to carrion, and feeding on all the filth that is found on the outskirts of a

* Francolinus vulgaris. † Francolinus pictus.
‡ Perdix Indicus.

native village. This habit generally makes most sportsmen exclude him from their bag.

Of quail, three varieties are most common, viz., the grey, or European quail,* the black-breasted quail,† and the bush quail.‡ The first two are the largest, and fit to grace the table of any *bon vivant*, though the little bush quail is by no means to be despised. These latter are found in the jungles, and are most provoking little creatures, squatting even in a road till almost trodden on, when up gets the whole bevy with a buzz all round you, startling you out of your senses, and often doing ditto to your horse should you be riding. They always presented to my mind a sort of 'catherine-wheel' of feathers, and they are so small that this makes them rather more than ordinarily difficult to make a bag of.

I once, however, had my revenge on the little rascals, though in rather a mean manner; still the circumstance of requiring something for the pot must be my excuse. I was strolling home one day after an unsuccessful beat for bears, with my smooth-bore loaded with number seven shot in my hand. Mechanically I had my eyes fixed on the dusty jungle road I was walking on, in the hopes of seeing a tiger's footprints, when a little

* Coturnix communis. † Coturnix coromandelica.
‡ Perdicula cambayensis.

puff of dust some ten yards ahead of me caught my eye, then the slight movement of a wing; so, stepping back some twenty yards, I fired at the spot, and on walking up to it found my shot had accounted for eleven of the little bush quail, and excellent eating they proved, placed for a few minutes in *boiling* water, and eaten with melted butter and green chilis.

I once shot five snipe at a shot under much the same circumstances. I was marching down country with some invalids and time-expired men, and was encamped half-way between Roorkee and Meerut. I was very hard-up for a dinner, and had had a fruitless search for game, when a native who accompanied me said he knew of a pond where doubtless I would find some 'moorghabi,' the generic native term for wild-fowl, in which they include paddy birds,* etc.,—in fact, every species of aquatic bird. The country for miles round was nothing but bare sandy plains with scant patches of cultivation, and I had not much faith in my black friend's assertions, but, nevertheless, went with him. We soon came to the spot, and looking over the bank cautiously I saw a small pool of muddy water about the size of an ordinary dining-table, not a patch of cover near it, not a rush or blade of grass, only round

* Or pond-heron (Ardeola leucoptera).

the edge of the water were the footprints of cattle made when the mud was soft, but they were now baked hard and dry by the sun. On the point of turning back, and roundly abusing my guide, I caught the glitter of an eye in one of these depressions made by cattle's feet, so out of mere wantonness, I suppose, I fired at it. Nothing moved, however; but, on going up to the spot, what was my delight to find five snipe all quite dead, and packed into the hole as if in a nest! Needless to add, my native guide did *not* get the 'bamboo backsheesh' with which I was so nearly threatening him.

To return to our quail, however. The grey, or 'rain' quail, is migratory, and comes in large numbers about August or September. It then affords very pretty shooting, and large bags are often made. They frequent the grain, and 'gram' fields, and are so numerous that three or four fields will often give you a good day's work to shoot. I remember when at Roorkee, in 1868, myself and two brother-officers in a couple of hours in one field of about thirty acres bagging seventy-two brace. Of course we lost a lot more which we did not pick up. The plan is to walk along in line, having two or three beaters between each gun. The great flight lasts about a fortnight or three weeks, and then they disappear, though a few odd brace may be generally found in a bag at the end of a day's shooting.

The black-breasted quail I have never seen in such large numbers, and my best bag of them was only nine brace. This was made near Kamptee, in the Central Provinces. In conclusion, as showing a fair mixed bag that may be obtained by average shots, I append the results of two days' shooting at Mongolpúr, nine miles out on the Rhotuk road, near Delhi, in 1869; myself and two other guns :

One ravine deer, or chikara, twelve pea-fowl, eleven hares, twenty-five black partridge, seven wild-duck, three teal, twenty-five quail, two pigeons (green), four bittern,* and one hundred and forty-three snipe. We had, besides, shot at black buck, but failed to get any.

As an illustration of the variety of game to be found around Delhi, I remember that in 1869, when encamped on the historical ridge near Hindu Rao's House, our mess larder-tent contained the following: Black buck, ravine deer, geese (both varieties), Brahmini duck, mallard, red-headed pochard, whistling teal, blue-winged teal,

---

* Botaurus stellaris.

common teal, sand-grouse * (two varieties), black partridge, bittern, sārus crane, hares,† quail (two varieties), snipe, green pigeon,‡ blue-rock pigeon, wild boar, and pea-fowl.

It was a pretty sight, and one that would delight a sportsman's eye. The deer and boar depending from the ridge-pole to which they were hung by their legs, and the small game in festoons all round. All this had been bagged in three or four days' shooting by officers in my regiment, and, *proh pudor!* the boar also; but he met an unworthy death at the hands of a youngster who knew nothing of the charms or the unwritten laws of hog-hunting. Can your game-larders, oh! sportsmen of Great Britain, boast such a show? I trow not.

* Common sand-grouse (**Pterocles exustus**). Painted sand-grouse (Pterocles fasciatus).

† Lepus enficaudatus. The Indian hare is much smaller than the English variety, rarely weighing more than 5 lbs., and being about eighteen to twenty inches in length. It goes to ground readily when pursued. The flesh is dry and tasteless, and only fit for soup. The black-naped hare (lepus nigricolis) is about the same size, and has the same habits, but is peculiar to the southern parts of India and Ceylon.

‡ Crocopus chlorigaster.

CHAPTER X.

TIGER-SHOOTING.*

Tiger-shooting—Expenses of Camp Equipage—Preliminary Arrangements—'Hailas'—Ringing the Tiger—The Beat—Following up wounded Tigers—Precautions to be Taken—My first Tiger—Death of a Villager—Successful Right and Left—Bag the Cubs—Tigers' Whiskers—Curious Anatomical Structure—An Impudent Kite—The Khandla Tiger—The Artful Dodger—Cannibalism of Tigers—Frogs as a Diet—Tigers' fondness of Bathing—Attacked by Red Ants—A Shot in the Water—Tigris Redivivus!

No narrative of Indian sport can be considered complete without some account of that most thrilling and exciting sport of tiger-shooting, but I must warn my readers that in these pages they will find no account of numbers of tigers slain, or hairbreadth escapes. I can only endeavour 'a round unvarnished tale to deliver,' and relate such incidents as came within the limits of my own personal experience; and any others that I may relate I can vouch for the truth of.

* Felis tigris.

My own personal experience of tiger-shooting was confined to two hot-weather trips, during which I shot, or assisted in shooting, some sixteen to twenty tigers. I had, however, the advantage of knowing intimately some well-known and thorough sportsmen, good men and true, whose word could be relied upon, and who would sooner have cut off their right hand than exaggerate (as so many are prone to) the result of their bags, or any incidents connected with them.

Tiger-shooting is popularly supposed to be an expensive sport, and generally beyond the reach of a man not blessed with much of this world's goods. It is supposed that it cannot be pursued without a large array of elephants and beaters, etc.: all of which cost money. No greater mistake. If a man's heart be in any pursuit, depend upon it he will pursue it, and often successfully under every disadvantage: at least I know such was the case with me, for as an impecunious, very impecunious, subaltern I managed to have my share of this individual sport, without incurring any debt which I was not justified in doing. In fact, I do not think it cost more than, if as much as, living in cantonments.

My first hot-weather trip was taken in company with a brother-officer, much my senior in age, and service, but, as far as 'shikar' was concerned, in no whit more experienced than myself. We thought to do it economically, and accordingly stinted ourselves in many creature comforts, even to limiting our cooking arrangements, and crockery to such as could be contained in a Crimean bucket apiece!

The following year I went with the friend to whom these pages are dedicated, a thorough sportsman, who had had much previous experience in all the different arrangements necessary for carrying out a 'shikar' trip successfully and comfortably. In the first instance the cost for a two months' trip was about fifty pounds apiece, in the latter I think fifty-five pounds, but then in that one we had an elephant, and took our horses and many of our servants down some one hundred miles by rail, which we did not do in the former trip. In addition we lived like 'fighting cocks,' and had the best of everything.

'How was it managed, and how do you account for such a discrepancy?' may be asked

Kind reader, I will explain it in three words, 'Experience and management.' These two adjuncts did the trick, and made all the difference.

It may not perhaps be here out of place to give the items of our suites, and the paraphernalia that accompanied us in both trips. I must, however, state that we shared all common expenses, and only our individual servants' wages and horses' food was excluded.

First trip: self, and Captain Clay, 79th Highlanders. One shikari, four bullock-carts, one horse each, one field-officer's tent, one hill tent for servants and cooking, one native blacksmith, one 'colassie,' or tent-pitcher, one 'chukler' (a native skin-dresser), one dhobie, or washerman, three dozen soda and tonic water, one dozen claret, six bottles of gin, and three of brandy, a few pots of jam, sardines, bacon in tins, etc., one Crimean bucket each.

Second trip: self, Lieutenants 'H.'* and 'D.'† R.A. Two shikaris, one peon, one native blacksmith, one butler, two colassies, or tent-pitchers, one elephant with 'mahout' and two attendants, one horse each, (Lieutenant Hebbert had two,) eight bullock-carts, twenty-four pack bullocks with Bunjara owners, two field-officers' tents, and one hill tent, one 'chukler,' one dhobie, ten dozen soda-water, eight dozen claret, six dozen beer, one dozen gin, one dozen brandy, crockery for breakfast, dinner, etc. The best of stores, comprising tea, coffee, chocolate, jam, sardines, bacon, hams, sausages, potted meats, etc., in fact all manner of 'Europe stores' that could add a little to the

---

* Lieutenant Hebbert, R.H.A., now Colonel, R.H.A.
† Lieutenant Davidson, now Lieutenant-Colonel, R.A. retired.

jungle fare obtained by our guns. If these two lists will be compared, it will be seen how much more comfortably three people could live on the latter than two on the former.

The cost of the maintenance of the elephant alone, and the pay of its three attendants, was no trifling item, and if in addition to this the railway fare for our three selves, four horses, and servants be taken into consideration, it will be seen how experience and management told in making the much larger outfit only exceed the lesser by so small a sum. Of course the remainder of the expenses in each trip was made up by payments to beaters, rewards for information of game, supplies, &c.

The *modus operandi* pursued was as follows: Our shikari was sent out over the ground we proposed traversing during the trip, some six weeks previous to our start. It was then his business to make all inquiries respecting the localities in which tigers were to be found, their habits, and the particular spots they were in the habit of frequenting, and of their *characters;* for, strange as it may seem, nearly every tiger has a certain character for ferocity, wiliness, or the reverse—of being a man-eater, cattle-killer, or game-killer— which are well known to the jungle folk.

At the end of the six weeks the shikari would

return and make his report, saying two tigers had taken up their abode near such and such a village, another near so and so, and so on. To these points in rotation, according as they presented the most convenience on our line of march, we directed our camp.

On arrival the shikari would, by inquiry and personal inspection of the jungle, satisfy himself that the tiger, or tigers, were still in the vicinity. This he would do by looking out for fresh tracks. It being assured that the animal was about, some half-dozen young, bull-buffalo calves would be purchased for a trifling sum from the villagers. These would then be tied up in the evening at different spots where the tiger was known to pass, and left there all night. These were termed 'hailas.'

The tiger, in his nocturnal rambles, would come across one of these 'baits,' promptly kill it, and carry it off to some secluded spot, where he would leave it, after gorging himself well, and then sleep off the effects of his heavy meal close by. In the morning the shikari, or perhaps one of the sportsmen, would go the round of these tied-up calves, and, if one was missing, the first thing he would do would be to cast his eyes round the surrounding trees. If on their tops he saw any number of vultures congregated, he might be assured of the truth of the scriptural statement that 'where the carcase is, there will the eagles be gathered together,' and sure enough the 'kill' would generally be lying close by, and near it, in all probability, Master 'Stripes' himself. Sometimes, however, tigers will leave the 'kill,' and go and take their mid-day siesta some distance off.

To ensure their not having done this, and to 'harbour' them—as is done to the red-deer on the breezy, purple-clad heights, and among the deep and wooded coombes of Exmoor—whoever is going round the 'hailas,' takes a wide circle round the 'kill,' assuring himself by a careful scrutiny of the ground that the tiger has not gone out of the proscribed circle. Being satisfied as to the exact locality of the tiger, the shikari returns to camp, having previously untied and brought in the 'hailas' that have not been killed, and makes his report to his masters, that is, if none of them have accompanied him in his rounds. Beaters are then collected, and a start made about eleven o'clock, when it is very hot. The object of deferring the beat till the intense heat of mid-day is, that tigers are very unwilling to travel far during heat; in fact it has a great effect on them, and I have seen a tiger's feet quite raw and blistered by having to pass much over burning rocks and sand during a beat.

The sportsmen then select a spot, either in a

tree, or behind one, in the line along which the tiger is most likely to advance. The former position is preferable, first, because there is less danger, as a rule, and secondly, because, if the sportsman keeps quite still, the tiger, who seldom if ever looks *up* when disturbed, will be less likely to observe him. Then the beat begins by much shouting, beating of drums, blowing of 'rumtoolahs,' or native horns, and fifes, by the beaters, perhaps half-a-mile away, accompanied by the noise of some twenty rattles, which all combine to create such a Pandemonium of sounds, that few decent-minded tigers will stand it for long. Generally, at the first shout the tiger, particularly if he has been hunted before, moves off noiselessly, and, passing one of the sportsmen's posts, affords a quiet shot. If the tiger be wounded only, *the beaters should never be sent in to beat again.* It is not fair to send in a lot of poor, half-naked wretches, armed only with sticks, to beat out a furious and enraged animal, suffering from the agonies of a wound and a burning sun. If not on the score of humanity, self-interest alone should prevent sportsmen taking this course; for, if one of the beaters be either killed or wounded, the news of the catastrophe will travel like wild-fire through the district, and he will not only have much difficulty in getting beaters in the future, but also 'khubber,' or news of tigers, will probably be withheld from him.

Besides I think, myself, that any man who goes in for tiger-shooting should make up his mind to consider it a point of honour to follow up, even alone if necessary, any tiger that he may *wound*, and follow him up until he either bags him or loses him, for a wounded tiger often takes heavy toll of human lives when left behind.

Far abler pens than mine have, however, given such accurate details of the method of pursuing this sport that I will add no more, except by referring anyone in search of further information to such writers as Sanderson, Shakespear, Newall, Gordon-Cumming, Burton, etc. I will now endeavour to give a few anecdotes regarding tigers, and relate my own personal encounters with the feline race in instances where their death has been attended with any details which may prove of interest to the sportsman who may honour me by casting an eye over these pages.

The first view of a tiger in its wild state is a sight which once seen will not by those who have witnessed it be soon forgotten. At least, I know the remembrance of my first tiger, though her death was unattended with any exciting incident, stands out in the vision of my memory, undimmed by the mists of time, as clear and lifelike as it was on the day it happened some sixteen years ago. It was on this wise:

Myself and a brother-officer (Captain Clay, above referred to) reached during our trip a place called Marouda, situated on the banks of a river, a tributary of the Wein Gunga, if I remember rightly, in the Chanda district. We here heard that a tiger, tigress, and three cubs frequented a strip of jungle on the banks of the river; the tigress, moreover, had by native report been magnified into 'a man-eater,' and was said to have killed a man the day previous to our arrival. This, indeed, proved to be the fact; but that the poor wretch lost his life was due entirely to his own carelessness and foolhardiness. The man in question had a small patch of cultivation bordering the cover in which the tigers generally lay up. The cubs in their gambols had done considerable damage to the crop, rolling about in it, and breaking down the plants. In order to prevent their making his field their playground, the owner, in spite of being advised to the contrary, announced his determination of setting fire to the long grass at the edge of the jungle. This intention he accordingly proceeded to carry into effect, and had hardly kindled the flames which were to ensure him from future damage when the tigress, who had been lying up within a few

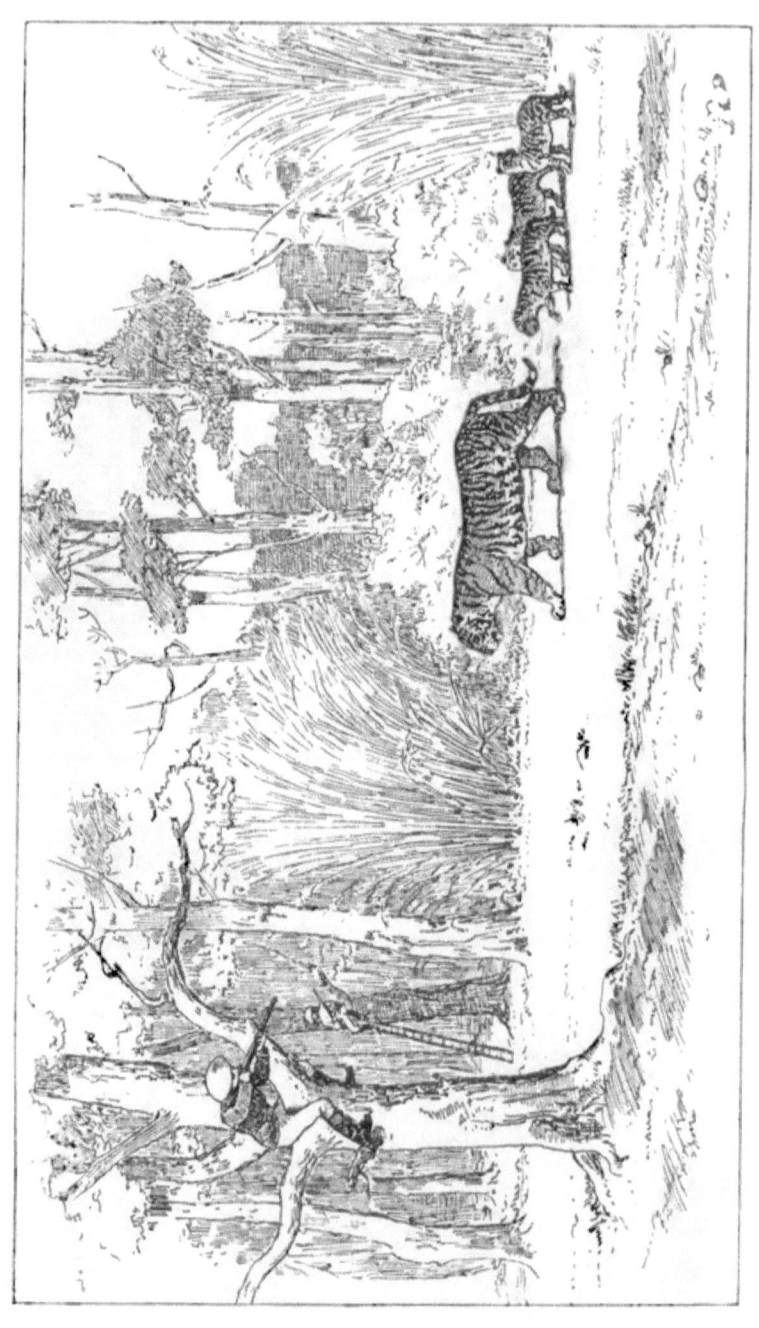

"SHE WAS SLOUCHING SULKILY ALONG."

p. 163.

yards of him, rushed out and knocked him over, killing him almost instanteously. She, however, left him, and never ate any of the body as she would have done had she been a real man-eater.

The evening of our arrival we had three or four 'hailas' tied out, and the following morning had the satisfaction of hearing one was killed.

Accordingly, about eleven o'clock, we started with some eighty beaters for the scene of action. The carcase of the calf had been dragged by the tigress into a small nullah that debouched into the main river; about half-a-mile further on there was a similar nullah, and between these two we took up our positions in trees, and some fifty yards apart. The beat had not commenced more than five minutes, and I was gazing eagerly to my front, when I saw the tigress followed by three cubs not quite half-grown, and about the size of big mastiffs, coming straight towards me.

She was slouching sulkily along, evidently much put out at being disturbed, and the cubs trotted after her, one of them every now and then stopping, with pricked ears, and gazing back towards the beaters; then it would scamper on after its mother. It was a pretty sylvan scene, and the sunlight, falling on their sleek-striped hides as they moved noiselessly over the dead leaves that carpeted the ground, glittered and quivered in fantastic rays. They came straight on for my post, and got within some ten yards of me, when with an upward curl of her lip and a twitching of the tip of her tail, that well-known sign of irritation which always means mischief on the part of the feline race, the tigress stopped to listen; and, as she turned her head back gazing towards the beaters, I aimed at her neck between its junction with the shoulders and the ears, and fired. She dropped in her tracks without a groan, and never stirred. It seemed as if in a twinkling the ground had, as it were, been cut from under her legs, at the same moment depriving her of life with the speed of electricity.

I only on one other occasion ever saw any large animal pass so suddenly from life to death, without even a twitch, or movement of a muscle. That was also a tigress which I shot, and oddly enough also the first tiger I got on my next year's trip. I observed at this time a curious instance of how close wild animals will sometimes lie. This tigress was shot on the edge of a nullah along which were some patches of grass. In stepping on one of these, not six inches from where the dead tigress's nose was resting, out jumped a hare, which had remained hitherto squatted in her form.

To resume, however. At the shot, the cubs

scattered right and left, one coming past me, which I knocked over, shattering its hind leg above the hock, and the remaining two going past Clay, who bagged one. We shouted to the beaters to come on, and, descending from our perches, went to despatch my cub, who could not go far. The vicious little beast snarled and spat at us like an angry cat, and even attempted to charge, but a bullet soon put him out of his misery.

Sending the beaters round we made them beat back to us, when Clay bagged the other cub. All endeavours to find the male tiger proved fruitless, and we had to be content with the three, and a very imposing spectacle it was to see them borne into camp slung on poles, the procession accompanied by native musicians making day hideous with the discordant sound of tom-toms, horns, and all 'manner of music,' that would have satisfied even Belshazzar. This tigress was a small one, only measuring seven feet eleven inches, but this was accounted for by her having lost some six inches of her tail from some cause. Her skin was however very rich in colour and beautifully marked.

Sportsmen should if possible always keep a keen look-out, or see their shikari does, that the tiger's whiskers are not stolen, as natives value them highly as a charm, and will, if they possibly can, purloin them. The absence of whiskers from the head of a tiger when stuffed, of course detracts much from its beauty and natural appearance. The best plan, therefore, is to pull out the whiskers *yourself* as soon as you have shot your tiger, and put them in your pocket.

I was much impressed with the enormous muscular development of a tiger on seeing this one skinned—but the stench was so awful that I was ere long driven from the spot where the operation was being carried on. Tiger fat is highly prized by natives as an application for rheumatism, etc., and they moreover eat pieces of the liver, by doing which they think they will be inspired with courage.

There is a peculiar anatomical structure about a tiger, and I believe in all the feline race, such as is found in no other animals, viz., two small bones, each about two and a half inches long, and about an inch in circumference. They are separate, and not connected with any other bone, being imbedded in the flesh of the chest, one on each side. These bones are highly prized by natives as charms, or amulets, and often fetch very high prices. The possession of one by a woman who has never borne children is considered to ensure pregnancy! Of course, though, it is only a superstition, but one firmly believed in by natives.

Whilst encamped at Marouda an instance occurred illustrating the audacity of the Indian kite.* Our breakfast was laid outside our tent under the shade of some giant mango-trees. We had just sat down, and I was pouring out the tea, when one of our table servants approached bearing a dish with a cold pea-chick on it, which was destined to form the *pièce-de-résistance* for our meal. He was in the act of placing it on the table when a kite swooped down under the branches, and making a dash at the plate, bore off its contents in his talons with triumph. The 'cheek' of the bird was so great that, after the first feeling of annoyance at having been deprived of the best part of our meal had passed off, we could not help laughing, and forgiving it.

The next tiger we got on this trip gave us rather harder work to bag.

It was at a place called Khandla, and, our 'haila' having been duly killed, we beat. Nothing, however, would induce this wily gentleman to face the guns. He would let the beaters almost tread on him, then jump up, and with a loud 'Wough-Wough,' would charge back through them. This game went on all day till five o'clock, when we had to give up. Again we 'tied out' for him, and again he killed; but the same thing was repeated;

* Milvus gorinda.

the tiger crossing backwards and forwards from one bank of the river to the other; but always out of shot. The third day we beat for a long time but did not succeed in finding him till late in the day, when he promptly took himself off to some adjoining hills and we saw no more of him. We then gave him up, and moved on to fresh ground. On our return journey, some three weeks after, we again heard of this tiger, and had another try for him, when he kindly disposed of two more calves for us, one being killed in broad daylight under our eyes, as he was making one of his dodgy trips across the river. As usual he beat us; but the following day I was fortunate enough to get a shot at him, and bag him. He was a very old, light-coloured tiger, and with the black stripes faintly marked; his skin had several long scars only half healed over, the wounds inflicted evidently by some other tiger with whom he had had a slight difference of opinion. He measured nine feet two inches before being skinned. We certainly were satisfied at getting him, as he had cost us five calves, and given us five days' beating.

That tigers do fight, and that occasionally the victor eats the vanquished, is a well-known fact. A friend of mine, a distinguished general officer,*

* Major-General W. C. Anderson, C.S.I.

and one who has had much experience in shikar, related the following incident to me:

'In Kandeish the Bheels one day brought "khubber" of two tigers. One was shot, but no amount of search with the elephants could discover the other. At length beaters were sent in to the cover, when the head and paws of the other tiger were found quite fresh, and the rest of his remains in the stomach of the tiger that had been shot. This happened to my brother, and P———.'

I have been told by the Gónds that tigers are very fond of frogs, and that they have been seen catching them by hooking them out of shallow pools with their claws.

This habit is corroborated by Jerdon in his 'Mammals of India.' At the place where I am now residing a villager has a cat, who whenever she has kittens to provide for (a pretty common occurrence) invariably goes to a little stream hard by, and catches trout and eels. I have never seen her in the act, but I have seen her returning across a field with a quarter-of-a-pound trout in her mouth! If a cat should do this, why should not a tiger eat frogs? They must be nice cool eating on a hot day, and to a tiger must taste much as oysters do to us! Anyhow tigers are no worse in their taste for this peculiar delicacy than our gallant neighbours across the Channel!

Tigers are very fond of a bath, and Hebbert (the friend before referred to) on two occasions shot them in the water. The first we were preparing to beat for; I had been posted, and Hebbert was going to his post, when he suddenly came on the tiger rolling about and splashing himself in a pool of water close to the 'kill,' and as the brute sat up in the shallow pool for a moment, gazing at the intruder, he shot him.

I shall never forget disturbing a nest of red ants on this occasion. I had been posted in a tree and Hebbert had just left me. First I felt a slight itching at the back of my neck, then as if a hot needle had been driven in; at last the irritation became so intense that I put my hand up and then discovered that my head, hair, and beard were covered with red ants. No philosophy could stand this; so flinging down my rifle, I jumped out of the tree, and rushed to the river, just as I heard the report of Hebbert's rifle, and heard his triumphant whoo-whoop announcing the tiger's death.

On the other occasion, Hebbert had been out after spotted deer, and returning home along the bank of a stream saw a tiger indulging in his ablutions. The tiger on seeing him swam away across the river, when Hebbert fired at, and knocked him over, the body turning feet uppermost, and floating down some little distance. It then grounded on a sand-bank, when it seemed to recover; and, springing up, bounded up the opposite bank, when Hebbert saluted him with two more shots ere he disappeared. On returning, and searching with the elephant, we found it stone-dead some fifty yards from where it was last seen.

CHAPTER XI.

TIGER-SHOOTING (CONTINUED.)

First Encounter on Foot with a Tiger—Apparent Failure of Beat—Sudden Appearance of the Tigress—Too Close to be Pleasant—What shall I do?—Close Quarters—In quest of Bears—A Blank—Unexpected Meeting with a Tigress—Wound Her—Follow Up—She charges—Her Death—Extraordinary vitality—Tiger's powers of Concealment—The Tandla Tiger—An awkward Predicament—He is very Sick—Precautions to be taken in Approaching dead Tigers—The Daba Tiger—' Independent Firing '—The Death-spring—Impotent rage of a wounded Tiger.

CERTAINLY the first time one meets a tiger close, and on foot, is I think calculated to shake even the stoutest nerves. I can at least answer for myself, and am not ashamed to own that the first time I met a tiger *close*, I was in what is commonly termed a blue funk! It happened thus:

I was out in the Berar jungles with my friends Hebbert and Davidson. We had bagged one tiger and a cub, and some days after camped at a place called Jarang-Jarur, where we heard there were three tigers. We 'tied out' as usual, but there was no 'kill' by eleven o'clock in the morning. However, about three p.m. one of our men came in with the news that one of our 'hailas' had been killed at a spot about two miles off. Hastily collecting some thirty beaters we sallied forth, but it was nearly 4.30 p.m. before we could commence operations. This, coupled with the difficult nature of the ground, was all in favour of the tigers; as by then the atmosphere had become cooler, and therefore the tigers would have less hesitation in facing the open. There was very little cover with the exception of a couple of small nullahs, which after tortuous course united in a larger one. Hebbert was placed on the right facing the beaters as they advanced, and about one hundred yards out in the open jungle, whilst my post was at the junction of the two nullahs, and Davidson was some fifty yards to my left. Almost at the first shout of the beaters, two tigers broke, and passed some one hundred and fifty yards to the right of Hebbert, who wisely did not fire. It looked rather hopeless to try and get a shot at them at such a late hour of the evening, but Lutchman, our second shikari, who was conducting the beat, was very anxious we should go after them, as he said some little distance ahead there was a nullah where they would probably lie up. Accordingly we acceded to his wishes, and Hebbert and I ran round about a mile as hard as we could, to post ourselves, leaving Lutchman to conduct the beat, and Davidson, who was feeling very unwell, to accompany him on the elephant. Goodness, what a run that was! I was feeling quite pumped out, and rather sick, when Hebbert selected a tree for me, and, giving me a hasty 'leg up,' went off to post himself accompanied by a native carrying his spare rifle. The tree I was posted in grew on the edge of a small shallow and tortuous nullah only some six feet wide (into which a lesser one, not wider than a ditch, debouched), and along it grew several large jamun* bushes whose dense gloomy foliage prevented my seeing where Hebbert had posted himself. The jungle to my immediate front, and from whence I imagined the tigers would advance, was perfectly bare under the large forest trees, which now in the hot weather were devoid of foliage, in fact one could have seen even a hare advancing.

I heard the beat approaching closer and closer, but not a sign of a tiger. At last, catching sight of the beaters, I removed the cartridges from my

---

* Eugenia jambulana. This shrub which sometimes attains the dignity of a tree is found in nearly all stream beds. It is evergreen, and therefore always affords shade, and thus is a favourite resort of tigers and bears.

rifle, and lowering it down to the ground by means of my 'cummerbund,' or waistcloth, slithered down the trunk of the tree, holloaing out to Hebbert, 'Where are you?' Not receiving any reply, I picked up my rifle, and was preparing to walk in the direction where I thought he was, when I caught sight of a tiger advancing round a bend of the nullah, and not fifty yards from me. She stopped for an instant, and began staring hard in the direction from whence the beaters were coming. I seized this moment to quietly and rapidly slip back behind the trunk of the tree, whose friendly branches I had lately occupied, and, squeezing myself flat behind the trunk, I, with the least possible motion, slipped in a couple of cartridges, and in great trepidation waited the turn of events. Oh! how my heart beat as I saw the tiger slip into the nullah, and creep stealthily along under the bank straight for me. A flood of thoughts rushed through my brain. What had I best do? I dared not shout, for that would probably have turned her right back among the beaters, some of whom might be mauled. At last when certainly not more than eight or ten yards from me, and if she had continued her course she must have passed within three feet of me, I determined to step out from behind my shelter, and take the opportunity of the surprise my sudden appearance would cause her, to fire both barrels into her. Circumstances, however, prevented my carrying this somewhat risky plan into operation, for, as I was on the point of doing so, I heard 'bang-bang' from Hebbert, accompanied by a surly roaring grunt, and *my* tiger whipped sharp round, sprang up the bank of the nullah opposite to the one I was standing on, and was bolting past when she caught sight of me, and stopped short, with ears back and that nasty upward curl of the lip which generally denotes no very amiable frame of mind. How my hand shook, and my heart beat, as raising my rifle quickly to my shoulder, I took the best aim at her heart that my excited feelings would allow, and pulled! She was not more than some twenty yards from me, and answered my shot by spinning round and round growling and biting at the wound, and tumbling about in a confused manner. Another shot, however, settled her, and I did just about feel thankful. This tigress measured eight feet, seven and-a-half inches, and was in good condition.

On rejoining Hebbert, I found he had fired at another tiger, which galloped past him, but had missed it, and though we beat another strip of jungle, where it might have stopped, darkness soon put a stop to any further proceedings, and we had to give it up.

It appeared that Hebbert from his post had seen the two tigers walking towards me along the bank of the nullah; the one I had shot leading by some sixty yards. My getting down from my tree had evidently attracted the attention of the hindermost tiger, who then had broken past Hebbert, and his shot had disturbed *my* tigress, and thus prevented her coming to such undesirable close quarters with me as she would otherwise have done.

We 'tied out' again that night and the following one, but no 'kill' was reported; however, my luck was in the ascendant, for I got another tigress the day but one after I had shot the one whose death has been described above. As it was rather an exciting bit of shikar, I will endeavour to describe the circumstances of finding her, and her subsequent death.

At four a.m. in the morning of the day in question, we all started for some isolated rocky hills about two miles off, taking our horses and spears, with a view of trying to ride and spear some bears which were said to frequent them; in this, however, we were unsuccessful, as Bruin was 'non est,' and we returned to camp very tired, and feeling decidedly lazy.

As there seemed no chance of any more tigers about, we determined to devote the evening to deer and small game. Hebbert started off by himself about three p.m., but only got a 'chikara,' or ravine deer, whilst Davidson and I did not go out till an hour later, riding our horses, and with our guns and rifles carried behind us. After proceeding some little distance I had to canter back to camp for something I had forgotten, and on rejoining Davidson at the edge of a large nullah that ran into the Kuni river, now nearly dry, he told me he had fired at, and thought he had wounded, a fine stag 'cheetal,' or spotted deer, which had then entered the nullah. We determined, therefore, to follow this up, though there were no signs of blood; still the thick cool patches of jumun bushes, that fringed the edges and bottom of the nullah, looked likely to hold game.

Separating accordingly, we took our rifles, and one went each side of the nullah, our horses being led some hundred yards behind us. We had gone but a short distance when an extra thick, cool, gamey-looking patch of cover in the bed of the nullah attracted my attention, so kicking up a large tuft of grass I hurled it in. This was answered by a loud 'wough-wough,' and out sprang a tigress, who was scrambling up the opposite bank when I fired at her. She flinched at the shot, and half fell back when I let her have the second barrel, yelling to Davidson to 'look out.' He heard me just soon enough, and had only time to get behind the trunk of a large 'mhowa-tree,' when the tigress galloped past him, within a few yards!

I heard him fire two shots in rapid succession, and soon made my way up to him. He said that, after his shots, the tigress went on, but very lame; and he had lost sight of her at a spot where the little plateau he was on sloped down to some open ground, covered with 'bhér'* bushes (a thorny plant that attains the size of a may-tree in England, and which bears a little round, yellowish fruit that has a bitter-sweet taste), around whose base patches of rumnah-grass, some three feet high, were scattered here and there.

On reaching the spot where the ground sloped downwards, we saw the tigress lying under a bhér-tree out in the open, some two hundred yards from us. Davidson was all for opening fire on her there and then, but I would not assent to this; and, after some argument as to the best course to pursue, we decided to walk up to her till within some thirty or forty yards before firing, that is, if she would allow us to take such liberties. This we did; and got up to within some thirty yards of where she was lying, gazing

* Zizyphus jujuba.

at us, with her head between her paws, and her tail sweeping the ground preparatory to charging. Davidson then fired, and, with that hoarse, coughing roar made by a charging tiger, which can never be recalled by those who have once heard it without a tingling of the blood and a quickening of the pulse, up she jumped, and came straight at us, the incarnation of fiendish rage; but, both firing in succession, she turned, and entered one of the patches of grass I have alluded to, where she stood for an instant, giving me a standing shot. I heard the 'thud' of my bullet, and the next instant she turned, and came roaring and charging down at us again.

During this charge through the dry, withered grass, she presented a most curious appearance; and the only thing I can liken the scene to is to an imaginary long, fiery, wriggling serpent advancing rapidly in a sinuous course. Davidson gave her another shot as she came on; and, as he did so, an old stump of a tree, some four feet high, and slightly out of her direct course, seemed to attract her attention, and *this* she attacked with great fury, giving it a couple of swift, lightning-like pats with her great, muscular paws.

This gave us time to put in three more shots, which, as they were delivered at only some fifteen yards distance, tumbled her over, to our intense

"CAME STRAIGHT AT US, THE INCARNATION OF FIENDISH RAGE." *p.* 180.

relief and satisfaction. Pelting the body well with clods of earth and stones, to make sure she was dead, we walked up to inspect our prize, and were surprised to find the vitality she had exhibited. We had fired twelve shots at her, and out of these ten were hits, as shown in the diagram. The shot marked 'A' was my first

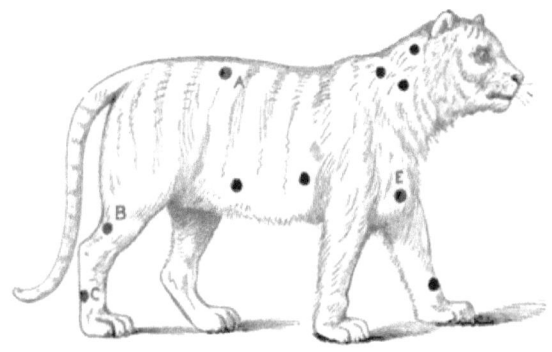

shot at her as she sprang up the bank, and had just missed breaking the vertebrae of the spine. 'B' and 'C' were Davidson's two shots, and had broken her off hind leg above and below the hock. 'E' was full in the chest. The other shots we could not individually account for; but one of the three between the head and the shoulder must have been the fatal one. It certainly seemed extraordinary that an animal with two legs broken, and wounded near such vital spots besides, could still have had the courage to show the fight she did!

Sending back to camp for the elephant to carry her there, we went to inspect the place where I had put her up, and there found the freshly-killed body of a stag cheetal, doubtless the one Davidson had fired at, but which he had evidently missed. On skinning and cutting open this tigress—whose skin lies before me as I write—we found three cubs in her womb. They were the size of kittens, and were distinctly marked; so would have been born in a few days.

Poor Hebbert's face, when he returned to camp and saw our bag, and heard all about the 'scuffle,' and what he had missed, fell sadly; but he was too good a sportsman to grudge us our good-fortune, and congratulated us heartily. This tigress was a large one, and measured eight feet nine inches.

It is extraordinary that an animal so large as a tiger should have such marvellous powers of concealing itself, even from the keenest vision; but this, like many another wise provision of Nature, has been, I suppose, given it to enable it to approach its prey the more easily, as well as to aid it in escaping from its enemy—man.

Who has not seen a hare squatting in a fallow-field, a hen pheasant among the dry underwood and dead leaves in a covert, or a grouse among the heather, and has not noticed how marvellously their fur or plumage harmonises with the surrounding ground? It is the same with a tiger; his tawny, striped hide is just the same shade as the dead grass and fallen leaves, amongst which he is often found in the hot weather. As an instance of how *very* close a tiger will lie, and remain concealed as long as he imagines he is undiscovered, I will relate the following incident which occurred during the same trip as that last related:

During a beat at a place called Tandla, Hebbert had wounded a large tiger, so, sending all the beaters away from the cover, we posted men in trees in a large circle to give us notice should the tiger sneak away. There were only Hebbert and myself out that day, Davidson being laid up with dysentery. All arrangements being made, we two mounted the elephant, and proceeded to look up the wounded animal. The spot where we expected to find him was a nullah about twenty feet wide, and about ten or twelve feet deep, and at a certain spot a smaller nullah joined it. They were both without any cover in them with the exception of a few tufts of stunted and withered grass not big enough to conceal a hare. We had carefully looked up the left bank which was opposite to the one where the small nullah debouched, and then turned and came down the opposite bank, intending to investigate the smaller nullah. We had got to the point of junction, and the elephant was standing close to the edge of the bank, whilst from our elevated position we were peering down into the nullah. Suddenly the elephant gave a loud 'phrew' (that well-known sign of alarm), and rapped the ground sharply with his trunk, drawing back slightly at the same time. The next instant we heard the deep roaring grunt of a charging tiger, saw a brindled mass of fur appear over the edge of the nullah, and the next moment the enraged tiger was on the elephant's head.

Such a scuffle as then ensued defies description from my poor pen. We dared not fire for fear of wounding the elephant, who was screaming with pain and rage, trying to kneel down, whilst the mahout, swearing, and expending all his choicest expletives on all the female relations of both tiger and elephant, was doing his best to retain his seat. Added to the confusion, we had our 'tiffin' basket in the howdah, into which I accidentally put my foot, driven out of my proper position by the violent shaking, and, slithering amongst edibles, soda-water, etc., I lost my balance, and nearly fell out of the howdah. At last the ele-

"THE NEXT MOMENT THE TIGER WAS ON THE ELEPHANT'S HEAD." *p.* 184.

phant, with a mighty effort, shook his assailant off, who came down to the ground with a resounding whack, and, turning tail, bolted off into the jungle. However, he was pulled up before going very far, and we returned to renew the fight. The tiger was sitting on his haunches, with his tongue out, and looking very sick, and three or four more shots finished him off. He was a fine tiger, and measured nine feet three inches. He was a very old one, evidently, as two of his large upper teeth and one of the lower ones were worn to stumps. This accounted for his not being able to retain his grip on the elephant's trunk. On skinning him, we found two slugs the size of peas imbedded in his flesh, so he must have been at some time wounded by a native.

On examining the spot from whence he charged out, we found that the bank projected very slightly, certainly not more than nine inches, and a few blades of withered grass hung down over this projection. The spot was perfectly visible from the opposite bank where we had begun our search, and it seemed unaccountable that we had not then detected the tiger. That the elephant did not do so was accounted for by the wind blowing *from* us towards the tiger.

Sportsmen cannot be too careful in approaching

a dead tiger, or dead as it may seem to them. Every precaution should be taken to make sure that life is extinct before the liberty of handling the body is taken. The neglect of this has often resulted in lives being lost, for it is astonishing how apparently dead animals sometimes recover.

I remember a few days previous to the death of the tiger recorded above, an incident illustrating this came under my notice. At a place called Dāba, Davidson had wounded a tiger which we were following up. That day, however, our elephant had, from some cause or other best known to himself, taken it into his head to reduce the howdah to splinters just before it was put on him. We had, therefore, to be content with only a pad, which is not the easiest thing to sit on and shoot from when occupied by three people. Our plan of operations was for Davidson and myself to be posted in trees, whilst Hebbert, on the elephant, should try to drive the tiger towards us, for, of course, as soon as we knew the animal was wounded, all the beaters had been withdrawn. With this end in view, and also with a view of safety in going to our posts, we all got on the pad, and from this more safe conveyance we intended to reach our respective trees. My tree had been selected, and I at once decided on occupying as my coign of vantage a convenient branch some ten feet from the ground. Below this tree the dry rumnah grass grew to a height of some two feet.

On our way thither the tiger jumped up about one hundred yards off, and charged down at us, roaring loudly. It was all brag on his part, however, for he dared not face the open, and the elephant stood like a rock. Turning back, he again repeated this manœuvre as we advanced, till he finally came to a standstill under the very tree in which it was intended I should be posted. Getting within about eighty yards of him, we saluted him with a volley, of which he took no notice. Hebbert then fired at him, and rolled him over. We saw him kicking about in the grass, then all was still, so we advanced a little closer, and treated him to a little 'independent firing,' to make sure (*proh pudor!* only one bullet hit him; but shooting off a pad is not calculated to ensure steadiness of aim), when he jumped up and sprang at the tree, scoring its trunk deeply with his claws to a height of some fourteen feet, and far above where I should have been sitting. This, however, was his expiring effort, and he fell back dead. He was a fine tiger, and measured nine feet, six inches. Had we dismounted, and gone up to him whilst lying apparently dead, the consequences might have proved serious to some of us.

There is no more striking incident connected with tiger-hunting than to witness the fearful and impotent rage of a wounded tiger. When out with Clay of my regiment, he fired at and hit a tiger in the back, so paralysing it. I then walked close up to it, and never shall I forget the wretched brute's mad but futile efforts to get at me till I put him out of his misery. He could only reach a short circle in front of him, but within this stones, sticks, and the earth were torn up with teeth and claws, and he even seized his own paws in his mouth, biting them through and through, whilst a mass of mingled foam and blood dripped from his jaws.

CHAPTER XII.

TIGER-SHOOTING (CONTINUED.)

Noiseless Motion of Tigers—Death of a Man-eater—Scene on the Neilgherry Hills—The Stalker Stalked—The Pipulkulti Tigress—A Good View of her Stalk—Apparent momentary Fascination of Cow—The Charge—Unconcern of Remainder of the Herd—The Cow Avenged—Tigers' Mode of Killing their Prey—Curious Incident with Black Buck—An Invulnerable Jackal—Assam Man-eater—Sitting Up as a ' Bait '—The Plan Succeeds, though not quite in the Manner Intended—Wonderful Presence of Mind—A Narrow Shave.

THE noiseless manner in which a tiger moves has always been to me one of the great marvels of nature, and, to those who have not witnessed it, it is difficult to convey an idea of how such a large animal can pass over dead leaves, twigs, &c., all dry and parched from the intense heat, and ready to crackle at the slightest touch, in such deadly silence ; for I can apply no other term. It may, however, be realised if any of my readers, who have not had the privilege of seeing a tiger in his native jungles, will watch the movements of a domestic tabby stalking a bird, and, further, if they will note the wonderful mechanism of a cat's foot, which causes the noiseless footfall. On those occasions on which I have seen a tiger approaching my post during a beat, I invariably found that he did so without the slightest noise. The first thing heard during a beat will be the patter of jungle-fowl and pea-fowl running over the dead leaves; then perhaps a hare will scamper past, followed, perhaps, by the frightened rush of a deer; and then, in striking contrast, will be seen the lord of the jungle approaching with noiseless tread, for he will not be heard unless he is alarmed, and is moving fast; *then*, caution seems thrown to the winds.

I cannot, I think, describe such a scene better than by quoting the words of a dear old friend to whom I am indebted for many hints of jungle-lore and much instruction in sport, *viz.*, the late Brigadier-General McMaster, a keen sportsman, good naturalist, and well-known man in the Madras Presidency.

He says: 'I was standing at the edge of a wood one burning day in April. The dry leaves and twigs with which the ground was covered rustled so audibly when moved by breeze, or living creature, that one might have fancied it impossible for a mouse to have passed unheard. I remembered afterwards that a hare, a jungle-hen, and some small lizard had each, as they ran by, attracted my attention, and that of the man beside me, by the crackling rustle of the dead leaves.

'Almost at the first distant shout of the beaters the large, man-eating tiger came out close to me, so noiselessly that, had not my eye caught him, he might have passed unobserved by me, as he was by the trained and trusty gun-carrier standing at my elbow, and who, looking in another direction and not seeing me raise my gun, had not, although his ears were from constant practice as keen to any noise on hillside or in forest as those of the wildest animal, an idea that game was on foot until he heard the angry growl with which the animal received his death-wound.'

Again he says, as an illustration of the cat-like tactics of the tiger:

'A few months ago, while going to look for ibex, I was passing over the large hill in front of the Avalanche bungalow on the Kondahs. Suddenly my gun-carrier asked me for my glass, and whispered that he could see a tiger crossing a bare ridge about half-a-mile off; his assistant corroborated this, but, even with the glass, I could not succeed in making out what these two men had discovered with the naked eye—and I own I thought the men were attempting to deceive me in order to restore my temper, which had been sorely ruffled by them the day before. They insisted that they saw a large tiger and not a panther, as I suggested it might be, and, when it passed out of view, agreed that we should probably come on it again by skirting another spur of the hill. I consented to this, although without placing the slightest faith in what they said.

'Presently, however, there was no doubt that they were right, for about five or six hundred yards from us appeared a tiger, a magnificent hill animal. He was quietly crossing a bare and rocky ridge, evidently looking out keenly for his breakfast, and taking advantage of every inch of cover, much as a cat in a cabbage garden looks out for sparrows. He sank nearly to a crouching position before attempting to top any ridge or hillock, and thus, with all but his head concealed, cautiously surveyed the ground in his front; to us on his flank he was perfectly visible. It may have been by chance, but, as he was then working, he was able to take as much advantage of the wind as the most scientific deer-stalker could have done. Twice he crouched in a half-sitting, half-recumbent posture, and gazed long and anxiously over the valley between us at the brow of the spur whereon my two men and I were stretched as flat as we could lay ourselves. He evidently suspected that there was something uncanny there, but luckily the wind was blowing strong from him to us, and moving the scanty grass sufficiently to puzzle his vision. The light shone full upon him, and in the clear mountain atmosphere which always causes objects to appear nearer than they really are, even without the glass, one could almost have counted the stripes on his sleek and glossy coat. He must have remained in view for many minutes as he quietly passed along the mountain side; and when he disappeared my men, with admirable knowledge of ground, took me as fast as we could run to a spot which would, they said, cross his path. He must have increased his pace during this interval, or he may have discovered there was something wrong in the air, for, notwithstanding that we had only a short way to go in comparison to his, he was at a rapid trot, or *run* would be a more correct term for the pace, and coming direct for us, just topping one hillock as our eyes rose to a level with the summit of the opposite one; we were in Indian file, and dropped down on the grass without a whisper. This attracted his attention—but he could not make us out, and, probably taking us in our grey shooting clothes for pigs, or ibex at rest, commenced stalking us

o

most carefully. He was about one hundred and thirty yards from us with one of the most beautiful Kondah glens between; on his hill, and about fifteen or twenty yards in his front, was a single rhododendron, about the same distance on mine was a small clump of three or four of those lovely shrubs, then glowing in all the glory of their deep red blossoms. He dropped on his belly at once, and thus crept onwards to his bush, while I, making myself as snake-like as possible, contrived to get forward to my clump.

'Thus stalking each other, so to speak, we mutually managed to decrease the distance between us. It was almost in vain, however, for the cunning brute kept his rhododendron stump so pertinaciously before him that, although I had a perfect view of his hind-quarters beyond it, and he was facing me, I could not, though in a most favourable position to aim, get a shot at his chest. I think he would have come on had not one of my men tried to crawl after me; this caused him to jump up; as he turned I fired, breaking his hind-leg, but although this stopped him so much that I managed to get up to him again, and have two shots—one of them a very bad miss—he still lives to prey on Todah buffaloes. I would rather, however, have seen what I did then, and have missed him altogether, than have killed him without such a rare opportunity of watching a tiger.'

In this latter expression of the writer I think all true sportsmen and lovers of nature will agree, and will envy him the opportunity he had of thus observing the animal's tactics in a stalk. It must have been intensely interesting, and the pure air and lovely scenery of the Neilgherry hills, where the adventure occurred, must have enhanced the pleasure considerably.

It is but seldom that the chance of seeing a tiger stalk his prey is afforded to the European sportsman, and, as such instances are rare, I feel I need offer no apology to my readers for again quoting from a friend of mine— Captain Pierson.*
He, Allen,† and Oxley.‡ were all quartered at Kamptee in the Central Provinces shortly before I was, and I was intimately acquainted with Captain Pierson. The account which was written by Captain Pierson appeared, I believe, in the *Indian Sporting Magazine*, and the incident occurred on the 11th of May, 1869, on the banks of the Peu Gunga river in Berar. It is as follows :—

'We had been tempted off our proposed line of route, while on the march on the 11th by the receipt of the news of a tiger which had killed

---

* Now Lieutenant-Colonel Pierson, retired, R.A.
† Lieutenant G. B. Allen, R.A.
‡ Captain C. R. Oxley, 38th M.N.I. (now dead).

two village cows in the bed of the river, near the village of Pipulkulti; and, encamping at Watoli, had sent our shikari to "tie up" near Pipulkulti, and also near Amba, a village in the opposite direction, close by which we had a "kill" a week previous.

'The news came in early from both directions, nothing from Amba, and "no kill" also from Pipulkulti; but "Shaikh Boden," our head shikari, who had inspected the latter place, had found fresh tracks, so we determined to try our luck, and started after breakfast with about twenty coolies for a beat.

'One mile below Pipulkulti the Pen Gunga averages about four hundred yards in breadth, where a larger nullah runs into it from the Berar side. In the bed of the river there are a large number of small, flat islands covered with a description of cyprus and grass, affording sufficient cover for a tiger to take refuge in.

'Shaikh Boden proposed beating diagonally up the bed of the river, and that we should post ourselves half-way down the bank behind some bushes on the *up* extremity of the cover, the dispositions of the islands, on which was the only cover, being such that the chances were greatly in favour of the tiger being forced within easy range. This plan we agreed to pursue, and were walking along the northern bank, on our way to our posts, when we were stopped by the cry of "Bagh hai," and, looking down to the bed of the river, saw what was apparently a very large tiger stalking a herd of cattle that had come down to water. We crouched down, and had the luck to see the whole business. The tigress, as she proved to be, when first seen, was stealthily stalking a white cow, which was some little way off from the main body of the herd, and, taking advantage of the slightly undulating bed of the river, had probably approached across an open space of perhaps five hundred yards, before this cow had seen her; the rest of the herd were behind one of the islands, and could not yet see the enemy.

'The white cow allowed the tigress to approach her within about eighty yards before she appeared to notice her danger, and at first seemed to be fascinated by the appearance of the brute creeping towards her, and it was only when the tigress commenced to increase her pace to a trot that the cow made off; the trot increased immediately to a lumbering gallop as the tigress had now got on to the firmer ground that surrounded the islands, and in a very short time she skirted 'over a small ridge into close proximity of the herd, which was then commencing to scatter on the news received from the white cow! The gallop turned into a charge, and in a few seconds the tigress had picked out a fine young cow, on whose back she sprang, and they both rolled over in a heap. When the two animals were still again, we could distinctly see the cow standing up with her neck embraced by the tigress, who was evidently sucking her jugular; the poor cow made a few feeble efforts to release herself, which the tigress resented by—breaking her neck!

'The remainder of the herd, some twenty in number, after rushing wildly away, now returned to within fifty yards of the tigress, who was silently slaking her thirst off the cow, and stood looking on, huddled up together, at the unexpected arrangement; finding, after a few minutes' survey, that the animal embracing the cow was probably a dangerous one, they scuttled up the south bank and commenced grazing immediately.

'Our first idea was to go down and try to stalk the tigress whilst still on the slaughtered animal, but Shaikh Boden recommended sitting still, as the ground was unfavourable, and we should certainly frighten her away before we could get within shot, even supposing she remained on the cow long enough to allow us time to walk round; so we sat quiet, and had the satisfaction, in a few minutes, of seeing the tigress leave her prey, and move slowly away. Creeping round the small bit of cover where she had killed, she walked back over her stalk to a pool of water at the east extremity of the islands, where we lost sight of her. As the tigress had retreated into the very part of the cover where Shaikh Boden had first expected to find her, we had merely to follow out the original idea of the beat, and we posted ourselves about half-way down the bank under a couple of trees.

'The tigress turned up almost at the first shout of the beaters, and made straight towards Allen, and, turning off when opposite to where he was sitting, moved nearly parallel to the bank in Oxley's and my direction (we were under the same tree), and brought up in a small crack between two islands opposite to us, about eighty yards off, and looked round in the direction of the beaters. As this seemed the best chance we were likely to get, we agreed to open fire. I fired first, and rolled her over, and Allen got two difficult shots as she was galloping up a small bank over which she disappeared. We then went down, and, after a short search found the tigress lying dead in the grass.'

I think the sight so graphically described by my friend has been seldom if ever equalled, as an example of the tiger's mode of taking its prey; and, as far as my limited knowledge and experience goes, it must have been a sight that seldom falls to the lot of any sportsman to witness.

Everything was complete: the sportsmen, unobserved themselves, looked on at the stalk, and could see the stalker and its victim; how the former took every advantage of ground and cover, the fascination produced on the cow by the tigress's stealthy approach, the terror of her fellow-kine, and then, when *they* were no longer threatened, their selfish and utter unconcern. The *finale*, too, was quite in keeping, and the successful shots that laid the tigress low, and the quiet and sportsmanlike manner in which the whole affair was carried out, without hurry or fuss, worthy of the actors in the sylvan scene; who were, I may safely assert, some of the best sportsmen, in or out of the saddle, with rifle or spear, of many that have been known in the sunny land of Ind.

There is a very prevalent notion that the tiger kills his prey with a crushing blow from his fore paw. This is decidedly a mistake, I think. A tiger certainly does use his fore paws to strike down his quarry, but the death-wound is administered by the teeth. The neck being seized in the powerful jaws, and bent back till it is dislocated. In every instance where I have had an opportunity of noticing an animal killed by a tiger, I have invariably found the fang-marks in the neck, though the shoulders and flanks of the victim might be scarred by the claws of the tiger.

Another incident showing how a tiger *will* charge on occasion was related to me by the same friend (Captain, now Lieutenant-Colonel, Pierson), which occurred during a subsequent trip, and, as it is a most exciting bit of sport, I give it in the words of his own journal, which he has kindly placed at my disposal:

'On the 22nd of April, Rawlins, Hebbert, Brough, and self were at Dāba,* a village consisting of some twenty thatched houses, where there was a strange story of a panther who was in the habit of visiting this and the neighbouring villages at night, making a hole in the roof or wall of a hut, and dragging off an unfortunate victim from the inside. In this way some thirteen men and women had been carried off during the past month. News arrived of a kill whilst we were at breakfast, so we started about ten a.m. with twenty beaters, and travelled four miles in a country cart, over, I think, the stoniest roads in Asia, thereby saving our horses and jolting ourselves.

'The first beat near the hill proved blank. Leaving our posts, we walked down the nullah

* Vide p. 186.

till we came across tracks which Shaikh Boden declared were quite fresh; so we arranged a fresh beat which also proved blank, though our shikari whilst conducting the beat, discovered by some very creditable tracking in the grass that the tiger had doubled back in the direction of our first beat. This he must have done in a most leary way on hearing us. His tracks were, however, soon lost; so, after deliberation, we resolved on trying our first beat (which ran along a nullah between two ranges of hills) again, only in the opposite direction to which we had beaten it previously.

'The tiger turned up at the very end of the beat, and trotted down a branch nullah towards Rawlins, who fired and hit, turning the tiger back into high grass, amongst which he disappeared. It was impossible to "walk him up," so, having posted markers in trees, we set fire to the grass, which we succeeded in burning all round a triangular patch in the fork between two nullahs. Although the markers saw him move, he refused to leave this, so Rawlins and Brough, being posted in trees, Hebbert and I went round to protect the beaters whilst firing this last remaining cover. In doing so I saw the tiger lying down under a bush, and fired; with several roars, and after some delay, during which the tiger appeared to be tumbling about in the grass, he galloped off past Rawlins and Brough, who emptied their rifles without stopping him. We then all joined together, and followed up in the direction he had gone, not very sanguine, as the tiger was apparently not very hard hit; the ground was jungly and the grass high. However, Hebbert soon saw him moving slowly through the grass, and fired. This was too much for him, and with a roar of warning he charged straight at our line, the long grass only showing his head as he galloped over the thirty yards of ground between us. Six shots met him *en route*, mostly hitting him about the head and neck. Hebbert fired *his* last shot almost in the brute's face, slightly checking and turning him; but, recovering, he, after clearing our flank, turned in on Hebbert (who was backing with empty rifle round the others), and was on the point of springing on him, when I fired the last remaining barrel left among us, and bowled him over. The pluckiest charge on record. Length, eight feet nine inches.'

It must indeed, as my friend says, have been one of 'the pluckiest charges on record,' and shows what determination *some* of these brutes possess, not to be stopped or even turned for a moment, except for a twinkling, as it were, by four determined men in line, armed with the best of rifles; and yet, although hit all over the head, chest, and neck, as subsequent examination proved, he still came on, and very nearly made good his charge. Anyhow, *he* died as a tiger *ought* to die —tracked, met face to face, and fought on his own ground by four *sportsmen*, and not done to death by that low, villainous system of poisoning, which, alas! I heard subsequently was the means of destroying many another tiger in India, and which poaching system of shikar was (*proh! puder*) I believe, invented and practised by an officer of Her Majesty's service, who dubbed himself 'Tiger slayer to the Government of India.' Let him be nameless, and let his cognomen sink into that oblivion amongst true sportsmen which is the only fitting resting-place for the name of one who could practise such vile arts, looked at from a sporting point of view.

With reference to the allusion made in a preceding page of how apparently dead animals will sometimes recover, I may perhaps here be pardoned for quoting one or two instances of the fact that came under my notice, and, though the game in these instances was more ignoble, I think they are none the less interesting.

A friend of mine once, after a successful stalk, knocked over a fine black buck, and walking up to him, as he was lying kicking convulsively on the ground, laid down his discharged rifle, and pulled out his shikar knife wherewith to cut his throat. Seizing the buck by the horns with his left hand, he bent back its throat, and, plunging the knife in, was just about to give it a turn, when with a mighty effort the buck sprang up, and, sending my astonished friend flying on to the broad of his back, made off, and was soon lost to view. He was never seen again, though tracked for a couple of miles by the blood. My friend supposed his bullet must have struck one of the buck's horns, and so stunned him for a moment.

When I was stationed at Roorkee, and had no time to make expeditions after larger game, I often used to go out for a ride in the evening with a few dogs, and have a course after jackals, foxes, or hares. My pack consisted of an English greyhound, three cross-bred terriers—but regular varmints—and often a well-bred bull-bitch belonging to a brother-officer. These generally managed to account for any animal they hunted of the three species above named. The greyhound generally ran down or turned the quarry into the mouths of the rest of the pack.

One day, when out with a brother-ensign near the hospital at Roorkee, we started a jackal, which was soon run into, and apparently killed. After the dogs had had a good worry at him, and I had given him a couple of cracks on his head with a hammer-headed hunting-whip to extinguish any spark of life, and finding we neither of us had any knife with us to take off his brush, my friend cantered off to the hospital to get one.

The dogs were all lying down panting some little distance off, and I had for the moment turned my back to what I supposed was a *dead* jackal. Suddenly the dogs jumped up in a great state of excitement, and the next moment I saw my supposed defunct quarry making off. He was, however, soon run into, and then the worry was repeated, and I hammered his skull into what I fancied must be a pulp; my friend reappearing shortly after, we deprived the jackal of his brush; but the knife was too blunt to cut his throat, so carrying his body to the Ganges Canal, which was only some two hundred yards distant, we flung it in.

We watched the body float down the rapid stream some little way, then it seemed to revive; presently the head came uppermost, and the next moment we saw our friend actually swimming, and after a minute or two the poor maimed brute gained the opposite bank, and, crawling under a bush, disappeared, and we never saw him again.

I trust that this may not be considered an Indian story, for I can vouch for the truth of every word, and so would, I know, my companion, if haply he were alive, which I regret to say he is not. I may be blamed for unnecessary brutality, but I knew very little of the habits of Indian wild animals at that time, and still less of the extraordinary vitality they will at times display, and in the innocence of my heart imagined I had taken every means to kill the animal. The result showed how mistaken I was.

Of man-eating tigers I have had no personal experience; but the following extraordinary story, which I believe has lately caused considerable sensation in India, was a few days ago related to me by my brother, who has just returned. In a certain planting district (Assam, I believe) there was a notorious man-eater. Two gentlemen, we will call them A. and B., residing together on an estate, had lost, besides other employés, two 'chowkedars,' or native watchmen, within a few days, and the unfortunate men had been actually carried off out of the verandah of the bungalow. A. and B. therefore determined to clothe themselves like natives, and sit during the night, armed, in the verandah, in the hopes they might be able to get a shot at the man-eater, who they thought might probably return to the spot which had already provided him with two victims.

They proceeded to carry out this intention, and

sat up till about two or three o'clock, a.m., but nothing appeared. A. then said he should not stay up any longer, as he did not believe the animal would come; but B. announced his intention of waiting half-an-hour longer by himself.

There were large windows opening down to the floor of the verandah, and through one of these A. retired, and, after entering his room, had just closed the window, and was gazing out for an instant, when he saw a dark mass land in the verandah, right on to his friend, then heard sounds of a scuffle, and a cry for help. Seizing his rifle, to which a sword-bayonet was attached, and flinging up the window, he rushed out, in time to see B. walking down the steps that led up to the verandah from the garden *alongside of the tiger with his hand in the latter's mouth!*

A. was afraid to fire lest he should hit his friend, so running after him he, with admirable presence of mind, went up to the tiger, and plunging his bayonet into the animal's body, at the same instant fired.

There was a roar and a scuffle, and B. took advantage of the moment to release his hand, and the tiger, after tumbling about for a moment or two, died. B.'s hand was terribly mauled, and he subsequently, I believe, had to have it amputated; but the loss of a hand was a comparatively cheap price to pay for saving his life, which was mainly owing to the wonderful coolness of himself and his friend.

From his narrative of the event, it appears that as soon as A. had closed the window, the tiger (who must have been all the time lying close by them) landed in the verandah with a mighty spring, and seized B. by the hand. He, with wonderful coolness, at once, on being seized, made no effort to extricate the limb, though the pain must have been excruciating, but, quietly rising, followed the tiger's movements, and actually walked some way by his side, with his hand in the brute's mouth, until A. by his prompt and determined action released him.

I regret being unable to give the names of the parties concerned, but my brother tells me he can vouch for the truth of the story, the events of which caused a great sensation at the time, only a few months ago.

It may not here be out of place to say a few words regarding the measurements of tigers. We constantly hear of twelve and thirteen feet tigers. This is all nonsense. A ten-feet tiger is an enormous brute. Nine feet five inches is the biggest I have ever seen, and nine feet four inches is about the average of a full-grown male, and about

P

eight feet four inches for a tigress. A tiger's skin may be stretched to measure any amount when *dry;* but the correct method is to measure the length from the point of the nose to the tip of the tail over the head and along the spine as soon after death as possible. Sportsmen should always do this themselves; for, as Captain Forsyth truly says, 'if natives are allowed to use the tape, they are certain to throw in a foot or two to please master. Master also, no doubt, sometimes pleases himself in a similar manner!'

CHAPTER XIII.

TIGER-SHOOTING (CONCLUDED).

Unlucky Days—Ningnur—I nearly make a Fatal Mistake—Folly of Changing One's Mind—Useless Pursuit—Blank Day—'If——' —Another Try for Bears—Galop after a Boar—Lose Him— Sold by a Panther—Tigers' and Panthers' Mode of Devouring their Prey—Start for the other Kill—Mistakes—The Tiger Roused—My Folly—Bad Luck with a Boar—A Chapter of Accidents.

> 'All hits are history,
> All misses are mystery.'

How true is the above quotation, for successful days in sport are certainly charming, both at the time, and when one looks back on them in after years; but days when everything seems to have gone wrong are certainly the reverse. Do we not all know the day when we were 'out of it' in a good gallop with hounds, owing perhaps to taking a wrong turn, or perhaps our heart failed us when we ought to have negotiated that awkward place in the corner, and we thought we

p 2

could find an easier place. Ah! those easier places are seldom found, and a little want of decision and determination at the right moment sends us home, put out, discontented, and inclined to pooh-pooh the accounts of our rivals, who, owing to doing the right thing at the right moment, have enjoyed all the delights of that fast forty minutes.

Or maybe we are anglers, and devote our time to the capture of the lordly salmon and the speckled trout. How many occasions are there when, owing to having put too much strain on our fish, or not caring to follow him over some nasty ground, or through tumbling into a hole when doing so, or by committing some of the hundred and one mistakes we are all prone to do sometimes, we have seen the delicious bend of our rod straighten out, and our line, perhaps, minus a cast, and a half-crown fly, floats back, slack and useless, whilst we mutter, below our breath, 'D—— it, he's broken me!'

Or we may have played our fish with consummate skill: have alternately fought with and humoured him, until he floats broadside helplessly in the shallow water beneath our feet. Cautiously we advance the deadly gaff or the landing-net; another moment, and he will be ours: and won't we just drink his health in a nip of pure

'Glenlivet!' But no, just one final wag of the broad tail, and he is off, gradually sinking and vanishing from our distracted gaze!

Yes, we have all gone through it: hunting, shooting, fishing, racing. In all sports there have been some days which would have been marked with a red letter in our sporting memory—*if only*—— Ah! that infernal 'if'; it is always that. That accounts for the 'slip betwixt the cup and the lip.'

As I have devoted some pages to narrating successful incidents in Indian sport, it is only fair that I should relate the result of some days, when all went wrong, and we came back to camp disheartened, disgusted, and out of temper, breathing anathemas at our bad luck, and vowing we would be more careful next time—and then, perhaps, next time we committed the same faults! It would only weary my readers to relate many of the unsuccessful days I had, so I shall content myself with the narration of two that stand out particularly clear in my memory. The first will show the folly of changing one's mind, and the second the folly of over-excitement and eagerness.

To begin with the first. During my second hot-weather trip, Hebbert, Davidson, and myself had arrived at a place called Tandla, situated on the borders of the Nizam of Hyderabad's territory.

Just before breakfast, 'khubber' arrived of a kill near the camp, (this tiger we subsequently bagged, and was the one who lay so close, as narrated in a previous chapter)*, and also of one near Ningnur. Now, at this latter place, Captain Preston, of Her Majesty's 44th Regiment (now Major-General Preston), had been badly mauled by a tiger the preceding year, so we determined to go and avenge him.

Davidson was still feeling very ill, and, as it necessitated an eight-mile ride on the elephant, he determined not to accompany us. This was the first piece of bad luck, as *if*—there it comes in —he had been with us, we should have had the third gun we so badly wanted. Hebbert and I accordingly started, and a precious hot ride we had. On arriving at Ningnur we found Lutchman, our second shikari, (who was worth twenty of our head 'boss,' a gentleman rejoicing in the name of Tooker-Ram, and who proved utterly useless) had made all necessary preparations, and had forty beaters collected, and all ready to start as soon as we should arrive. The ground we were to beat was very bare, part of it having lately been burnt by a jungle-fire, with the exception of a deepish nullah, which, after winding about, branched off in two directions.

* Vide page 183.

It was a blazing hot day, and, as the villagers had been out with Captain Preston the previous year, and knew the road these tigers (for there were two) travelled, we left the posting of the guns to them. I was placed in a tree at the spot where the nullah branched out, whilst Hebbert was taken to a small tree right out on the bare, burnt ground. I was intently watching the big nullah down which the beat was advancing, and heard the tigers roar, when a rustle among some dead leaves to my left rear caught my ear. Peering cautiously round, I saw a movement amid the brushwood, then a sun-ray fell for a moment on, as I thought, a yellow hide. Raising my rifle very cautiously, I covered the spot, only waiting for the next movement to pull the trigger, when, to my horror, I saw Hebbert's *face* as a slight gust of wind stirred some of the foliage amongst which he was hidden!

I shall never forget the cold, creepy sensation that came over me when I thought how near I had been to shooting my best friend. It appeared, subsequently, that he, on reaching the spot where he was advised to post himself, right out in the open in the re-entering angle formed by the nullah, had come to the conclusion that for a gun to be posted in such an open spot was useless, for, as he said, he felt no tiger would face such an open piece, devoid of any shade or cover, on such a broiling hot day. He had, accordingly, left his post, and come back to post himself in what *he* thought would be a better place.

Here was mistake number two, for, as it turned out afterwards, both tigers passed right under the very tree he had originally been in, and went away up into some bare, rocky hills. Here we followed them, attracted by the chattering of some monkeys, but failed to find them. On our return, on jumping down from a rock, I fell and dented one barrel of my rifle rather badly. Bit of bad luck number three. Soon after we came on fresh footprints and a spot under an overhanging rock showing plainly that one of the tigers, at least, had lain up in a little corrie not fifty yards out of the line of our beat up the hill. We had been in too great a hurry, and had passed him by, and this he took advantage of by doubling back to his original cover. Mistake number four.

To make a long story short, we tried every dodge to circumvent these wily brutes, but ineffectually; at last, being past five o'clock, we had given it up, and were on our way back to the village where the elephant was awaiting us, when we saw one of the tigers drinking at a pool below us, some hundred yards off. She was too quick, however, for, hearing the chattering of the beaters, she jumped up the opposite bank and disappeared, and, though we tried another beat, it was unavailing. Another bit of bad luck. Then the weary, jolting ride home had to be faced, and poor Hebbert was feeling miserably seedy from the combined effects of hard work under a blazing sun and an empty stomach, and I was not much better—for, thinking the distance to Ningnur was only about half what it eventually turned out to be, and thinking we should be back in camp at three p.m., at the latest, we had taken no lunch with us. As it was, we did not get back till past nine p.m.; too done up and tired to eat anything, and, after a 'B. and S.' (a truly grateful draught), we tumbled into bed, weary and disgusted, and our last words, I think, to each other, ere the drowsy god claimed us, was ' If we had only——' Again that fatal 'if.'

Now nearly all these mistakes might and should have been avoided, and we might have had a successful termination to our expeditions, if we had only been content to take things a little more quietly, and trusted more to the knowledge of men who knew far more of the habits of these individual tigers than we possibly could do: but no, with the overweening confidence of Britons in our own powers, we neglected advice and precautions which, had they been taken, would have caused us to remember the day with pleasure instead of numbering it among one's black-letter days.

Now for incident No. 2. We were, a few days after the fruitless expedition just related, encamped at a place called Mehal Kini.

Early in the morning, in fact before daylight, we had all gone to some small conical hills out on an open plain, on the chance of meeting bears, and riding and spearing them—a feat I never had the good fortune to perform; for, though I often tried, I never had the chance to come across one on rideable ground. Hebbert had, however, speared several himself, and described the sport as a very fine one. However, on this occasion, like on many others, we were unsuccessful, for 'divil a bear' came near us, though from pretty fresh tracks they evidently had been in the habit of lying among the boulders and overhanging rocks with which the hill-sides were strewn.

After leaving the hills, we saw a couple of hyænas go into a small 'sind-bund,' or grove of 'sindee' palms, and, *faute de mieux*, determined to have a gallop after them. On beating the cover, a sounder of eight or nine hog broke, containing a fairish boar, so of course we elected to ride them instead of the more ignoble game. We had a good spin over rather rough ground, plentifully covered with stones and sheet rock, which of course was all in favour of the boar, who eventually beat us by getting into a very large sind-bund from which we found it impossible to dislodge him. We had just 'scratched' him with our spears as he reached the cover; but this was all. On our way back to camp I had a shot at a fine buck chikara, or ravine deer, which jumped up close to me, and bowled him over, and this was the only bit of good fortune we had during the day.

Whilst at breakfast, news arrived of two kills in opposite directions—one about four miles off, and the other about six. We determined to go to the nearest, and, on arriving at the place, proceeded to go and look at the 'kill' (a village bullock), which we found lying under a tree on a rocky hill-side, very sparsely clothed with a few trees. One glance was sufficient to show us it was the work of a panther, and not of a tiger, for the only parts devoured were the stomach and flanks, which had been neatly eaten out all round, whereas a tiger *invariably*, as far as my experience goes, begins with the hind leg, and eats upwards. In this statement I am corroborated by many Indian sportsmen of far greater experience than myself.

I am induced here to make allusion to this

matter of a tiger's mode of eating his prey, as there have lately been several letters in the *Field* on the subject, brought forth by a statement in Colonel Barras' book, 'India and Tiger-Hunting,' in which a tiger is said to *always begin with the stomach*. With all due deference to the gallant colonel, I must beg to differ from him *in toto* on this point, which is, I think, an important one, and the observance of which will in many instances save sportsmen not only much fruitless beating, but also disappointment, for a panther is as a rule a far more difficult animal to rouse during a beat than a tiger.

To resume, however. When we found the 'kill' was the work of a panther, and saw the nature of the ground, we determined to go and visit the other kill which Lutchman had personally inspected, and which he assured us was certainly the work of a tiger, and that, moreover, he had tracked him.

Accordingly we returned to camp, but Davidson, who was still weak from his illness, did not feel up to any further exertion, and decided to stay at home, so Hebbert and I started with some thirty beaters. On arriving at the scene of action, the Huiri nullah, we found it was almost a small river running through a gorge in the hills, which rose steeply on either side, and were devoid of grass and brushwood, though there were some fine forest trees about which at that season, however, were bare and leafless, with one or two exceptions. It was a somewhat difficult place to beat, so we thought our best plan was to walk up to the kill, which we found lying under a jamun-bush overhanging the left bank of the river, and close to one of the few little pools of water left in it, in the hopes the tiger might be lying close by, and thus afford us a shot.

This proceeding was in itself a mistake, as subsequent events proved; still, had it not been for my own inexcusable over-eagerness and stupidity, we might eventually have bagged this tiger. Lutchman assented to our suggested plan of attack to a certain extent, but said, if we did not find the tiger in the close vicinity of the kill, we might walk up the nullah and look at some thin cover that lay a short distance beyond. Then, if we did not find there, that we should make a *détour*, and, posting ourselves, beat up the nullah from this spot.

This plan we proceeded to carry out, and had hardly gone some three hundred yards from the kill, when the tiger jumped up from under the left bank of the nullah from under a jamun bush, looked at us for a second, then, turning, trotted up the nullah, and, springing up the right bank, stood for a moment as if undetermined what to do. Hebbert happened to be a little in front of me; we had each been examining one bank of the nullah, he taking the left, whilst I looked along the right. I had got slightly behind, owing to having stopped to examine more minutely a 'pug' in the sand with a view to determine its freshness, when the tiger got up; so—running up to Hebbert, as the tiger stood on the bank, some hundred and fifty yards, gazing at us—like an idiot I fired at him! Needless to say I missed, and he only acknowledged the salute with a surly grunt, and galloped up the hillside when Hebbert fired at him with a like result. Running round, we posted ourselves, leaving Lutchman to head the beat towards us. It was no use, however; the tiger was thoroughly alarmed, the day was getting on, and the ground was so rocky that tracking was almost impossible, and we never saw him again. Hebbert of course was excessively put out with me, and rightly attributed the losing of this tiger entirely to my over-eagerness, though on thinking matters over subsequently I came to the conclusion that if—there comes in the fatal little word again—we had *begun* by beating we should have been more successful; still, I could not conceal from myself that the fiasco was entirely owing to my thoughtless hurry.

To atone, what more can I do than even now, after the lapse of many years, relate the fact of my folly and exclaim, 'Mea culpa, mea culpa'?

This, I think, was an instance of a day when all went wrong. First we got up in the dark, and had a longish ride in search of bears which we never saw. Secondly, after a good gallop after a boar, we failed at the last moment to bag him. Thirdly, a hot and weary ride to a place after a mythical tiger, and finally, when we did find a real one, a successful termination to our 'chasse' was spoiled through stupidity!

At the risk of wearying my readers I cannot refrain from quoting another day, which for a real chapter of accidents I never knew beaten, and, though it was not connected with tiger-shooting, it may perhaps not be out of place to relate it here.

A large party of us were out on a pig-sticking expedition, and we had heard of an enormous boar, which by native report was said to be the size of a bullock! His stronghold was a sind-bund, not very big, but very thick and dense. Well, we beat for this boar from eleven a.m. till four p.m., and tried every stratagem that ingenuity could devise to induce him to break, but in vain, and we had to give him up. On our way home, I was behind the rest of the party leading my horse. I remember putting my foot in the stirrup on mounting, to catch up the rest of the party, and then all was a blank till I woke up next morning with a fearful headache. I had been picked up insensible that night amongst some high grass, and brought into camp—but how the fall happened I have never been able to fathom to this day. Then my unfortunate 'boy,' or native servant, lost an eye through the bursting of a bottle of soda-water which he was placing to cool for me, and a servant belonging to another of the party got badly stung by a scorpion!

This, I think, was a pretty good conglomeration of unlucky incidents, none of which were attributable to any want of precaution on anyone's part. These few anecdotes will be fair evidence that in the pursuit of large game in the East everything is not always *couleur de rose*.

CHAPTER XIV.

ABOUT SOME DEER.

The Poetry of Sport—Long Shots to be Avoided—Varieties of Deer —Sambur—Beating—Stalking—Amongst the Sewalik Hills— The Twelve-tined Deer—Spotted Deer—Their Habits—An Imaginary Stalk—A Wounded Stag shows Fight—Good Bag out of a Herd—Riding down Spotted Deer—Para, or Hog-deer —Shoot One in a Snipe Jheel—The Muntjak—Description— Their curious Bark—'Paloo'—A Shot in the Hills—Jungle Fare—The Four-horned Antelope—Description.

IF, as 'Hawkeye' (that good sportsman and charming writer who has contributed such delightful articles to the *South of India Observer*) remarks, *beating* for deer on the hills and dense forests of India may be termed the prose of sport, surely he is right in dubbing *stalking* the poetry of sport?

There are numerous Indian field-sports more exciting than stalking the 'bonnie dun deer,' but few that bring back more delightful recollections of hours passed in the solitary grandeur of the hills and jungles but seldom trod by the foot of a white man. We love to remember the day when we saw the lordly stag, accompanied by his harem, browsing in some open glade of the forest, or perhaps standing out in bold relief on the top of a hill, against the skyline at the first flush of dawn; we love to remember the pains we took to circumvent him, and match our human reasoning powers against his marvellous sense of smell and keen vision; and still more dearly do we love to recall that, to a sportsman's ear, most delicious sound, the answering 'thud' of our bullet, and perhaps the long weary tramp after our wounded quarry, and then to picture our delight at finding him dead perhaps some miles off from where we had fired at him, and we found our toil and perseverance rewarded by a noble pair of antlers.

There are dozens of men good and true sportsmen, with both rifle and spear, on foot or mounted, who yet will not be bothered with the (to them) tediousness attending stalking. How much they miss seeing many of the glories of nature, only those know who have participated in this, the poetry of sport.

To such men I can only say that beating for deer bears as much comparison to stalking them, as shooting a home-bred pheasant in England does to knocking over a wily, twisting snipe on a bright frosty day when 'Scolopax' is more than usually on the alert.

And I must warn my readers that they will find no records here of wonderful long shots —of deer knocked over at three hundred yards, etc. In the first place, I do not believe in long shots at *any* kind of game, and secondly, I think it is unsportsmanlike; for, if a man does hit his game, the poor brute will probably go off to die a lingering and painful death, and secondly if he misses, as he probably will, he only frightens the game unnecessarily. No shot I think ought to be fired with a rifle at a distance beyond one hundred and fifty yards, for preference say from eighty to one hundred yards.

However, as both methods are pursued, I will endeavour to give a slight sketch of each, as well as of the varieties of deer that a sportsman may expect to meet with, viz., the sambur, twelve-tined deer, spotted deer, hog deer, munt-jak, and four-horned antelope. All these I have shot myself, with the exception of the twelve-tined or swamp deer, in the valley of the Doon, or in the jungles of the Central Provinces.

To commence with beating. A stag sambur is a grand-looking beast. Larger and more massive than the British red-deer, he stands some four feet eight inches at the shoulder—his colour is a dark brown, darker and without the red tinge that pervades our red deer at home. He has at some seasons a coarse sort of mane on his neck, and round his throat, which is often erected when the animal is excited by pain, or from other causes. He has three points on each horn, and a good pair will measure over three feet along the sweep, and about eight to nine inches round the burr—where they spring from the frontal bone.

Sambur * love the hill-sides and table-lands which are often clothed with long grass, and, though they will travel a long way during the night for food and water, are seldom found during the day-time on the more level portions of the forests they inhabit. Having reached the spot where they intend to lie up for the day, and having first taken a good look round to assure themselves that no enemy is in their vicinity, they proceed to make a form very like a hare's in the long grass, generally under the shade of a tree. These forms are usually made when the grass is green, and resorted to daily by the sambur, as long as they frequent that particular locality, and remain undisturbed. This fact is well known by the jungle tribes, and they can make pretty certain of the whereabouts of the animal, and the usual route he pursues going from and returning to his

* Rusa Aristotelis.

form. All that has to be done, therefore, is to obtain a sufficient number of beaters, and post the guns accordingly. This method, however, is open to the great objection of disturbing a large extent of country, a great drawback in the eyes of sportsmen who are in pursuit of nobler game; and besides, the shooting of such an animal driven up to you, calls forth but little skill and ingenuity on the part of the sportsman partaking of the sport.

Far different will be the feelings of the sportsman who obtains a noble pair of antlers, without the aid of beaters, and by exercising all his own powers of endurance and skill in woodcraft. I say *antlers* advisedly, for no one pretending to the name of sportsman would disgrace himself by shooting a hind, except when meat was urgently required in his camp. Alas, though, I am afraid there are many calling themselves sportsmen who do resort to such vile practices, and prefer the quantity to quality as far as their bag is concerned. To such the best term that can be applied is one used by my dear old friend the late General McMaster, to whom I have alluded in a preceding page, who always called them 'fleshers,' the Scotch term for butchers, and well it suits such men.

Stalking can be pursued by the sportsman going out himself with one attendant, and searching silently the spots sambur are known to frequent. For this sport a good pair of binoculars is indispensable, for it is astonishing how easily a sambur may be mistaken for an old tree-stump, or rock.

In pursuing this method the sportsman should endeavour to be just below the sky-line of a ridge of hills, so that the deer which always travel upwards should have less chance of detecting him. He then will have the chance of meeting any stags that may be returning to their forms, or, should he be unsuccessful in this, he may come across stags lying down after the sun is up.

Another method is to send out some of the jungle-men in couples, long before daylight; these should post themselves where they can command a good view of the surrounding country. Some spot may be appointed as a rendezvous to which the sportsman may proceed when it suits him. Probably one or more of these couples will have marked down a stag, then one man will remain behind to see that the deer has not moved, whilst the other returns to bring the sportsman news, and guide him to the spot. This being indicated, all will then depend on his own knowledge of venerie whether he obtains a shot or not, and it is often no easy task to approach the wary animal, for dead leaves, dry as tinder, and rotten sticks abound, and a slight crackle made by incautiously stepping on one of these is quite enough to rouse the deer's attention, and send him off clattering down the hill-side.

In stalking, I found a pair of racquet shoes most useful. These I had carried by my gun-bearer, and exchanged my shooting boots for them on beginning the stalk.

I was never fortunate enough myself to obtain a really good head, but I got a very fair one once, and the description of the stalk may be worth recalling, more perhaps because it was typical of the sport than for any of the incidents which were by no means out of the common. I had got a few days' leave, and had gone out to the valley of the Doon, and pitched my camp at a place called Kansaro, about midway between the native town of Hurdwar and the English station of Dehra Doon. I had met with a shikari called Juggoo, a capital tracker, and a wonderful shot. I once saw him knock over with my twelve-bore rifle a jungle-fowl sitting on the branch of a tree some eighty yards off. However, I must not digress by enumerating Mr. Juggoo's good qualities and accomplishments. Suffice it to say that I had undertaken this expedition on the strength of his assurance that I should have good sport, and as far as the truth of his assertions went I had no fault to find, and only my want of experience in woodcraft and my bad shooting were to blame that I did not secure very handsome trophies.

On the morning in question, Juggoo and I had started some two hours before dawn bent on searching the Sewalik hills for sambur. We had a tramp for about three miles along the road that led from Hurdwar to Dehra Doon, and then turning off at right angles commenced the ascent of the Sewalik hills, which here were of no very great height, though steep enough to try one's powers of endurance. Numerous spurs jutted out into the plain from the main hills. Up one of these spurs we made the ascent, and gained the summit, which consisted of a table-land, or slightly undulating plateau, just as the sun rose, and a flood of greenish yellow light streaked with crimson and pearly-grey gradually melted away into all the glories of an Eastern sunrise. Some rain had fallen during the earlier part of the night, and the smell of damp earth and the cooler air of the elevated spot were most refreshing and delightful.

The rain, too, had laid the dust, and so made tracking easier, and every branch and blade of grass glittered and twinkled as if 'tipped with diamond dew.' We had proceeded some little distance along the plateau, and had carefully scrutinized the ground on the side by which we had ascended, and were preparing to examine the other side where the spurs ran down into a thick, thorny jungle, composed mostly of bamboo and bhér bushes, the fruit of which all wild animals of the herbivorous order delight in, when Juggoo suggested that he should go and examine a salt lick down below, and endeavour to take up a track from there, whilst I should remain where I was, and await his return. This course I assented to, and he departed; in about an hour he returned with the intelligence that he had seen the fresh tracks of a fine stag that had visited the salt lick, and that the tracks led towards a spot on one of the spurs where he knew sambur often made their forms. He had, therefore, thought it best to return to me at once, and lead me to the spot.

We had reached a ridge within about half-a-mile of the spot, and I was sweeping the opposite spur to the one we were standing on with my glasses when Juggoo nudged me, and in a low whisper said, ' Wo hai, sahib,' ('There he is, sir'), and, directing my glasses to the spot he indicated, I saw a noble stag lying down at the foot of a tree, and had it not been for his occasionally throwing back his head, and brushing the flies off his broad back with his antlers, I should have had considerable difficulty in distinguishing him from a rock.

He lay in a pretty favourable position for a stalk, being some forty yards below the ridge of the spur; but, alas! in a few moments another head appeared coming over the ridge from the opposite side, that of a hind; then another, and another, till at last five appeared, and began moving about in a suspicious, uneasy manner, occasionally stopping to browse off a branch of a tree, or a mouthful of the short sweet grass just springing up after a jungle fire. At length they all but one lay down at various distances from their lord and master, and luckily below him, on the slope of the hill. The last hind, however, seemed of a more suspicious frame of mind, and kept sauntering backwards and forwards along the ridge. Once she stopped, and gazed long and steadfastly in the direction in which we were lying motionless behind a clump of rock, as if she thought something was not all quite right. Perhaps she caught for an instant the glint of the sun on my glasses.

After watching her for about an hour, at last, to our relief, she stretched herself out, and, taking one more searching look, joined her companions, and went and lay down nearly on the same level as the stag, but considerably to his left, as if to guard the flank.

We waited for about half-an-hour, and then gradually, inch by inch, crawled away till we reached the friendly shelter of a clump of bamboos, where we could once more stand upright. Then, walking away, we made a considerable détour, which necessitated an abrupt descent over some very rough ground, the crossing of a little stream knee-deep, and then another ascent up the spur in the direction we had seen the hinds advancing from. All this took time, for the slope was steep, covered with boulders, loose stones, and dead leaves that, if stepped on, would crackle at the slightest touch. Bending low, we advanced just under the brow of the hill, towards the spot which we had marked as being just above where the stag was lying; and then Juggoo wriggles himself, snake-like, up a rock, and his quick eye catches sight of an ear. Alas! it is that of the last sentinel hind, so we have to retrace our steps. At last, however, we reach the spot immediately above the stag, and I creep up.

I think few moments ever seemed longer to me than those in which I was engaged crawling and squirming myself over the rocks and loose stones, with my heart in my mouth. Just as I gain the summit, however, and raise my head inch by inch, a large stone slips from under my feet, and goes rolling down the hill, and in a moment the whole of the deer are up and on their feet, gazing steadily towards us. I am well hidden, however, and only some fifty yards off, so a miss is impossible; and, covering the stag's shoulder, I fire. There is a tremendous clatter, as the deer rush down the declivity, and plunge into the forest below—all but one, at least: my stag, who is rolling over and over down the hillside in the last agonies of death. Juggoo, however, rushes after him, and soon the 'hāl-hāl' is performed, which makes his flesh fit food for all orthodox Mahomedans.

I had many another stalk in these hills, but never got another decent head. Once or twice I bagged stags with a snap-shot, only to find their horns in velvet; for, in firing at running deer through thick cover, it is almost impossible to distinguish whether their horns are in velvet or not.

Unlike their brethren at home, I believe deer in India have no regular time for shedding their antlers. I have shot two stag cheetal out of the same herd, one of whose horns were in perfect order, whilst his companion's were in velvet. The loud and metallic sounding bellow of a stag sambur can be heard for a long distance, reverberating among the hills in which he loves to dwell. The call of the hind is much fainter, and is a faint, grunting sort of bark. There is another sort of cry, however, used by both sexes—a short, sharp, ringing snort, which I myself have never heard till after sunset.

I only once came across the swamp,* or twelve-tined deer, commonly known as the bara singha (twelve horns) of Central India, (which must not be confounded with the Kashmir stag—cervus Cashmeriensis—also known as bara singha.) This was at a spot near Kikri, in the Doon valley. A herd of seven, comprising two good stags, galloped across the road I was walking on one evening whilst returning to camp. I had a snap shot at them, but missed, and never again came across them.

Jerdon describes them as standing about forty-four to forty-six inches high, six feet in length, tail about eight inches; form lighter than the sambur, colour dull, yellowish-brown in winter, light chestnut in summer; horns about three feet in length, with often fourteen or fifteen points; and says they used to be found, sparingly, through Central India, to be rare south of the Narbadà, but to have been killed between that river and

* Rucervus Duvaucelli.

Nagpore. It is also found in the open forest between Mandla and Omarkantak. A brother-officer of mine shot a fine specimen of this deer in the jungles north-east of Seoni in the Satpura Hills.

From the fleeting glimpse I had of them, their hides were distinctly different from sambur in colour, and the rays of the setting sun, as it glanced on their sleek coats, made them glisten like bronze, with a golden tint pervading it. I believe they do not lie up so long during the day as the sambur does.

Next in order we come to that graceful animal the cheetal,* or spotted deer, whose colouring much resembles the fallow deer, only that it is far more vivid and brilliant, and the whole shape and bearing of the animal is more game-looking.

Its colour is a bright chestnut, tinged with red, and a black, or very dark brown stripe running down the back; the belly is white, and the whole body beautifully flecked horizontally with large white spots. The tail is generally rather long, and somewhat bushy. There is, however, a wide and very marked difference between the cheetal and the fallow deer, and that is in the shape of their horns; for, whilst a fallow deer's horns are *palmated*, a cheetal's are exactly the reverse. They

* Axis maculatus.

have, as a rule, only six points, though I have shot them with seven, and even eight points. Two in my possession, which I shot in the Chanda district, in the Central Provinces, have seven and eight points respectively. The one with the seven points has the extra tine singularly well developed; in fact, it is nearly as big as the brow antler, immediately above which it projects. The female, or hind cheetal, is of a much lighter build than the stag. She is also lighter in colour, and the white spots are not so well developed as in the stag. Cheetal generally are found in herds of from ten to forty or fifty, and I have seen herds which must have numbered over a hundred. They love shade and cover, and water is indispensable to them. They are therefore always found in the vicinity of water and in the valleys; the banks of a river being their favourite resort. On the banks of the Pen Gunga and Wein Gunga, rivers in Berar, I have seen very large herds, and in the Doon valley they also abounded. I do not think, however, that they ascend to any great elevation, and are more generally found in the forests at the base of mountain ranges. During the heat of the day, they lie up in thick cover, and sally forth at sunset to feed and drink. They may generally be found up to about ten o'clock, when the sun begins to assert its power, and again from about four o'clock in the afternoon. When alarmed, the cheetal utters a short, sharp bark, and this often betrays the presence of a tiger or panther to the sportsman.

To my mind the pursuit of cheetal has an indescribable charm, and the surroundings and the time at which it is conducted all tend to endear it to the sportsman. Come with me, kind reader, and in imagination we will try to shoot one of these graceful animals.

We have wandered forth from our camp say about four o'clock in the afternoon, and have entered a large tract of jungle composed of forest trees, and clumps of the feathery, graceful bamboo which, meeting overhead, form arches, through which charming vistas of nature are visible. To our right a little rivulet meanders through a grassy glade, and the sound of running water falls with pleasing cadence on our ears, whilst the glitter and sparkle of the tiny wavelets, as the evening sun falls on them, enhances the beauty of the sylvan scene. Stop, though! what is this? A collection of hard kernels of the bhér fruit, undigested and piled in a heap—in fact, fresh droppings of cheetal. We know, therefore, that the object of our search must be near, so let us proceed cautiously, keeping a good look-out, for it is extraordinary how difficult cheetal often are to detect, though they may be all round you. Mind you do not step on those dead leaves or that rotten stick—or else our presence will be betrayed.

Hold hard! there they are, a herd of at least sixteen. Do you see that handsome stag, wandering about in the midst of his harem, stopping now and then to browse on some succulent morsel, and anon butting some of his female kind who may have perhaps not shown due regard for his lordship's wishes, and perhaps punting into some 'buckeen' who may have been guilty of some infringement of cervine etiquette. Just watch him for a moment (the wind is all right for us, and we are safe from detection) as he prepares to drive off that younger stag whose attentions to some of his ladies have annoyed him. Mark how he advances gingerly as on tip-toe—his hair all standing on end, when, with a tremendous and sudden rush, he drives away the offender, and then comes swaggering back in all the masterly pride of superiority!

But see! he suddenly wheels round, and is gazing at something. The sound of an axe wielded perhaps half-a-mile away has doubtless caught his ears, and the hinds too are suspicious,—so take your shot whilst you can. I will take the younger stag. One moment more, though, just one more look at him. Is he not a quarry worthy of your notice. See his head erect, his antlers thrown back, with his white neck plainly visible, and, as, sniffing the air, his tail standing out, his whole body gathered together, he is ready to spring off at a second's notice. The sunlight falls and flickers in fantastic rays of light and shadow on his glossy spotted hide—and we are almost tempted to let him go; but no! man's selfish animal nature asserts itself. We *must* have those noble antlers—even at the sacrifice of that innocent life; and we can scarce wait longer, or he may be off, so take him steadily but quickly just behind the shoulder. Bang! All right, he is down. I have missed mine clean, but, as the smoke clears away, the bonnie stag is kicking convulsively on the ground, and the rest of the herd has vanished like magic, a dappled hide now and again gleaming in the sunlight, and glancing through the openings of the bamboo and forest trees, is all that is seen.

Take care, however, how you go up to your victim to cut his throat. I once got a very nasty cut from a wounded stag. I had laid hold of his antlers, when he struggled up, and we had a regular tussle till Juggoo came up to my assistance. The stag had, however, in the scuffle managed to strike me with one of his fore feet with such violence that it cut through the thick leather of a stout English shooting-boot, and penetrated to the bone of my ankle, laying me up for several days.

Cheetal, like all other deer, are very fond of salt, and are in the habit of constantly visiting salt licks, or spots where the earth is strongly impregnated with saline matter. This fact, and their most frequented spots, are well known to the jungle-men. At one of these salt licks I once got five cheetal out of seven shots. I must, however, plead guilty to having shot two hinds, though the other three were stags. It was on this wise. During one of my first trips to the Doon valley, I was out with Juggoo before mentioned, and he took me to one of these salt licks. It lay between two spurs that projected out from the main range of the Sewalik Hills. The ground ran into a sort of *cul de sac*, the end terminating abruptly in a mass of rock that rose sheer up for some forty feet. At the base of this was the salt lick.

Creeping cautiously up to the summit of one of these spurs early one morning, and concealing ourselves behind an old fallen tree, we peered over, and such a sight as met my eyes I shall not easily forget. The whole of the little valley seemed alive with cheetal. There must, I fancy, have been close on a hundred. I was so bewildered by such a concourse of game that it was some time before I could select the best stag as the herd lay unconsciously below, some lying down, some browsing, whilst others were licking the salt-red soil. At last, selecting a stag, I fired, and rolled him over. The rest of the herd sprang to their feet, and huddling up bewildered, gazed around to detect their hidden foe. Again I fired right and left, knocking over a stag, and missing another. The herd then dashed up towards the sheet of rock I have described, which of course arrested their progress, giving me time to put in a couple more shots, this time resulting in the death of two hinds. Then they turned back, and scattering, came racing past below me, and whilst some kept straight on, others, separating, climbed the face of the opposite spur, affording me another couple of shots. All my shots were at distances varying from forty to sixty yards, and the last one I got was also a stag.

It is wonderful how hard they are to kill, and what distances they will often travel after being hit. I have put four twelve-bore bullets into a cheetal besides breaking his fore-leg, and yet had to follow him quite three miles ere I got him. I should be ashamed almost to say how many I have wounded and lost. I never had, however, the advantage of using an Express rifle, and with such a weapon I believe the chances of losing deer would be considerably minimised.

March, April, and May are the best months for shooting the spotted deer as well as most other game, for at this season most of the grass has been burnt, and the deer are then more easily found. Still I have had good days in the cold weather; but the chance of finding one's game is greatly lessened owing to the greater density of the cover. Cheetal form a very staple article of food for tigers, and a tiger may often be found in a tract of jungle much frequented by cheetal, for water is a necessity to them *both* in the hot weather, and they therefore congregate where it is easily attainable.

Of course in a trip for big game cheetal are only pursued in a part of the jungle which the sportsman has ascertained not to contain tigers, or in which he may have killed the tiger or tigress who frequented it.

Anyhow, it is a charming sport to my mind, and, though a less lordly animal than the noble sambur, the cheetal is far more graceful, and affords opportunities of stalking on varieties of ground. His flesh is, however, coarse and unpalatable.

I believe that cheetal could easily be ridden down and speared on fairly open ground. I once had a gallop after a stag and a hind in Berar. I rode them for about half-a-mile in tolerably open jungle, and had got almost within spearing distance when my horse came down a regular 'buster' with me in a small nullah hidden by the long grass through which I was galloping. Had it not been for this *contretemps*, I verily believe I should have succeeded.

The para,[*] or hog-deer, comes next on our list; but as they are not an interesting animal I shall devote but few lines to their description. They are of a dark reddish-brown colour, the hide plentifully besprinkled with white hair. The texture of the hair is somewhat like a roe-deer's, only, if anything, rather coarser. The hog-deer is heavily made, and has derived its name from its curious pig-like action in galloping with its head carried low as it rushes headlong through the long grass in which it loves to dwell. The horns have, like the cheetal, only three tines, but are much smaller, and lack the graceful sweep of a spotted deer's. To a tyro their mad rush through the grass as they get up is to a certain extent alarming, as it gives one the idea of being made by a much larger animal.

They are not, I believe, gregarious, and I have

[*] Axis Porcinus.

never seen more than two together. I have seen them amid the long grass and low jungles on the banks of the Indus, and also near Delhi, on the banks of the Jumna. They abound in the valley of the Doon, but are there very difficult to get a shot at, except from the back of an elephant. I remember on two occasions shooting them with shot, once in the Barrara jungle, near Delhi, when beating for black partridges, and once at the close of a day's snipe-shooting in a large swamp near Roorkee. On this occasion I was passing through some high grass and reeds that fringed the swamp, when a something rushed past me only a few yards off, and I blazed at it, not knowing what it was, until I discovered a dead para lying out in the open some forty yards beyond the cover, shot through the neck.

I have never seen any hog-deer in the Central Provinces, and I believe their habitat is confined to the Punjab, Scinde, and the Gangetic valley, in India proper. It is, I believe, very abundant in Assam and Burmah, but I never had an opportunity of visiting those favoured regions. I have been told that they are often speared by members of the Meerut Tent Club, when out pig-sticking in the Kadir, or old bed of the Ganges, that celebrated spot in the pig-sticking world. A para stands about twenty-seven inches at the shoulder, and the horns, which are a true stag's, average about fifteen inches in length.

I think few animals for their size are capable of uttering a more alarming noise or presenting a more ferocious aspect than the rib-faced deer,* more commonly known as the muntják, or barking deer. This little animal, which I think may be almost described as the roe-deer of India, only stands some eighteen to twenty inches high. The colour of the hair is a bright chestnut red, smooth and glossy. The under parts are white, and the tail, for the size of the animal, rather long. When running away, the tail is carried curled over its quarters, much in the same manner as a rabbit carries its scut when bolting from a gun or dog. It is wonderfully active, and seems to be possessed of a marvellous flexibility of spine, and limbs which enable it to squeeze through and under brushwood that even a dog might have some difficulty in forcing a passage through. Doubtless this power is given to enable it to escape from their great enemy the wild dog, of whom more anon.

Its great peculiarity, however, is the curious formation of its head, and the fact of its being furnished with a pair of teeth resembling boar's

* Cervulus Aureus.

tusks in miniature. I cannot better describe the animal than by quoting the words of that well-known Indian sportsman, Colonel Kinloch, of the 60th Rifles, in his charming book entitled, 'Large Game Shooting in Thibet and the North-west,' and, should he deem these pages worthy of perusal, I trust he will excuse the liberty I have taken in using his description, but it is so lifelike that I trust this apology may be deemed sufficient. He says:

'Two grooves or folds in the skin, in the form of a V, give a curious expression to the face, which is heightened by black tufts of hair over the eyebrows. Above the folds in the face are two pedestals of bone covered with hair, on the summit of which the horns are situated; they fork near the top, the outer branches bending inwards in the form of hooks. In adult specimens there is also a small tine near the base of the horn. The male is also furnished with two small, strong, and sharp tusks in the upper jaw; these are formidable weapons, and, small as the karkur* is, he can make uncommonly good use of them. I have heard on the best authority of powerful dogs being badly injured, and even killed, by a wounded buck. When the karkur runs, a curious rattling sound is sometimes heard,

* Karkur is the Hindi name for the rib-faced deer.

and various theories have been adduced to account for it. I have not succeeded in solving the problem to my entire satisfaction, but I *believe* the sound is produced either by the jaws being closed with a clash, or by the tongue being struck sharply against the roof of the mouth. The sound is not produced by the tusks, for I have heard it made by a female karkur which I kept for some time.'

This certainly is a most graphic description of this curious little deer. That it can do considerable damage to dogs is borne out by the testimony of many Ceylon sportsmen, who, when hunting sambur or 'elk' (as they are there called) frequently come across them, and their pack, generally composed of foxhounds, Scotch deer-hounds, and Australian kangaroo-hounds, often suffer considerable loss from the determination with which this little deer defends itself with horns and tusks when brought to bay. In Ceylon it is called the 'red-deer.'

Its gait when not alarmed is very peculiar, and is somewhat ludicrous. It steps daintily along, lifting each leg alternately high above the ground, as if treading on hot iron, and yet it moves noiselessly along, glancing right and left, and keenly alive to the slightest noise or indication of danger.

Its bark, or rather hoarse, discordant roar, is

most peculiar, and when first heard gives one the idea of being produced by some ferocious wild beast, rather than by such a timid, graceful little animal; and how the little body can produce such an alarming volume of sound is a mystery which it is hard to fathom. This bark will generally be heard during the morning and evening, or if the animal is alarmed either by the presence of tigers, panthers, wild-dogs, or their common enemy, man. To the latter, however, he often betrays his presence by this means, for he will continue barking at intervals for a long time.

He is, from his size, a most difficult animal to shoot with a rifle, and his movements, when running, are so rapid that the chances of bagging him by a snap shot as he rushes with lightning-like rapidity from one patch of cover to another are considerably multiplied. He may be often bagged, however, with a charge of shot as I have mentioned at another page in this work.* Still, stalking is the most sportsmanlike method of pursuing him, and the difficulties attending this method of pursuit will enhance the pleasure of success.

They are pretty common, though by no means numerous, in all the large jungle tracks, and, like the cheetal, they do not ascend, I believe, to

* Vide p. 41.

any great elevation, though they show a partiality for any wooded hills where there is plenty of cover.

They are not gregarious, and are generally seen in pairs, but, as often as not, singly. The horns are shed annually, but I do not think there is any regular period for their doing so. The tongue is peculiarly long and extensile, enabling the animal to lick its own face with it. As venison the flesh of the barking-deer surpasses all other in India, with the exception, perhaps, of the four-horned antelope—and if roasted, well wrapped-up in mutton fat, is excellent. If possible, however, it should be hung for a few days, not an easy task except in the cold weather.

The best muntjâk head I ever got was in the Sewalik hills, and in a very unexpected manner.

I was encamped at a place called Peree, at the base of the Sewalik hills, and intended to devote the day to elephants, or rather, to endeavouring to obtain a shot at them, for as yet my efforts to bag one of the pachyderms had been unsuccessful. It was a clear, cold morning in January, and the air was keen and crisp when I started at about two a.m., accompanied by a very smart young shikari named Paloo, and two villagers. A six-miles ride in the clear starlight brought us to our ground, when, tethering my pony and leaving my syce, or horse-keeper, in charge, we ascended the hills, and, on reaching the summit, lit a fire, and waited for dawn. Well, to make a long story short, we wandered about all day following up elephant-tracks, which were numerous enough, but not one did we see, so at last we gave it up, and turned for home, weary and disgusted. On the way I shot a stag cheetal, and, whilst Paloo and his companions were gralloching him, I sat down and lit a pipe, some little distance off. Presently a savoury odour as of cooking meat smote upon my nostrils, and going down to the spot where the cheetal had fallen, at the bottom of a small ravine that ran up the hills, I found a fire lit and culinary operations going on.

Paloo had taken out the cheetal's liver, and, cutting it into small, square pieces called 'kabobs,' had skewered them on a splinter of bamboo, and then put them on the fire to cook, or rather scorch.

Some of this delicacy was offered to me, but at first my stomach revolted. However, at last the pangs of hunger (for I had had nothing but a couple of hard biscuits since my very early breakfast) began to assert themselves, and I changed my mind. Cutting open a cartridge, I sprinkled a little gunpowder over the charred morsel, and found it not unpalatable with the addition of that excellent sauce, 'hunger.'

Whilst engaged in this *al fresco* meal, the harsh roar of a karkur rang out close to us, and with such suddenness that it made me jump up and instinctively seize my rifle that was lying by me. Looking in the direction from which the sound emanated, I saw a fine buck standing staring at us, not thirty yards off. He was end on by the side of a clump of bamboos, and so presented a somewhat difficult shot. Aiming at his chest, however, I fired, and had the satisfaction to see him tumble over. It was curious that such a shy animal should have approached us so close, and that, even after detecting our presence, he should have remained long enough to afford me a shot. I can only account for the fact of his having come to drink at a little spring close to which I was sitting, and then had become fascinated by the sight that met his eyes.

At the risk of posing as a gourmand, I cannot refrain from giving the *menu* of one of my jungle dinners during this trip, and it will thus be seen that the Indian forests afford no contemptible meal to the sportsman. My dinner on one occasion I find, on referring to my old shikar diary, consisted of hare soup, salmi of green pigeons, roast jungle-fowl, deer's brain curry, cheetal kidneys on toast, and stewed fruit of the bhér. A dinner not to be despised, I think!

I have often noticed the curious noise made by barking-deer when running, alluded to by Colonel Kinloch. The noise resembles that made by a pair of castanets; I cannot, however, quite agree with him in his theory as to how the noise is produced, though he is more likely to be right than I am. I have heard, on two occasions, a very similar noise made by cheetal when running, and I was always under the impression that the sound was produced in a totally different manner. All the cervidæ have immediately above their hoofs small false hoofs, as it were (I am not naturalist enough to give their scientific name). These have the appearance of a hoof divided, each half being some little distance apart. We all know how a horse in trotting ' plays the castanets ;' now my theory is that this noise is produced by these hoofs in deer having grown abnormally long, and so, as the animal is moving quickly, they clash together, producing this peculiar sound. Of course this is only theory, and I offer it in the hopes that some more experienced sportsman and naturalist may be able to evolve something more definite from the suggestion.

Last of all on my list comes the four-horned antelope,* which, though a true antelope, is only found in jungle which antelope do not frequent,

* Tetraceros Quadricornis.

with the exception, perhaps, of the chikara or ravine deer. It is one of the smallest of the antelope tribe. In height it seldom exceeds eighteen inches, and is more of a fawn colour than a muntjâk. The hoofs, like those of this latter species, are long, slender, and upright, and it resembles it also in its peculiar, stilted gait; the hair, however, is much coarser in texture. The buck has four distinct sheathed horns, while the female is hornless. The posterior horns are about four and a half to five inches in length, whilst the anterior ones seldom exceed one and a half inches in length, but more frequently they are mere horny knobs. The animal seems to be pretty evenly distributed all over India, wherever the jungle is thick enough to afford them the seclusion they seem to delight in. Females seem to preponderate, and to kill a buck is rare, and to get one with the four horns perfectly developed rarer still. I never succeeded in getting one myself, but Captain Clay of my regiment, with whom I was out in the Chanda district, one hot weather, shot two, one a nearly perfect head, and the other a very fair one.

They seem very shy and retiring in their habits, and may generally be found near some water-hole, lying in a patch of grass, in which they make forms like a hare, and are often nearly trodden on before they jump up. For a short distance they run with wonderful swiftness with their heads carried low, and making themselves as small as possible; then they suddenly pull up, and stare at you, but always choose such a position to do so that their body is partially concealed by the trunk of a tree, clump of bamboo, rock, or some other obstacle that prevents your getting a fair shot; then they dash on, make another short halt, and so on till out of sight. They may be generally found in the same spot on several consecutive days.

They are generally found alone, though occasionally in pairs, and I only can recall two instances in which I have seen more than one at a time. They are frequently seen when beating for tigers, but of course are then allowed to go unmolested. The venison is excellent, and is always highly prized as an addition to the table whilst out in the jungle.

I think that these few rough notes and remarks on the variety of deer that any sportsman may expect to meet with in a trip to the jungles will be enough to satisfy the most exacting for variety of game. If he be a lover of natural history, the study of the habits of the animal, will afford him a subject of great interest, whilst even if he is no naturalist, and only pursues his game for the

s

pleasure of killing it, he will yet find much that will appeal to his sense of admiration in the beauty of the surroundings in which the game will be found, and may have cause to congratulate himself on the dexterity with which he has found, followed up, and bagged them. All this will, I venture to hope, make him think that stalking is the real 'poetry of sport.'

CHAPTER XV.

WILD DOGS AND HYÆNAS.

Wild Dogs—Description—A Jungle Course—Native Belief in **Wild Dogs** killing Tigers—Their supposed **Method of** Doing so—Deserted Temples—Wild Dogs attacking Tiger—Curious Scene on the Neilgherries—The Madras Hounds run with a Panther—The Kill—Names of Hounds—'Evangeline'—'Hawk-eye's' Description of Sambur Hunted by Wild Dogs—The Striped Hyæna—Spearing Hyænas—A **Startling** Adventure—Relief!—Cowardice of Hyænas—A Hyæna 'Leaps before he Looks'—A Mixed Bag.

THIS description of Indian sport would, I think, be incomplete without a reference to two animals that are occasionally met with, and, though they do not exactly come under the head of game, they often afford the sportsman objects of pursuit and sport with rifle and spear. I allude to the wild dog* and the striped hyæna.†

To begin with the former. Jerdon's description is so accurate that I cannot do better than

* Kuon Rutilans.   † Hyæna Striata.

avail myself of it. He says, 'The general colour is bright rusty red or rufous fawn—paler beneath; tail moderately brushed, reaching to the heels, usually tipped blackish: limbs strong: body lengthened—head and body thirty-two to thirty-six inches: tail about sixteen inches: height, seventeen to twenty inches.'

The wild dog is, I believe, pretty evenly distributed amongst the large forest tracts that abound in India, and are often a cause of considerable annoyance to the sportsmen, owing to the way they harry the game he is in pursuit of, rendering it wild, and more than usually unapproachable.

They generally hunt in packs from five to twenty, and run by scent as well as by sight, and their strength, speed, and endurance render them formidable foes to all the deer tribe. I never succeeded in bagging one myself, but have come across them on two or three occasions in the jungles of Berar and in the Chanda District. My friend Lieutenant-Colonel Hebbert shot a very fine specimen when I was with him at a place called Daba (alluded to in a former chapter), and I once had a shot at them, but missed.

I was out one morning taking a stroll with my rifle, when my attention was attracted by a low sort of whimper, and, looking round, I saw a four-horned antelope defending itself against what I at first sight took for a couple of jackals. Concealing myself behind a tree, further observation showed the supposed jackals to be wild dogs. What I saw was as follows: the little deer would make a short, rapid rush, and then pull up, facing its assailants, one of whom would make a snarling, snapping sort of feint at it in front, whilst the other sneaked round behind, and made snatches at the deer's flank and quarters whilst it was engaged butting at its assailant in front. Then the proceedings would begin *da capo*. I saw the deer make three consecutive rushes, and then I thought it time to interfere; and put an end to the matter by firing at one of the dogs, which, however, I missed. The dogs then went off in one direction, and the antelope in another, and I saw no more of them. Whether these two dogs were only 'unentered puppies' hunting on their own account, or whether the rest of the pack were in the vicinity waiting to make their final rush on the antelope when it had been worried into a state of exhaustion, I know not, but I am inclined to favour the former theory.

It is commonly believed and reported by natives in *all* parts of India that the wild dog will even attack and kill tigers, and when questioned as to the method in which they manage to overpower such a large animal, the answer is always the same. They say that, 'Super caudes micantes in occulos tigris urinam jactant!!'

It is extraordinary how implicitly this is believed in by the natives, and how the fact of the legend (for I can term it nothing else) seems to have been handed down from father to son. In one of the earliest works on Indian sport (*viz.*, 'Oriental Field Sports,' by Captain Williamson), mention is made of this stratagem, and Dr. John Fryer, an old writer, in his account of 'East India and Bombain,' says:

'Wild Beasts frequent there; Wild Dogs, which they say thus put out the Eyes of Venison as they feed in the Woods, and so Venom them that they become their Prey.'

The natives also of Burmah, I have heard, believe that wild dogs destroy elephants by means of the same stratagem. I can only ask my reader to take the report for what it is worth. It is impossible to credit, but yet it is extraordinary that the belief in it should be so universal!

It is a well-known fact that tigers are but seldom found in a part of the jungle frequented by wild dogs, but I believe that this is accounted for by the fact that the dogs so harry the deer and disturb the jungle, that they forsake it, and, naturally enough, the tiger will not stay in a place where he cannot obtain food.

That wild dogs will, however, attack a tiger—not to kill him, but to drive him away from his prey—I do believe; and the following extract from a letter which appeared in the *South of India Observer* of the 25th of March, 1869, corroborates this. It was sent me by my old friend, the late General McMaster, to whom I have before alluded. He was at Ootacamund at the time, and had the facts of the case related to him by an eye-witness of the scene. The letter is signed 'A Deer-stalker,' but I regret that I am unable to identify the writer. He was, however, well known to General McMaster, and was not one likely to relate anything the truth of which he had doubts about. He says:

'I venture to write on a subject that has puzzled me for many a year, *viz.*, the statement so often made by native shikaris that wild dogs will attack and *kill* a tiger. I never could believe that they would even attack him, and was under the impression that, by driving the deer from their accustomed haunts, they drove away the tiger also. However, I have recently heard from a friend a most interesting account of a scene that he witnessed between a pack of wild dogs and a tiger. My friend, not many weeks ago, was passing through a jungle in Wynaad, when he heard, close to him, a curious, snapping noise. He fancied it was parroquets, or some such birds, having a row among themselves; but, on taking a few steps forward, to his no small astonishment, he found himself in the presence of a tiger, surrounded by a pack of wild dogs, snapping and barking at him, but, at the same time, keeping well out of reach of the terrible forepaw.

'The tiger was lashing his tail from side to side, and showing great excitement, or, as I feel inclined to put it, *funk*: he was standing with his back to the new arrival, and consequently did not see him; but, as he was not more than twenty yards distant, my friend wisely decided on beating a quiet retreat, shortly returning, however, with some of his friends, when they found the tiger had disappeared; but the pack of wild dogs feasting on a sambur fresh killed by the tiger.

'There was no mistake about this, for the marks of the tiger's teeth were distinctly visible in the throat of the deer. Ten dogs were counted, but there might have been, and probably were, more. This to a certain extent corroborates the shikari's statements that wild dogs will attack a tiger, but I still think that they never attempt to lay hold of him, for that would be nearly certain death; their sole object is, I imagine, to drive the tiger away. They may, when in sufficient numbers, be able to kill a leopard; but even this I doubt. I know, however, of two instances where wild dogs have been seen following them. In one instance they had 'treed' the leopard, which certainly looked like mischief; possibly they may have chased it as dogs would a cat, for I have heard of both tigers and leopards being fairly chased on the hills* by a pack of spaniels, and such-like dogs, when parties have been out beating the woods for game, but, like their wild brethren, they generally kept at a respectful distance. If a pack of wild dogs were to attempt to close in on a tiger to kill him, they must leave some of their number dead on the battle-ground before they succeeded. Yet I have never heard of anyone meeting with such a sign. The tiger, like all the cat tribe, is not naturally a bold animal, and, though both he and the leopard will not hesitate to steal on and kill the largest dog, yet they have not the courage to fairly face a pack of the smallest curs. The instinct of the wild dog has taught him this, and hence, I imagine, the cause of the scene my friend witnessed.'

Apropos of the writer's reference to dogs tack-

* The Neilgherries.

ling a leopard or panther, a well-authenticated instance is on record of a pack of fox-hounds doing so. It was narrated in the *Field* of September 24, 1869, and there was a spirited sketch of the scene in the *Illustrated London News* of October 9, 1869. The pack who thus distinguished themselves were the Madras hounds, which during the hot weather are always sent up to the cooler atmosphere of the Neilgherry Hills. The pack, with one or two exceptions, had been imported from England some six months previously, and was largely composed of drafts from the Pytchley kennels, sent by Colonel Anstruther Thomson, who was then master of the Pytchley hounds, and in whose possession I saw the stuffed head of the panther.

On June 22, 1869, the hounds had had a run after a jackal, and accounted for him by themselves, not, as our old friend Mr. Jorrocks would say, 'by losin' 'im,' but by killing him, when a full-grown panther jumped up out of a 'sholah,' or wooded ravine, and the pack broke away after him full cry. They soon came up with him, and rolled him over in the open on a grassy hillside. The panther, however, managed to get away, and entered a small patch of cover with a stream at the bottom. Into this the pack followed, and panther and hounds rolled over in a confused heap into the stream. Again the panther freed himself, and again was brought to bay. After considerable difficulty, **in** about half-an-hour the pack **was whipped** off, **and the whole** thirteen couple turned up all safe, **though some three couple were** badly **wounded.**

Mr. R. A. Dalyell was master of the Madras hounds at this time, which were mainly recruited by drafts from the Pytchley kennels. The names of the hounds out this day were Tarquin, Gaiety, Goneril, Fleecer, Harriet, Gilder, Dimity, Marksman, Sampson, Prowler, Clovis, Shiner, Gaudy, Boscobel, Limner, Lively, Bouncer, Purity, Darter, Driver, Royster, Hasty, Druid, and three others names forgotten. The hounds that particularly distinguished themselves were Royster and Marksman, Driver and Purity. The latter was bred at Madras. Driver was by Fifeshire Sportsman, **out** of their Dairy-Maid. An interesting account of this extraordinary incident will be found in the 'Records of the Fife Hunt,' by Colonel Babington.

In the meanwhile, guns **had been sent for, and** the panther **was eventually shot.** The number of the hounds, and their attacking the panther simultaneously from all sides, seems the only explanation why they did **not suffer more.**

Now, if fox-hounds would thus tackle a full-grown panther, why should not wild dogs do the same to a tiger? However, I must leave this point to be decided by better naturalists than myself; but, for my own part, I confidently believe that, even if they do not attack a tiger with a view to killing and eating him, they do so to bully him, and make him leave any game he may have killed.

The skin of a wild dog makes a handsome rug, the fur being very thick in the cold weather, and this, combined with the fact that he is an arrant poacher, should always induce the sportsman to have a shot at him whenever he has a chance.

I believe they are untameable. My friend the late General McMaster had one which he kept for some time, and whom, on account of her diabolical temper and untameable savageness, he had named Evangeline! Her wild instincts could never, however, be subdued, and she eventually died.

'Hawkeye,' that charming writer previously alluded to, gives the following graphic description of a stag sambur being chased by five wild dogs, and apparently escaping:

'When they first appeared they were observed spread out like a fan, and pressing the stag at his best pace. It may, I think, be assumed that this disposition of the pack is a matter of instinct, so that in case the deer is forced to turn to either flank during the flight the outer dogs would have the opportunity for a rush to seize him. On the occasion in question the stag kept on straight, and the ground being very precipitous, and intersected with 'sholahs,' he contrived to elude his fierce and hungry enemies. He was observed, on reaching a slab of rock, to double back down its precipitous side into the sholah beneath; this was the first check to the pack, who craned over the spot, and seemed to be bewildered for a time; however, taking up the scent, and apparently assured that the deer was below, they too got down after their prey. Meanwhile, the deer getting clear of the wood, obtained a good start; only three dogs came out of the sholah and resumed the chase; another wood favoured the stag, and on his reappearance two of the dogs alone followed at a long interval, so it is to be hoped the stag escaped.

'At another time a gentleman saw a pack in chase of a sambur close to him, and noticed that the dogs, in their rushes at the deer, attempted to seize the animal at the flank; and we can well understand how easily, with their peculiarly sharp fangs, they are enabled to tear through the flesh and skin, causing the entrails to protrude, and thus soon despatch their victim. On this occasion, after pulling down the deer, two if not three of the pack paid forfeit with their lives from the rifle of the looker-on.'

The hyæna is, I think, one of the most repulsive-looking animals in creation, with his great gaunt head, powerful jaws, high withers, and narrow quarters; and were it not for the evil reputation he has of occasionally carrying off children, and sometimes affording a good run with horse and spear, would, I think, generally remain unnoticed by Indian sportsmen. He stands about twenty-eight to thirty inches high. The hair, which is long and coarse, is of a dirty light-brown with black stripes. He is a cowardly brute, and hardly ever shows fight. I seldom troubled myself about them, and, though I have had two or three gallops after them, I never got the first spear, though on one occasion my horse pursued the brute, as will be related later on. They sometimes give good runs, not from possessing any great powers of speed or endurance, but because they have a marvellous power of turning and twisting just as the horseman imagines he is going to spear.

On one occasion I remember, near Kamptee, a hyæna giving us a run of over two miles after being speared (which he was within a field or two of the start) over very bad ground, and under a burning sun before he was despatched.

One of the greatest starts I ever got in my life was occasioned by a hyæna, and the scene to anyone who could have been a spectator must have been intensely ludicrous.

When out with Captain Clay of my regiment during the hot weather of 1870, we were encamped at a place called Pangurjerrie—at least, we dined and slept there, having sent on the tents to another place called Seoni. We had some panther-traps with us, enormous gins, which we used occasionally to bait with offal of any deer we might have shot, in the hopes of catching a panther. In this, however, we were unsuccessful, though we had caught three or four hyænas. On the night in question one of these traps had been set in a nullah one hundred and fifty yards from our beds. At about twelve o'clock, when it was pitch dark, I was awoke by the clanking of a chain, accompanied by much snarling and growling, proceeding from the spot where the trap had been set. Immediately fancying that this time it must be a panther in the trap, I jumped out of bed, and hastily putting on my slippers, and catching up a hog-spear, I shouted to Clay to follow me with some of our servants, and a torch. I got to the spot, and just distinguished a dark mass tumbling about in the nullah, and soon after Clay and the servants were seen approaching with a light, so, not waiting till they arrived, I jumped into the nullah, and advanced with my spear at the charge towards, as I imagined, the trapped panther. There was a great scuffle, and a good deal of growling as I drove my spear into the struggling form. Suddenly the torches carried by our servants were thrown down, and with loud cries of 'Bagh, bagh,' ('Tiger, tiger,') they fled. My quarry selected this moment to seize the shaft of the spear in his teeth, and I at the same time, catching my foot in the chain by which the trap was attached to a log of wood, tumbled over right on top of, as I fancied, the infuriated panther, losing hold of my spear in the fall.

Clay said my agonised cry of 'Good God, man, get a light,' was most piteous, and he really thought for the moment I must be hurt. However, he soon ran back, and fetched a torch, when its light revealed me squatting under one bank of the nullah with my nightshirt all torn and covered with mud, whilst some ten yards further lay a huge hyæna, fast in the trap, with my spear sticking in him! Needless to say we had a good laugh over the absurdity of the situation, but I must confess that for the time being I was in what is commonly called a 'blue funk!'

Hyænas are, however, sometimes tamed, and are then as gentle as a dog. I think I cannot close this chapter more appropriately than by quoting the words of the dear old friend so often alluded to in these pages—General McMaster—for the two instances he gives of the cowardice of the hyæna are so vivid that any attempt of mine to describe it would pale before his more powerful pen. In the first instance I was the unlucky wight who got the fall, and the hyæna, though speared, eventually got into a big earth where we had to leave him.

'The most ludicrous instances of animal cowardice I have ever seen have been displayed by hyænas. Once, whilst beating a hill for hog, a hyæna broke past us; in despair of more noble game we rode at him, and, after a long and fast run, I had slightly speared the ungainly brute, hardly drawing blood, and merely "ruffling the feathers," so to speak, when one of the other horses rolled over with his rider in the black cotton ground we were then crossing; the rider lost his reins, and the Arab, an old hog-hunter, picked himself up and forthwith pursued the hyæna, whose abject fear and efforts to escape as he shuffled along with tail between his legs, and quarters more tucked in and drooped than ever, when the old horse bit at them, made him look the most miserable creature I have ever seen, and a wonderful contrast to the game old Arab, who, with ears well laid back and tail aloft, pursued the enemy at a long trot, every now and then striking at it with one of his forefeet.

'Another case was nearly as illustrative of the faint-heartedness of the animal. Shortly after daybreak I had fired at a bear, that died almost immediately. Ere long a large hyæna blundered up the same path the bear had taken. I did not wish to waste a shot on him, and he stumbled on for some distance in the vacant-looking, undecided way of his race; suddenly, having caught the scent of blood or dead flesh, he became a different and rather fine-looking creature, as he rushed with head and tail well up—the latter waving almost in the style of a foxhound's stern while drawing—direct to the spot, and in his hungry haste he jumped on a stone beside which lay the dead bear, and almost on the carcase. All at once matters changed, and I shall not soon forget the horror-struck look of the hyæna as, stiffened as if by magic, too frightened to move back or forward, and with every bristle erect like a worried cat, he stood quivering over the body. Although I had spared him before, I could not resist taking his worthless life as he stood.

'That was a red-letter day, one of those that reward an Indian sportsman for his numberless unrecorded blank excursions. The time was January, the most delightful month everywhere in India. I left my friends' tents about three o'clock one cold morning, and under a beautiful full moon had a pleasant ride to my ground, which I had not long reached before I got the bear and hyæna just mentioned, both fine specimens; within a couple of hours after, perhaps much less, I killed two more good bears, both of which gave me some trouble. I then shot my way back to the tents, going for many miles along one of the salt marshes of the upper part of the Northern Circas, and getting a large and diversified bag of small game, among them my three first specimens of the flamingo, some red-crested pochards, a very beautiful teal (the 'clucking teal,' Querquedula Glocitans), which I have never seen before or since, and seeing what I think were specimens of the scaup pochard, (too wary to bag, however,) and winding up when near the tents with an antelope, which, notwithstanding a ball through his body, gave my active Deccanee galloway, a long and uncommonly fast gallop before the spear blade was blooded.'

There, kind reader, I think that though you may be the owner of the best deer-forest or grouse moor in bonnie Scotland, or the best coverts and partridge-ground in England, you will find it hård, nay, impossible to beat such a day's sport as above described. And yet, an you be disposed, it is within your reach; and, if you will deign to cast your eye over the succeeding chapter, I will venture to offer you a few hints how to do so.

CHAPTER XVI.

ON RIFLES, GROUND AND OUTFIT.

India as a Field for Sport—Comparison with other Countries—Indian v. African Sport—Where to Go—Cost of a Shikar Trip—Rifles and Guns best Adapted for Indian Sport—Outfit—Arrangements for Supplies—Beaters to be Paid Personally—Conclusion.

IT has often been a matter of surprise to me that British sportsmen, with the means to gratify the love of sport that is inherent in most Englishmen, do not oftener go in for a shikar trip to the sunny land of the East. In other countries, no doubt, game of every description is to be found in as great variety and in as great numbers, but in most of these countries the pursuit of sport is attended with far greater expense, and many more difficulties. Servants are not so easily obtained, means of transport for large supplies has to be provided, and many comforts cannot be taken. Much rough and dirty work has to be done by the sportsman himself, and, in the event of sickness or accident, medical aid is unattainable—and no approximate estimate of the expenses of the trip can be formed.

Now, in India none of these objections exist. Servants are easily obtainable, and at comparatively low wages. Transport is abundant in the shape of pack-bullocks and ponies, or country carts. Large supplies need not be taken, owing to the numerous villages, where the ordinary food for servants is easily got, and, moreover, the British stations or cantonments are thickly studded over the country, and in most of these there is either a skilled military or civilian doctor, whose services can be relied on in case of illness or accident. There is now a largely extended railway system that traverses the country in all directions, and makes locomotion from one part to another comparatively easy, and, lastly, the sportsman knows that he is pursuing his sport in a part of the British empire, and that, as one of dominant race, his wishes will be more likely to be forwarded by the native inhabitants, than they would be in any other part of the world.

I may, perhaps, be met with the objection that Africa affords a better field for the sportsman, and that there a larger variety of game will be found. This I deny. In mere numbers, perhaps, a sportsman may bag more, but, after all, the man who really cares for sport will think more of the nature of the animal he pursues and the difficulty of obtaining it; its fighting powers; the scenery amid which it is found, and its wildness; than of the actual numbers: and I venture to express the opinion that a sportsman, returning from a successful shikar trip to India, will be able to show trophies which Africa cannot match.

Africa and India have both elephants, but the Indian elephant is a far finer-looking animal, better bred, quite as, if not more, intelligent, and, as a fighter, better, I believe. In India, certainly, we have no hippopotami, giraffes, or zebras, but the pursuit of these animals, as far as their utility goes in the shape of affording food or handsome trophies, may be dismissed as *nil*. In the Northern parts of Hindoostan, on the borders of Thibet, the kyang, or wild ass, may be found, which afford about as much sport as a zebra would, but they are generally unmolested, except, perhaps, by one or two being shot, merely for the sake of the sportsman being able to say that he has done so. In Assam and Bhootan, rhinoceros will be found whose fighting powers are quite equal to his African cousin's. The Indian wild buffalo has far superior horns to the African one, and is quite as savage. In India, too, we can boast of other bovines, in the shape of the bison (so-called), gayal, and yâk. Africa may boast of its lions, panthers, and leopards. So can India (for the lion is found in Kattywar), and boast, besides, of tigers, which are not known on the 'dark continent.'

For beauty and symmetry the black buck of the Indian plains can rival any of its African congeners; and, besides them, there are some twelve or thirteen other varieties of antelope obtainable. Ovis ammon, markhoor, ibex, oorial, thár, and numerous other wild sheep and goats afford such opportunities of stalking as will not be found in Africa, nor do these animals exist there. India has nine species of antlered deer, varying from the lordly Kashmir stag or bara-singha to the little muntjâk. Africa has but one or two varieties, and those not found where other large game abound. In India there are three varieties of bears. In Africa they are unknown—and, as far as small game goes, India is far ahead with its swarms of pea-fowl, jungle-fowl, wild-fowl; snipe, quail, partridge, etc.; to say nothing of that most magnificent game-bird, the bustard, and the numerous varieties of pheasant found amid the slopes and valleys of the Himalayas. And all this is obtainable within little more, perhaps, than a three weeks' journey from England!

I never had any experience of shooting in the

hills—by which I mean in Kashmir, or on the Himalayas and Neilgherries, and so I do not propose to offer any remarks on this phase of Indian sport, but I shall confine myself to drawing the outline of a trip which would cost a comparatively small sum for one sportsman, and, if three or four combined, the cost would be considerably reduced. We will suppose our party is going out for the purpose of getting as much pig-sticking, tiger, bear, panther, bison, deer, antelope, and small-game shooting as could be compressed into a nine months' trip. Leaving England in November, they will reach Bombay about the end of the month. Here they will be able to fit themselves out with tents, camp-equipage, etc., purchase horses, and engage servants. They (mind, I speak of what *I* should do) could then take the rail to Nagpore, which they could make their head-quarters. During December, January, and February, they could enjoy capital pig-sticking by becoming members of the Nagpore Hunt Club; and a house could be rented for about eight pounds a month that would put up four sportsmen very comfortably. They would find in the vicinity of Nagpore black-buck, chikara, bustard, and numerous varieties of small game; all within a day's ride. If fond of coursing, and they took out a brace or two of greyhounds, jackals, wolves, hyænas, foxes, and hares would offer numerous opportunities of indulging in this form of sport.

Then, about the end of February, having decided on the district they were going to hunt for big game, they could make a start either for the jungles of Chanda and Berar (where I should go), and which would lie within some eighty or one hundred miles of Nagpore, the greater part of which distance could be travered by rail; or they might hunt the Assirghur jungles in the province of Nimar, and thence to the Bhétul country; or they might proceed to the Puchmurree Hills, where they would have fine sport with bison and sambur, and would get a few tigers, bears, and panthers; and then explore the regions of Mandlá and the sources of the Narbadà. The middle of May would find our party back at Nagpore, the rains having then begun. Here they could dispose of their horses, surplus kit, etc., and then proceed by rail to Bombay, and thence by sea to Calicut. They might go direct by rail to Madras, if they wished to visit that presidency town. Then on either to Ootacamund or Bangalore, where they could again establish their headquarters, and from whence they could explore the Annamully Hills and the great forests of the Wynaad. Here they would meet with sport of the most varied description, and to anyone proposing to hunt this part of the country—which, alas! I never was able to do—I would recommend a perusal of Mr. Sanderson's charming book, entitled, 'Thirteen Years among the Wild Beasts of India,' one of the best, if not the very best book, ever written on Indian sport.

The sportsmen could then return home by the end of July, and be in time for the grouse campaign, unless they preferred to spend a few extra weeks in visiting various places interesting from historical, archeological, or other points. If, however, they did not care to face the constant wet weather they would probably have during the months of May, June, and July, they could, after their hot-weather trip, return straight to Bombay, and be back for the London season.

The cost of such an expedition would not exceed the rent of a good grouse-moor in Scotland, and be far less than that of a deer-forest. The return ticket to Bombay would cost about one hundred pounds. A hill-tent and a small 'pál' tent, capable of accommodating two sportsmen, could be obtained at Jubbulpore, new, for about thirty pounds, but, of course, could be bought for much less second-hand. If our party is going in for pig-sticking, they could buy plenty of good horses in Bombay, both Arabs and Walers, at prices varying from fifty to one hundred and twenty pounds, and a good pony apiece for about fifteen to twenty pounds. If they can arrange for the loan of a good shooting elephant, all the better, but, if they had to buy one, they would have to pay at least three hundred pounds. However, this latter course, unless our friends should be Crœsus, I should not recommend. Kit, etc., which can be purchased at Bombay, would not cost more than about fifty pounds apiece. Saddlery, ammunition, and boots should be taken out from England. Hog-spears are best obtained in India. Arnachellum of Salem is the best maker. After providing for all these items, about thirty to forty pounds a head per month ought to cover all extra expenses.

As regards rifles, every man must suit himself, but, were I going out to my old hunting-grounds, and had the means of providing myself with a *thoroughly* efficient battery, I should take a ·500 Express rifle for deer and antelope, a 12 bore rifle for tigers, bears, etc., and, if I expected to get elephants and bison, I should also have a single-barrel 8 bore. I should, of course, have, besides, a 12 smooth-bore gun.

I bagged all my game with a twelve-bore rifle by Henry, of Edinburgh, and for all-round shooting it is as good as any. Of course, a rifle of this calibre has not the low trajectory of an Express, and for antelope and deer shooting the latter weapon is preferable, as it gives a point-blank trajectory of some two hundred yards, and firing shots at longer distances than this is to be deprecated for several reasons, to which I have alluded in a former chapter. I have never used an Express myself on tigers, but, from all I have heard of the results attained by using one for this particular sport, I am led to believe that they do not possess the 'bone-smashing' effect, nor do they administer such a shock to the system as a spherical ball, which is so essential in shooting dangerous animals.

Of course, a sportsman using an eight-bore would have even a greater advantage; but the exertion of carrying such a heavy rifle over rough ground would be a considerable drawback, and tend to unsteady his nerves when coolness and precision were most required. In the pursuit of elephant and bison, as well as buffalo and rhinoceros, an eight-bore would be invaluable. It could be carried by the sportsman's gun-bearer until he got close to his game, and be used for the first shot, when the wound inflicted by such a heavy weapon would considerably 'take the kick out of' any animal struck.

It cannot be too strongly borne in mind that,

in the pursuit of large and dangerous game, the great object is to inflict a wound that will *break bones*, and to a certain extent cripple the animal, and so avoid accidents. Now an Express bullet has not this power, nor has it penetration enough to reach a vital part, and, when it is considered what a mass of bone, muscle, and sinew a tiger possesses, it will, I think, readily be conceded that what is wanted is a projectile that will penetrate all this. The penetrating power of an Express bullet can, however, be considerably increased by omitting the hollow in the point; but then, of course, all advantages obtained by the bullet being hollow, and which causes it to expand in an animal, is lost.

Many sportsmen will doubtless disagree with these remarks, and may bring forward numerous instances of tigers, bears, etc., and even the elephant, being killed by a single Express bullet. No doubt such instances have occurred; but do they prove that it is the best weapon? I myself know of an instance where a full-grown panther was killed by a charge of shot fired at random into a bush in which it lay concealed. One pellet alone entered the ear, and penetrating the brain, caused death; but I think if I were on this account to advocate the using of *shot* to shoot panthers with, I should at once qualify myself for lodgings in Hanwell Lunatic Asylum.

In shooting large game no precaution that tends to ensure the safety of the sportsman and his attendants should be omitted, and a man is no worse sportsman for exercising a little care. I have jotted down from memory and some rough notes a few things that, were I organizing a shooting-trip and had the management of the commissariat and general arrangements, I should take with me. These are for a two months' hot-weather trip for a party of three:

Ten dozen of soda water,* five dozen of tonic water, five dozen of claret, five dozen of beer, half-a-dozen of brandy, half-a-dozen of gin, half-a-dozen of champagne, two dozen of tinned soups, one dozen tins of sardines, half-a-dozen tins of bacon, half-a-dozen rolled tongues, three bottles of chutnee, three bottles of pickles, one dozen pots of jam, two pocket filters, three pounds of alum (for skins), three tins of preserved vegetables, half-a-dozen tins of biscuits, three flasks of oil, two bottles of vinegar, flavouring essences, anchovy paste, half-a-dozen of Worcester sauce, four pounds of coffee, four pounds of tea, twelve pounds of sugar, six pounds of candles,

* Or a couple of gazogenes and supply of powders.

cocoa, four dozen boxes of fusees, four pounds of soda, soap, baking powder, one bottle of ink, isinglass, vermicelli, six pounds of native tobacco for presents, one measuring tape, carbolic acid, chloroform, quinine, Warburgh's fever drops, Holloway's ointment, laudanum, ammonia, hyasymus, one lancet, one pair of forceps, two dozen of Indian solution, large tin of arsenical soap, heavy hammer and two hundred long iron nails for pegging-out skins, clyster pipe, two sets of shoes and nails for each horse, three packing-needles and thread, one burning-glass, binoculars, one set of tools in leather case to roll up, three chaguls, or leather water-bottles,* rods and spinning tackle, four skinning knives, vaseline and camphorated-vaseline, several books, *not* of a too light literature.

Clothes, etc. (for each person) : three pairs of sambur skin boots, two pairs of English shooting boots, three suits of shikar clothes, two hats (one helmet and one topee), six pairs of woollen socks, two dozen of handkerchiefs, six towels, six pairs of pyjamas, two kummerbunds, one pair of gaiters, eight flannel shirts—the coats to be wadded down the spine and across the shoulders; two lanterns, one cot, broad, long, and as light as possible; two waterproof sheets to cover the cot, camp wash-stand and basin, one wicker-chair for dinner, one

---

* The chaguls should be well seasoned but *not* greased.

easy-chair, both to travel on the cot, one camp-stool.

Cooking, etc., utensils for common use: six soup plates, six large plates, six small plates, six cups and saucers, three ashets, two vegetable dishes, three hot-water plates, candlesticks and glass shades, twelve knives and forks and spoons, six tea-spoons, six dessert-spoons, one gridiron, one frying-pan, three saucepans, three small dekshis.

In going into a native state, it would be desirable to provide oneself with a 'purwunah,' an official document which will greatly facilitate procuring supplies, beaters, etc.

These are a few of the things that occur to me. I am, it must be understood, calculating for a party of three, and doing everything *comfortably;* for I believe in comfort tending much to preserve one's health during the time spent in the enervating climate of an Indian summer. Of course, in the latter part of the trip, such a large kit and so many supplies would not be necessary, for the sportsman would make shorter trips, say, of a week or ten days at a time, from the place he selected as his head-quarters, and in giving the list I have, I am calculating on the party being away for two months, and being often in places where they cannot supplement their supplies as they diminish.

It will be a good plan also to endeavour to ascertain if the villages on the route chosen are capable of affording plenty of supplies for the native servants and camp-followers. Often much disagreeableness is occasioned by the native following of a sportsman literally 'eating up' the supplies of some poor jungle village who have only sufficient for their own wants. Of course this is distasteful, to say the least of it, to the villagers concerned, and, if they think they will be subject to such treatment, they will withhold information regarding game, for fear of bringing the 'sahib log' and their harpies of servants down on them. If, therefore, supplies are unlikely to be met with in abundance, it will be as well to take plenty of rice, flour, curry stuff, etc., for the servants. This may entail extra transport arrangement, but it will be found to pay in the long run.

Information of game, if proved correct, should always be liberally rewarded, and, in case of success, an extra douceur may be given with good effect. Beaters should always be paid *personally* by one of the party, to ensure their receiving their wages. It is but a mite, each man getting a sum equivalent to about twopence to fourpence, but it is much to them, and, if left to your shikari to pay the beaters, however good he may be in other ways, he probably will not be able to resist the temptation of feathering his own nest at the expense of the wretched beaters. A little attention to such apparently trivial matters will go far towards making the excursion a success, instead of resulting in failure.

Of course sportsmen going out to India cannot be expected to know the language or customs of the country, and therefore they should endeavour to have among their number one who does do so, and generally some one who has this knowledge may be found among the officers of the regiments, European or native, quartered in most cantonments, who would be glad to join the party. Any introductions to the head civilian of the district will be found of great use, and tend much towards smoothing the way for the party.

In conclusion, I will only add that I trust these few lines may prove of some slight interest and use to any sportsman who is going to attempt 'shikar' for the first time. The veteran sportsman will doubtless find many faults and imperfections in what I have written, but sportsmen are usually generous, and I would therefore throw myself on his mercy and ask him to be

> 'To my virtues ever kind,
> To my faults a little blind.'

Finally, I have added a few Indian sporting songs and verses, all of them, with a few exceptions, culled from the old *Oriental Sporting Magazine*. The names of their authors I have been unable to ascertain, except in a few isolated instances, and so I have appended the *nom de plume* under which each one wrote. I am induced to do this from constantly having heard the words of such songs asked for, both in the sporting papers and verbally; and, knowing the pleasure it has afforded me to peruse the spirited lines of many of these songs, I have thought that presenting them in a collected form may prove not unacceptable to my readers—if haply I should find any. To their authors, should they fortunately be alive, I must tender my most humble apologies for quoting them, and can only ask them to let the perusal of their charming lines afford as much pleasure to others as they have to me.

And now, kind reader, farewell. If through reading these lines you may be induced for a season to forego the pleasures and luxuries of sport at home, and direct your steps to the far East, I think you will say that 'the game was worth the candle,' and that in future days you will look back with pleasure to the time spent in jungle, on hill-side, and plain, and often drink a toast to rifle, as well as to

'Saddle, spur, and spear!'

INDIAN SPORTING SONGS.

INDIAN SPORTING SONGS.

HURRAH FOR THE SPUR AND THE SPEAR!

Tune—' Hurrah for the Bonnets o' Blue!'

I.

Here's a bumper to spur and to spear,
    A bumper to challenge a song,
A bumper to those who, where'er the boar goes,
    Are spearing and spurring along!
'Tis good to be steady and cool,
    'Tis better to dare than to doubt;
'Tis best to be clear of the funks in the rear,
    And be always thrown in than thrown out.
        Then hurrah for the spur and the spear!
          Hurrah for the zest of my song!
        Hurrah for all those, who where'er the boar goes,
          Are spearing and spurring along!

II.

Here's a cheer for the charms of the chase,
    A cheer for a glorious burst;
And who wouldn't cheer when the bold win the 'spear,'
    For the fearless are always the first.
There are some ever in the right place,
    There are some who just toddle and trot,
There are many who love every danger to face,
    And many I swear who do not.
        Then hurrah for the spur and the spear! etc.

III.

There's a joy when the boar makes his rush,
    There's a joy when the monster first bleeds,
There's a joy though *to-day* has now glided away,
    For *to-morrow* shall double our deeds.
Here's a sigh for the sportsman afar,
    A welcome to those who are here,
A health to the whole who in spirit and soul
    Are friends of the spur and the spear!
        Then hurrah for the spur and the spear! etc.

S. Y. S.

'Oriental Sporting Magazine,'
    August, 1830.

THE MIDNIGHT BOAR.

Tune—'The Glass is Sparkling on the Board.'

I.

No more of daring deeds by day
   The song shall pass my lips;
The chase beneath the moon's bright ray
   Doth every sport eclipse.
      When o'er the stream
      The silver gleam
Hath spread from shore to shore,
      With spear in hand
      We firmly stand
To meet the Midnight Boar.

II.

Oh! deep we'll drain the brimming bowl
   To toast that jungle glen,
When forth like some grey ghost there stole
   The monster from his den.
      His dark brown eye
      Hath watched the sky
For the cloud that's passing o'er;
      While spear in hand
      We sternly stand
To meet the Midnight Boar.

III.

Away! away! the boar hath been
  Some moments now on foot—
Hath cleared the river and ravine,
  And challenges pursuit.
    Yet cautious still
    He climbs the hill,
Nor deems the danger o'er;
    With spear in hand
    No more we stand,
But chase the Midnight Boar.

IV.

Hurrah! hurrah! the chase is done—
  What will not sportsmen dare?
The tuskied trophies too are won,
  And boldly won they were.
    Then let us drain
    The bowl again,
And its wine to the *next night* pour,
    When spear in hand
    We sternly stand
To meet the Midnight Boar.

                    S. Y. S.

'Oriental Sporting Magazine,'
  August, 1831.

MEET ME WHEN DAYLIGHT MAY DAWN.

Tune—'Meet me by Moonlight Alone.'

I.

Meet me when daylight may dawn,
    And then I will show you a boar,
Who will lead us, thro' thicket and thorn,
    To the hills where he beat us before.
Then remember be there, tho' you dread
    To meet such a monster alone;
For I *must*, and I *will*, win that head,
    'Tis the greyest that ever was known.
        Then meet me when daylight may dawn,
        And follow thro' thicket and thorn!

II.

Moonlight may do for the 'spoons'
    Who at balls pass their moments away,
But what are a million of moons
    To one bright little hour of day?
Oh! then fail not to be at your post,
    For tho' hunting's my pleasure and pride,
Yet the charm of the chase is half lost
    If we have not a rival to ride.
        So meet me when daylight may dawn,
        And follow thro' thicket and thorn!

                            S. Y. S.

'Oriental Sporting Magazine,'
    August, 1831.

HURRAH! HURRAH! ONE BUMPER MORE!

I.

Fill the goblet to the brim—
Fill with me and drink to him
Who the mountain sport pursues,
Speed the boar where'er he choose.
Hurrah! hurrah! one bumper more—
A bumper to the bristly boar!

II.

Hark! the beater's shout on high—
Hark! the sportsman's shrill reply;
Echo leaps from hill to hill,
There the chase is challenged still.
Hurrah! hurrah! one bumper more—
A bumper to the bristly boar!

III.

Ride—for now the sounder breaks;
Ride—where'er the grey boar takes;
Struggle through the desperate chase,
Fearless, death itself to face.
Hurrah! hurrah! one bumper more—
A bumper to the bristly boar!

IV.

See, the jungle verge is won ;
See, the grey boar dashing on ;
Bold and brave ones now are nigh ;
See him stagger, charge—and die !
Hurrah ! hurrah ! one bumper more—
A bumper to the bristly boar !

S. Y. S.

'Oriental Sporting Magazine,'
October, 1830.

DASH ONWARD, MY STEED!

I.

Dash onward, my steed, while the crowd creeps behind us,
The boar leads the way, and we're bound to pursue ;
Tho' vengeful and swift, never doubt but he'll find us
Both able and willing to dare and to do.
Like the lightning that flies from its home in the heaven,
And strikes into ashes the tower and tree,
So deep in his heart shall our spear-blade be driven ;
Then onward, my Arab, bound onward with me.

II.

Fly onward, my steed; see, the monster before us,
   Still struggling right upward the hill-top to clear;
And hark to the 'tinkers' all roaring in chorus,
   They view him, they press him—shall *they* win the 'spear'?
Heed not the broad river. Oh, well we've got thro' it;
   Now strain for the steep, though a mountain it be;
And *now* for the nullah! I knew we could do it;
   Then onward, my Arab, bound onward with me.

III.

Now gently, my steed, for we're close to his quarters,
   I hear his gruff grunt as he slow lobs along;
Full soon shall he add to the list of our slaughters—
   Full soon shall his death be recorded in song.
There! *that's* thro' and thro' him—he staggers—he stops—
   He sinks to the dust with his blood flowing free;
And here come the 'tinkers' in time for the chops—
   Hurrah! then, my Arab, now homeward with me!

                                    S. Y. S.

'Oriental Sporting Magazine,'
   August, 1832.

'TIS THE BOAR.

Tune—'C'est L'Amour.'

I.

'Tis the boar, the grim grey boar,
 The boar with the foamy tusk,
That bursts o'er hills at 'the pace that kills,'
 From dewy morn till dusk—
That leads the throng of the chase along,
 With their spurs all dashed with gore,
And tries the speed of the fleetest steed
 Who ne'er was tried before.
And it's hey! over the jungle plain,
 With the tall spears glancing bright,
And it's hey! over the mountain top
 Morning, noon, or night!
   'Tis the boar, etc.

II.

And what can make the spouse forsake
 The blush of his blooming bride,
And leave the bliss of smile and kiss
 For the joys of the jungle side!
And oh! what lures the wise and brave
 From their tomes of learned lore,
The toils and the care of the chase to dare,
 As bold ones dared of yore?
   'Tis the boar, etc.

III.

And what, in sooth, can tempt each youth
    To forget his failing purse,
To laugh at his debts and the bailiff's threats,
    While his pay grows worse and worse?
For 'tentage' and 'full batta,' too,
    No longer now we care,
But dash aside the tear of pride,
    Man's tribute to despair.
        'Tis the boar, etc.

IV.

Since nerve and health win love and wealth,
    The hopes we chiefly prize,
Let's seek the field and the bright spear wield,
    For *there* the elixir lies.
While it's hey! over the jungle green,
    When the game is once in sight;
And it's hey! over the deep ravine
    Morning, noon, or night!
        'Tis the boar, etc.

                S. Y. S.

'Oriental Sporting Magazine,'
    February, 1832.

SADDLE, SPUR, AND SPEAR

Air—'My Harp and Lute.'

I.

Let others boast and proudly toast
   The light of ladies' eyes,
And swear the rose less perfume throws
   Than beauty's fragrant sighs;
That ripe-red lips in hue eclipse
   The ruby's radiant gem;
That woman's far the brightest star
   In Nature's diadem:
But since for me no charms I see
   In all the sex can show,
And smile and tear alike appear
   Unheeded flash or flow—
I'll change my theme and fondly dream,
   True sportsmen pledge me here,
And fill my cup and drain it up
   To Saddle, Spur, and Spear!

II.

When dayspring's light first crowns each height,
   And tips the diamond dew,
We quick bestride our steeds of pride
   To scour the jungle through;

With loosened rein the jovial train
    Slow to the cover throng,
And wouldn't stir without a spur
    To coax their nags along.
We high uprear the glittering spear,
    Far flashing to the sky,
With hope elate anticipate
    To see the wild boar die.
To such bright hopes e'en misanthropes
    Would pledge a bumper here,
And fill their cup and drain it up
    To Saddle, Spur, and Spear!

III.

'Twere vain to tell the magic spell
    That fires the hunter's eye,
When shout and roar have roused the boar,
    And stirred him from his sty:
His rage at first, his glorious burst,
    Dark dashing through the flood,
His bristly might, his meteor flight,
    And his death of foam and blood!
Oh! who hath been in such a scene,
    That scene can e'er forget?
In sorrow's mood, in solitude,
    Its dream will haunt him yet;

'Mid festal times, in other climes,
   He'll think of days so dear,
And fill his cup and drain it up
   To Saddle, Spur, and Spear!

IV.

But, while I sing, Time's rapid wing
   This lesson seems to teach:
The joy and bliss of sport like this
   Are still within our reach:
Then let's away at break of day,
   Ride vale and hill-top o'er,
Scale mountains' side or stem the tide
   To spear the flying boar;
And Time may *then* bring eve again,
   The while, at Pleasure's shrine,
To check his flight for one gay night
   We'll wet his wing with wine;
And ere we part pledge hand and heart
   Once more to rally here,
To fill the cup and drain it up
   To Saddle, Spur, and Spear!

                               S. Y. S.

THE BOAR.

Tune—'My Love is like the Red, Red Rose.'

I.

The boar, the mighty boar's my theme,
    Whate'er the wise may say,
My morning thought, my midnight dream,
    My hope throughout the day.
Youth's daring spirit, manhood's fire,
    Firm hand and eagle eye,
Must they acquire who do aspire
    To see the grey boar die.
        Then pledge the boar, the mighty boar,
            Fill high the cup with me,
        Here's a health to all who fear no fall,
            And the next grey boar we see.

II.

We envy not the rich their state,
    Nor kings their crowned career,
For the saddle is our throne of health,
    Our sceptre is the spear!
We rival too the warrior's pride,
    Dress stained with purple gore,
For our field of fame is the jungle-side,
    Our foe—the jungle boar!
        Then pledge the boar, etc.

III.

When age hath weakened manhood's powers,
    And every nerve unbraced,
Those scenes of joy will still be ours,
    On mem'ry's tablets traced,
When with the friends whom death hath spared,
    When youth's career is run,
We'll talk of the chases we have shared,
    And the tushes we have won.
        Then pledge the boar, etc.

S. Y. S.*

SONG.

Air—'The Days when we went Gipsying.'

I.

In the days when we went hog-hunting,
    A long time ago,
With every hunter clad aright,
    We made a goodly show.
We scorned the suit of russet brown,
    Likewise of Lincoln green,

---

* The author writing under the initials of S. Y. S. was Captain Morris, of the 9th Bombay Native Infantry, a well-known Indian sportsman. He succeeded the world-famed and chivalrous James Outram in command of the Bheel Corps—and may certainly be termed the poet-laureate of Indian sport.

And never was a scarlet coat
    Amongst us to be seen.
'Twas thus we passed the merry time,
    Nor thought of care or woe,
In the days when we went hog-hunting,
    A long time ago.

II.

Our custom was at early dawn,
    When dewdrops glittered fair,
To track the grey and grisly boar,
    And rouse him from his lair.
Our steeds the noblest and the best
    That e'er Arabia knew,
Well strung each nerve, and in each hand
    Was poised a weapon true.
      'Twas thus, etc.

III.

Now beating high is every pulse,
    Now fired is every eye,
And, answering to their riders' haste,
    The noble coursers fly.
Wide fame be his who ne'er turns back,
    But presses to the fore,
And foremost ranked be he who first
    Shall pierce the old grey boar.
      'Twas thus, etc.

IV.

With foaming tusk and fiery eye,
  Indignant—undismayed,
Regardless of the shock of steel,
  The foe now meets the blade.
What headlong strength can e'er withstand
  You well-directed thrust?
One moment's space—he reels—he falls,
  He's level with the dust!
    'Twas thus, etc.

V.

Then let not sage or moralist
  Our much-loved sport decry;
We claim a warrant for the fame
  From all antiquity.
'Twas thus that **Melaeger's** prowess
  In the chase was tried;
'Twas thus **Ascanius'** youth was fired;
'Twas thus **Adonis** died!
    Then thus we'll pass the merry time,
      Nor think of care or woe,
    In the days when we go hog-hunting,
      Now—as in days of yore;
    In the days when we go hog-hunting,
      Now—as in days of yore.

KURRAMORE.

I.

You ask me for a song;
To refuse you would be wrong,
   So of pig-sticking I'll sing once more:
A break in the monsoon
Had dispelled the season's gloom,
   Though the clouds still at intervals would pour;
So to Joe I said one morning,
'Both wind and weather scorning,
   Let's go and have a beat for a boar.'

II.

Said Joe, 'I'd have much pleasure,
But I really haven't leisure;'
   (And, turning on his bed, he gave a snore,)
'I'd like to go shikarin',
But you know the rains we are in;
   And the country's such a swamp—what a bore!'

III.

I found it was in vain
To arouse my friend again,
   For a drowsy appearance he bore;
Though my very heart was beating
With the hopes I had of meeting
   With such sport as I'd enjoyed before.

IV.

With grief I say the rain
Had returned in floods again;
  So my spirits were depressed, and I swore
That, though it rained both 'cats and dogs,'
I'd put on my hunting togs,
  And go and have a beat for a boar!

V.

To my niggers' consternation,
I sent in an application
  For twenty days' leave—or more;
And, though the clouds were very dense,
I soon was out in tents,
  On my way to have a beat for a boar.

VI.

Now, when blank I drew three places,
And yet blanker grew the faces
  Of my servants when I came back at four;
In a rage, as I'm a sinner,
For there was no pork for dinner,
  As I hadn't had the luck to meet a boar!

VII.

To one I cried, 'You lubber,
You had better bring me "khubber,"
  Or else come near me no more;

For the spears that are reclining
Seem to taunt me with their shining,
   And to say, " Where's the blood of the boar ?" '

VIII.

The shikaris, fearing hidings,
One morning came with tidings
   That near a village called Kurramore,
An old woman had seen a sounder;
The hogs had run all round her,
   And she'd got a rip behind from the boar!

IX.

Then my spear so brightly gleaming
I seized with savage meaning,
   And away across country I tore!
Till, on riding o'er a hillock,
I saw, as I thought—a bullock,
   But it proved to be a huge grey boar!

X.

Then onward to attack him
I spurred—when, slightly backing,
   My enemy prepared for the war;
He charged!—but the power
Of ten hunters in that hour
   Nerved my arm to slay that noble boar!

XI.

We met in mid career;
Loud crashed my shiver'd spear—
    One shock—and I knew no more:
Till, on rising from the heath,
There side by side in death
    Lay my steed and that noble boar!

XII.

Now all true sportsmen hail!
And may ye never fail
    To have luck and good sport to the fore:
May ye never lose a horse,
Or else, what is far worse,
    May ye never lose an old grey boar!

COLONEL NIGHTINGALE,
Hyderabad Contingent.

NOTE.—These lines were written by a celebrated Indian sportsman—the late Colonel Nightingale, who commanded a regiment of irregular cavalry in the Hyderabad Contingent. He has seldom been excelled, or even equalled, as a shot or spear, and, I suppose, shot more tigers and speared more panthers, bears, and hog than any man of his time. He died very suddenly in October, 1868, at Secunderabad, in the Deccan. A panther had been caught and turned out on the race-course before several sportsmen to ride with spears. Colonel Nightingale and a young native officer were leading, when he was seen to sway in his saddle, and his spear dropped. His companions were just in time to catch him as he fell from his saddle—but he never recovered consciousness, and was buried the following day. His death was caused by the bursting of a vessel on the brain—and, oddly enough, he had at times expressed a wish that he might die in the hunting-field or in action. His wish, alas! was only too truly realized. I never had the pleasure of meeting him personally, but I knew several of his friends, from one of whom I heard the above humorous lines, which, in places, show great ability and *power* of expression most worthy of the man who wrote them. Colonel Nightingale was credited with having killed over three hundred tigers, and also of having, alone and unaided, ridden, speared, and killed sixty-four bears off horseback in the space of about two months! More than a bear a day!

OH! REST THEE, MY HUNTER.

I.

Oh! rest thee, my hunter, oh! sleep while you may,
To-morrow I ride thee the wild boar to slay;
So thick are the covers, the country so strong,
So swift are the wild boars, the chase will be long.

II.

Then rest well, my hunter, oh! sound may you sleep,
For high are the hills, and the nullahs are deep;
When once on thee mounted, and the boar in full
    view,
Then where is the country we will not get through?

III.

So sure is thy footing, so good is thy speed,
Nor nullahs, nor rocks, nor holes do I heed;

So firm is thy courage that nought can dismay,
But sealed is the boar's fate when once brought to
   bay.

IV.

Then carry me swiftly, and, when thou art old,
I swear not to sell thee for silver or gold;
Thou shalt range at thy pleasure the rest of thy days,
Thou best of all hunters, thou brightest of bays!

G.

'Oriental Sporting Magazine,'
   August, 1831.

LET OTHERS WASTE.

I.

Let others waste their life away
In stirring strife or calm decay;
Let others seek in beauty's eye
The pleasing pains of ecstasy,
And wile their time from lip to lip,
Now here to feast, now there to sip;
Let others by loud, thund'ring war
From home and friends and love afar
Be led, or by ambition curst,
For place, for rank, and riches thirst:

Give me my Arab nag and spear,
A boar from out yon thorny 'bheer,'
I want no other pleasures here.

II.

'Tis sweet to see an infant smile,
So tender, soft, and void of guile;
'Tis sweet to view a mother's joy,
When gently sleeps her only boy;
'Tis sweet to see two lovers kiss,
And dream this life a life of bliss;
But oh! 'tis passing sweet to rear
The boar from out his grassy 'bheer,'
Undaunted meet his frenzied eye,
And all his savage might defy.

So give me my Arab nag and spear,
A boar from out yon thorny 'bheer,'
I want no other pleasures here.

C.

'Oriental Sporting Magazine,'
August, 1832.

AWAY, AWAY.

I.

Away! away, like lightning's flash,
O'er yon hills and nullah dash,
The 'baubul' branches round us crash,
  A rattling boar is gone ahead.

II.

Away, away, nor jungles heed,
Ply well the spear, increase your speed,
For glory's in the daring deed,
    The path where fame and honour tread.

III.

Near and more near's the panting nag,
The weary boar begins to lag,
Unceasing still, he yet does fag,
    To gain the covert of yon 'bheer.'

IV.

His vicious eye is backward cast,
And views his foes approaching fast;
Soon must the monster breathe his last
    Without a shade of dread or fear.

V.

The dusty soil is tinged with red,
For true and strong the spear has sped
That sent him to his gory bed,
    E'en in his strength and savage might.

VI.

But did he die alone, that boar?
The gallant steed that swiftly bore
His master on—he ripped and tore,
    Before his vengeful soul took flight.

                                    C.

'Oriental Sporting Magazine,'
  August, 1832.

THE HUNTER'S SONG.

I.

We value not false woman's kiss,
We value not the miser's bliss,
We care not for the gourmand's joy,
The rich ragoût or savoury soy;
'Tis claret cool and Hodgson's ale,
'Tis the steep hill and rocky dale,
The deep ravine, the thorny ' bheer,'
The Arab nag, the small sharp spear,
The glorious burst, the savage roar,
The madness of the maddened boar,
That makes us value life alone;
Nor love, nor wealth, nor despot's throne
Could tempt us from these joys to roam.

II.

Let fools with women wile away
The precious hours of youthful day;
Let sots with drink their senses drown;
Let bays the studious temple crown;
Let plodding souls heap up their dross,
And nightly dream of gain, or loss—
A boar to us is comlier far
Than Venus in her dove-drawn car;

The spicy bowl we only **drain,**
That o'er it we may hunt again :
If laurel leaves some temples twine,
'Tis with many **a furrowed line ;**
But **give us health and game in store,**
The savage panther, tuskied boar,
We wish, nor hope, nor pray for more.

III.

And some **there are** who pass **their lives**
Like captives chained, with snarling wives,
Happy in their home-made **toys,**
Great sprawling girls and **troublesome boys ;**
Some take a pleasure in their **drill,**
In hot mulled port, or **devilled grill ;**
Some **live to drive the mettled steed ;**
Some **love to smoke the fragrant weed ;**
And some there are who all night long,
With hideous **howls their mirth prolong.**
Let every man his taste enjoy,
For life, alas ! **flies speedily ;**
But **give us health and game in store,**
The savage **panther, tuskied boar,**
We wish, **nor hope, nor pray for more.**

C.

'Oriental Sporting Magazine,'
    March, 1833.

THE BOAR OF THE SOUNDER.

I.

The sun was just tingeing the Bheema's broad tide,
When the boar of the sounder stood close to its side;
And nothing was heard save the water's low moan,
As swiftly it rushed o'er the time-eaten stone.

II.

As he stooped him to drink at the clear, flowing stream,
On the high bank above him five horsemen were seen;
Gruffly grunted that boar as their forms met his eye,
And he dashed through the flood as the hunters drew nigh.

II.

'Woh jata! woh jata!' the hills echo back
Old Duttoo's loud shout as they pressed on his track,
And each heart beat high as they plunged in the wave,
Those riders of Nugger the bold and the brave.

IV.

He swam the wide river, he crosses the plain,
But the steep 'ghât' before him he never shall gain;
For those now are near him who mean not to part
Till the blades of their long spears are thrust thro' his heart.

V.

Like the whirlwind that sweeps over **mountain and mead,**
Thro' the jungle of thorn **is the rush of each steed;**
Yet *one* shoots ahead like a shaft from a **bow,**
And the hunter's sharp **weapon is poised o'er his foe.**

VI.

It is done—he is speared, and the flank of **that boar**
So lately unscarred, is dripping with gore;
He turns and he charges, but charges in vain,
For the next moment he lies a corpse on the plain.

VII.

Now, our sport being over, let us drink **to the day,**
When once more we assemble **a** grey **boar to slay.**
May his pluck **be as good, and** his **speed as well tried,**
As his who but now by the Bheema has died!

SCREW.

'Oriental Sporting Magazine,'
March, 1833.

I'LL LEND THEE THESE.

Tune—'I'll give thee All.'

I.

I'll lend thee these, for luck attends
    The aged sportsman's loan,
My spurs and spear, the truest friends
    I e'er could call my own.
The spur whose gentlest touch could coax
    The dullest steed to go,
And better far the spear whose pokes
    Have many a boar laid low.

II.

Though hogs may hide and steeds may swerve,
    And blank may prove the day,
Yet still the search itself will serve
    This lesson to convey:
If ever care should bring thee pain,
    Or sorrow dim thine eye,
Let spur and spear be used again,
    And see how grief will fly!

D.

'Oriental Sporting Magazine,'
    February, 1832.

PARODY.

I.

Farewell! but whenever you open your beer
And feast upon oysters or any such cheer,
Oh! think upon him who has gorged on them too,
And forgot his own grills to eat oysters with you!

II.

When of hog you get 'khubber' and Duttoo appears,
When it's 'Saddle your horses, make ready your spears,'
Oh! think upon him who, though luckless he be,
Has charged nullahs and fences whilst riding with thee.

III.

When out from the jungle starts the grey boar,
And 'Dehk dooker jata hai!' loud is the roar,
Oh! think upon him who, if wishes held sway,
Would have rode by your side on that glorious day.

IV.

And when you have killed, having taken 'first spear,'
To your tent have returned and drunk Bass' beer,
Oh! think upon him who, had he been there,
In 'spear' and in 'mug' would have tried for his share!

V.

Then farewell! and, though we may ne'er meet again
By hill or by jungle, by river or plain,
Yet think upon one who, where'er he may be,
Will ever bestow his best wishes on thee!

YESSAM.

'Oriental Sporting Magazine,'
August, 1830.

SONG.

Air—'Oh! think not my Spirits are always so Light.'

I.

Oh! think not our spear-blades are always as bright
And as free from a stain as they now may appear,
Nor expect that the steel, all so glittering to-night,
Will return back to-morrow unsullied and clear:
No! daylight shall see us, all dangers disdaining,
Our untainted weapons to purple with gore,
For the man that is last to debate about craning
Is always the first—for a touch at the boar!
Then off with each glass, 'twill be pleasure indeed
To bumper our toast when the pleasure is o'er;
Here's 'The boar that has bottom to puzzle the steed,
And the steed who will carry us up to the boar!'

II.

The chase of the hog would be dull, Heaven knows,
If we had not some raspers to vary the hunt,
And we care not o'er what sort of ground our horse
    goes,
While we see the grey boar dashing on in our front.
Oh! ride as you will, but, the bolder and truer,
More certain you are your hearts wish to obtain;
For the hog, though once he fairly beat his pursuer,
Is a rare one indeed if he beat him again.
Then off with each glass, while a 'sounder' shall stray
In mountain or jungle, let's drink with delight
That the chase which begins at the first flush of day
May be crowned with success ere the first shade of
    night!

'Oriental Sporting Magazine,'
    January, 1829.

SONG.

Air—' The Harp that once through Tara's Halls.'

I.

The spear that once o'er Deccan dust
  The blood of wild boars shed
Now stands as stained in Deccan rust
  As if all boars had fled;
So dies each spirit-stirring thought,
  And they who would have flown
With wild hogs bristly forms to sport
  Now ride to sport their own!

II.

No youth—so hunting zeal doth fade—
  The idle weapon heeds!
The gore alone that taints its blade
  Tells of its former deeds;
And thus that flush which taints each face
  Tells its own story too,
And proves the spirit of the chase
  Once found a home with you.

III.

Then bid that spirit welcome home,
  High pledge the joyous guest,
And join my song, while bumpers foam
  To give the toast a zest.
Here's bottom to the horse we ride,
  Size to the boar we rear,
And nerve and skill to aid and guide
  The arm that wields the spear.

' Oriental Sporting Magazine,'
  January, 1829.

THE BOAR'S DEATH.

Air—' There came to the beach a poor Exile of Erin.'

I.

There came to the stream a boar breathless and jaded,
The gore from his deep wounds empurpled the mud,
From his tusks dropped the foam as he, staggering,
    waded,
To strengthen his fast-failing limbs in the flood;
But the hunters' cry reached him, now sinking, now
    swelling,
As it came on the gale his death-hour foretelling,
While red from his ribs was the vital tide welling.
Loud cursing his rashness, thus murmured the boar:

II.

' Oh, where is the fame, the distinction I tried for?
Father, pig-prophet, thy warning was true,
And where art thou, dearest sow, that I sighed for?
And where's my friend "Dooker," who sighed for her
    too?
The hunter's wild shout will be my "ull-ulla";
They rode me from "Waree" down, down to this
    nullah,
Reined up for no rasper, they came with a "hullah;"
Oh! little I dreamt what such devils could do.

III.

'" Waree," once more could thine echoes awake me,
Up to thy hill-top, oh! would I could fly;
But, alas! had I wings, still these chaps would o'er-
   take me;
I'm done for, I'm dished, I can feel my chops fry:
Singe, singe, my head bald for this hour of sadness,
My spirit, my speed, were my pride and my gladness;
And *thus* to be foiled! Oh! it goads me to madness—
Yet, damn it! I'll die as a boar ought to die.'

IV.

Then, every hope of revenge swift returning,
This one bloody wish did the grey monster roar:
' Hog spirits behold me, at death itself spurning,
Waree, record the last deed of thy boar.'
Then up came a rider, exultingly dashing,
And forth rushed the boar, his tusks wildly gnashing,
And deep sped the spear through his heart as in
   clashing—
He ripped the horse dead; and thus died the old boar!

'Oriental Sporting Magazine,'
   October, 1829.

Note.—I regret that I have lost the proper names of places, etc., given in the original; I have therefore substituted others.

A FRAGMENT.

Know you the land where the jungle thick growing
Gives promise of sport, the true huntsman's aim,
Where the track of the panther and dark, tusky boar
Now startles to chillness, now maddens to fame?
Know you the land of the 'baubul' and 'bheer,'
Where the fruit never tempts you, the thorns never
    spare,
Where the 'mhowa' sweet-scented in solitude yields
Its perfume unsought o'er untenanted fields;
Where the palate unpampered's ne'er greeted with
    fruit,
And the voice of the jackal scarce ever is mute;
Where the grass aromatic waves high in the air,
And the sun's ever shining—incessant its glare;
Where the virgins are scarce as the rose on their
    cheek,
And all, save the sportsman's dear spot, seems a bleak?
    *   *   *   *   *   *   *   *

'Oriental Sporting Magazine,' October, 1829.

SONG.
I.

The hunter came down like the storm in its speed,
And the foam was all white on the flanks of his steed;
When he passed in his course there was trembling
    and fear,
And the mighty boar shrank from the gleam of his spear!

II.

When the hill's brighten'd o'er with the first glance of day,
The grim monster secure in his mountain lair lay,
And the blade of the spear flashed unstained to the light,
That was dulled o'er with blood ere the coming of night.

III.

Fear never till then chilled the heart of the boar,
And he ne'er had met man, the destroyer, before,
Who came down to meet him with spear and with steed,
With a hand for the blow, and a heart for the deed.

IV.

He fled as the hurricane swoops in its flight,
He charged as the storm rushes forth in its might;
But his strength was but weak, and his speed was but slow,
To fly from or cope with the arm of his foe.

V.

He dashed thro' the stream, he rushed down the hill,
But man, the destroyer, was close on him still;
There was fame to be gained, and a deed to be done,
The blow has been dealt, and the tushes are won!

'Oriental Sporting Magazine,'
November, 1831.

THE NAGPORE HUNT.

Air.—'The Hardy Norseman.'

I.

The hardy sportsman's post of yore
　　Was by the jungle-side;
For there he speared the mighty boar,
　　And pierced his brawny hide.
Oh! ne'er shall we forget the day,
　　Wherever we may be,
When first we heard the 'Gone away,'
　　And waving flags did see.

II.

A moment more,—and then we view
　　The boar break from his lair
(And sows there were, and squeakers too;
　　For these we did not care).
For then it was ambition's height
　　To spear the tusky boar,
And slay him fair in open fight,
　　As others had before.

III.

From Kamptee oft we sallied out
　　And met in good array,
With speedy hogs to have a bout
　　And spend a jovial day.

'Chandkee's' bheer was then well-known,
  And 'Gojee's' rumnah high,
At 'Baila' where the pán is grown
  Big boars were wont to lie.

IV.

There's 'Nagri,' too, of well-known fame,
  With 'Jamnee' to its right,
And 'Khoppa,' too, has earned a name
  For boars that run—and fight!
And oft o'er 'Karlee's' stony hill
  We've laid into a hog,
At 'Waree,' too, we've had a kill,
  And soused into its bog!

V.

And in 'Mahadoola's' corries deep
  We've roused our stubborn foe,
Though now to 'Ghirur's' hill so steep
  We can no longer go.
And 'Ghonee,' too, has shown us sport
  With panther as with boar;
Near Khootki's sindbund thick we've fought,
  And stained our spears with gore.

VI.

Then of those days we'll often think,
  And run our runs once more;
To old companions let us drink,
  And toast the mighty boar!

> But though grey Time shall make us old,
>   Nor fit to poise the spear,
> We'll still recall from memory's mould
>   Those days that were so dear.
>
> J. M. B.

Kamptee,
   September, 1871.

With regard to the songs and verses given, I have in the two instances where I have been able to identify the writers given their names. To some of the others initials have only been appended, and to some no signature at all. At any rate, for this *I* am not responsible. I have merely given them exactly as I copied them out of some old numbers of the *Oriental Sporting Magazine*, dating back as far as fifty-seven years ago! But 'there were giants in those days,' and my poor attempt at versifying, written after my last day's hunting, must, if at all worthy of being included in these songs of shikar, occupy the only fitting place for it, viz., the very fag end!

THE END.

HURST & BLACKETT'S

STANDARD LIBRARY.

LONDON:

13, GREAT MARLBOROUGH STREET, W.

HURST & BLACKETT'S STANDARD LIBRARY
OF CHEAP EDITIONS OF
POPULAR MODERN WORKS.
ILLUSTRATED BY
Sir J. E. Millais, Sir J. Gilbert, Holman Hunt, Birket Foster, John Leech, John Tenniel, J. Laslett Pott, etc.

Each in a Single Volume, with Frontispiece, price 5s.

I.—SAM SLICK'S NATURE AND HUMAN NATURE.

"The first volume of Messrs. Hurst and Blackett's Standard Library of Cheap Editions forms a very good beginning to what will doubtless be a very successful undertaking. 'Nature and Human Nature' is one of the best of Sam Slick's witty and humorous productions, and well entitled to the large circulation which it cannot fail to obtain in its present convenient and cheap shape. The volume combines with the great recommendations of a clear, bold type and good paper, the lesser, but attractive merits of being well illustrated and elegantly bound."—*Morning Post.*

II.—JOHN HALIFAX, GENTLEMAN.

"The new and cheaper edition of this interesting work will doubtless meet with great success. John Halifax, the hero of this most beautiful story, is no ordinary hero, and this his history is no ordinary book. It is a full-length portrait of a true gentleman, one of nature's own nobility. It is also the history of a home, and a thoroughly English one. The work abounds in incident, and many of the scenes are full of graphic power and true pathos. It is a book that few will read without becoming wiser and better."—*Scotsman.*

"This story is very interesting. The attachment between John Halifax and his wife is beautifully painted, as are the pictures of their domestic life, and the growing up of their children; and the conclusion of the book is beautiful and touching."—*Athenæum.*

III.—THE CRESCENT AND THE CROSS.
BY ELIOT WARBURTON.

"Independent of its value as an original narrative, and its useful and interesting information, this work is remarkable for the colouring power and play of fancy with which its descriptions are enlivened. Among its greatest and most lasting charms is its reverent and serious spirit."—*Quarterly Review.*

"Mr. Warburton has fulfilled the promise of his title-page. The 'Realities of Eastern Travel' are described with a vividness which invests them with deep and abiding interest; while the 'Romantic' adventures which the enterprising tourist met with in his course are narrated with a spirit which shows how much he enjoyed these reliefs from the ennui of every-day life."—*Globe.*

IV.—NATHALIE.
BY JULIA KAVANAGH.

"'Nathalie' is Miss Kavanagh's best imaginative effort. Its manner is gracious and attractive. Its matter is good. A sentiment, a tenderness, are commanded by her which are as individual as they are elegant. We should not soon come to an end were we to specify all the delicate touches and attractive pictures which place 'Nathalie' high among books of its class."—*Athenæum.*

V.—A WOMAN'S THOUGHTS ABOUT WOMEN.
BY THE AUTHOR OF "JOHN HALIFAX, GENTLEMAN."

"These thoughts are good and humane. They are thoughts we would wish women to think: they are much more to the purpose than the treatises upon the women and daughters of England, which were fashionable some years ago, and these thoughts mark the progress of opinion, and indicate a higher tone of character, and a juster estimate of woman's position."—*Athenæum.*

"This excellent book is characterised by good sense, good taste, and feeling, and is written in an earnest, philanthropic, as well as practical spirit."—*Morning Post.*

HURST & BLACKETT'S STANDARD LIBRARY

VI.—ADAM GRAEME OF MOSSGRAY.
BY MRS. OLIPHANT.

"'Adam Graeme' is a story awakening genuine emotions of interest and delight by its admirable pictures of Scottish life and scenery. The plot is cleverly complicated, and there is great vitality in the dialogue, and remarkable brilliancy in the descriptive passages, as who that has read 'Margaret Maitland' would not be prepared to expect? But the story has a 'mightier magnet still,' in the healthy tone which pervades it, in its feminine delicacy of thought and diction, and in the truly womanly tenderness of its sentiments. The eloquent author sets before us the essential attributes of Christian virtue, their deep and silent workings in the heart, and their beautiful manifestations in the life, with a delicacy, a power, and a truth which can hardly be surpassed."—*Morning Post.*

VII.—SAM SLICK'S WISE SAWS AND MODERN INSTANCES.

"We have not the slightest intention to criticise this book. Its reputation is made, and will stand as long as that of Scott's or Bulwer's novels. The remarkable originality of its purpose, and the happy description it affords of American life and manners, still continue the subject of universal admiration. To say thus much is to say enough, though we must just mention that the new edition forms a part of the Publishers' Cheap Standard Library, which has included some of the very best specimens of light literature that ever have been written."—*Messenger.*

VIII.—CARDINAL WISEMAN'S RECOLLECTIONS OF THE LAST FOUR POPES.

"A picturesque book on Rome and its ecclesiastical sovereigns, by an eloquent Roman Catholic. Cardinal Wiseman has here treated a special subject with so much generality and geniality that his recollections will excite no ill-feeling in those who are most conscientiously opposed to every idea of human infallibility represented in Papal domination."—*Athenæum.*

IX.—A LIFE FOR A LIFE.
BY THE AUTHOR OF "JOHN HALIFAX, GENTLEMAN."

"We are always glad to welcome Mrs. Craik. She writes from her own convictions, and she has the power not only to conceive clearly what it is that she wishes to say, but to express it in language effective and vigorous. In 'A Life for a Life' she is fortunate in a good subject, and she has produced a work of strong effect. The reader, having read the book through for the story, will be apt (if he be of our persuasion) to return and read again many pages and passages with greater pleasure than on a first perusal. The whole book is replete with a graceful, tender delicacy; and, in addition to its other merits, it is written in good careful English."—*Athenæum.*

"'A Life for a Life' is a book of a high class. The characters are depicted with a masterly hand; the events are dramatically set forth; the descriptions of scenery and sketches of society are admirably penned; moreover, the work has an object—a clearly defined moral—most poetically, most beautifully drawn, and through all there is that strong, reflective mind visible which lays bare the human heart and human mind to the very core."—*Morning Post.*

X.—THE OLD COURT SUBURB.
BY LEIGH HUNT.

"A book which has afforded us no slight gratification."—*Athenæum.*
"From the mixture of description, anecdote, biography, and criticism, this book is very pleasant reading."—*Spectator.*
"A more agreeable and entertaining book has not been published since Boswell produced his reminiscences of Johnson."—*Observer.*

HURST & BLACKETT'S STANDARD LIBRARY

XI.—MARGARET AND HER BRIDESMAIDS.
BY THE AUTHOR OF "THE VALLEY OF A HUNDRED FIRES."

"We recommend all who are in search of a fascinating novel to read this work for themselves. They will find it well worth their while. There are a freshness and originality about it quite charming, and there is a certain nobleness in the treatment both of sentiment and incident which is not often found."—*Athenæum.*

XII.—THE OLD JUDGE; OR, LIFE IN A COLONY.
BY SAM SLICK.

"A peculiar interest attaches to sketches of colonial life, and readers could not have a safer guide than the talented author of this work, who, by a residence of half a century, has practically grasped the habits, manners, and social conditions of the colonists he describes. All who wish to form a fair idea of the difficulties and pleasures of life in a new country, unlike England in some respects, yet like it in many, should read this book." *John Bull.*

XIII.—DARIEN; OR, THE MERCHANT PRINCE.
BY ELIOT WARBURTON.

"This last production of the author of 'The Crescent and the Cross' has the same elements of a very wide popularity. It will please its thousands."—*Globe.*

"Eliot Warburton's active and productive genius is amply exemplified in the present book. We have seldom met with any work in which the realities of history and the poetry of fiction were more happily interwoven."—*Illustrated News.*

XIV.—FAMILY ROMANCE; OR, DOMESTIC ANNALS OF THE ARISTOCRACY.
BY SIR BERNARD BURKE, ULSTER KING OF ARMS.

"It were impossible to praise too highly this most interesting book, whether we should have regard to its excellent plan or its not less excellent execution. It ought to be found on every drawing-room table. Here you have nearly fifty captivating romances with the pith of all their interest preserved in undiminished poignancy, and any one may be read in half an hour. It is not the least of their merits that the romances are founded on fact —or what, at least, has been handed down for truth by long tradition—and the romance of reality far exceeds the romance of fiction."—*Standard.*

XV.—THE LAIRD OF NORLAW.
BY MRS. OLIPHANT.

"We have had frequent opportunities of commending Messrs. Hurst and Blackett's Standard Library. For neatness, elegance, and distinctness the volumes in this series surpass anything with which we are familiar. 'The Laird of Norlaw' will fully sustain the author's high reputation. The reader is carried on from first to last with an energy of sympathy that never flags."—*Sunday Times.*

"'The Laird of Norlaw' is worthy of the author's reputation. It is one of the most exquisite of modern novels."—*Observer.*

XVI.—THE ENGLISHWOMAN IN ITALY.
BY MRS. G. GRETTON.

"Mrs. Gretton had opportunities which rarely fall to the lot of strangers of becoming acquainted with the inner life and habits of a part of the Italian peninsula which is the very centre of the national crisis. We can praise her performance as interesting, unexaggerated, and full of opportune instruction."—*The Times.*

"Mrs. Gretton's book is timely, life-like, and for every reason to be recommended It is impossible to close the book without liking the writer as well as the subject. The work is engaging, because real."—*Athenæum.*

HURST & BLACKETT'S STANDARD LIBRARY

XVII.—NOTHING NEW.
BY THE AUTHOR OF "JOHN HALIFAX, GENTLEMAN."

"'Nothing New' displays all those superior merits which have made 'John Halifax' one of the most popular works of the day. There is a force and truthfulness about these tales which mark them as the production of no ordinary mind, and we cordially recommend them to the perusal of all lovers of fiction."—*Morning Post.*

XVIII.—LIFE OF JEANNE D'ALBRET, QUEEN OF NAVARRE.
BY MISS FREER.

"We have read this book with great pleasure, and have no hesitation in recommending it to general perusal. It reflects the highest credit on the industry and ability of Miss Freer. Nothing can be more interesting than her story of the life of Jeanne D'Albret, and the narrative is as trustworthy as it is attractive."—*Morning Post.*

XIX.—THE VALLEY OF A HUNDRED FIRES.
BY THE AUTHOR OF "MARGARET AND HER BRIDESMAIDS."

"If asked to classify this work, we should give it a place between 'John Halifax' and 'The Caxtons.'"—*Standard.*
"The spirit in which the whole book is written is refined and good."—*Athenæum.*
"This is in every sense a charming novel."—*Messenger.*

XX.—THE ROMANCE OF THE FORUM; OR, NARRATIVES, SCENES, AND ANECDOTES FROM COURTS OF JUSTICE.
BY PETER BURKE, SERJEANT AT LAW.

"This attractive book will be perused with much interest. It contains a great variety of singular and highly romantic stories."—*John Bull.*
"A work of singular interest, which can never fail to charm and absorb the reader's attention. The present cheap and elegant edition includes the true story of the Colleen Bawn."—*Illustrated News.*

XXI.—ADÈLE.
BY JULIA KAVANAGH.

"'Adèle' is the best work we have read by Miss Kavanagh; it is a charming story, full of delicate character-painting. The interest kindled in the first chapter burns brightly to the close."—*Athenæum.*
"'Adèle' will fully sustain the reputation of Miss Kavanagh, high as it already ranks."—*John Bull.*
"'Adèle' is a love-story of very considerable pathos and power. It is a very clever novel."—*Daily News.*

XXII.—STUDIES FROM LIFE.
BY THE AUTHOR OF "JOHN HALIFAX, GENTLEMAN."

"These 'Studies' are truthful and vivid pictures of life, often earnest, always full of right feeling, and occasionally lightened by touches of quiet, genial humour. The volume is remarkable for thought, sound sense, shrewd observation, and kind and sympathetic feeling for all things good and beautiful."—*Morning Post.*
"These 'Studies from Life' are remarkable for graphic power and observation. The book will not diminish the reputation of the accomplished author."—*Saturday Review.*

HURST & BLACKETT'S STANDARD LIBRARY

XXIII.—GRANDMOTHER'S MONEY.
BY F. W. ROBINSON.
"We commend 'Grandmother's Money' to readers in search of a good novel. The characters are true to human nature, and the story is interesting."—*Athenæum.*

XXIV.—A BOOK ABOUT DOCTORS.
BY JOHN CORDY JEAFFRESON.
"A book to be read and re-read; fit for the study as well as the drawing-room table and the circulating library."—*Lancet.*

"This is a pleasant book for the fireside season, and for the seaside season. Mr. Jeaffreson has, out of hundreds of volumes, collected thousands of good things, adding thereto much that appears in print for the first time, and which, of course, gives increased value to this very readable book."—*Athenæum.*

XXV.—NO CHURCH.
BY F. W. ROBINSON.
"We advise all who have the opportunity to read this book. It is well worth the study."—*Athenæum.*

"A work of great originality, merit, and power."—*Standard.*

XXVI.—MISTRESS AND MAID.
BY THE AUTHOR OF "JOHN HALIFAX, GENTLEMAN."
"A good wholesome book, gracefully written, and as pleasant to read as it is instructive."—*Athenæum.*

"A charming tale, charmingly told."—*Standard.*

"All lovers of a good novel will hail with delight another of Mrs. Craik's charming stories."—*John Bull.*

XXVII.—LOST AND SAVED.
BY THE HON. MRS. NORTON.
"'Lost and Saved' will be read with eager interest by those who love a touching story. It is a vigorous novel."—*Times.*

"This story is animated, full of exciting situations and stirring incidents. The characters are delineated with great power. Above and beyond these elements of a good novel, there is that indefinable charm with which true genius invests all it touches."—*Daily News.*

XXVIII.—LES MISERABLES.
BY VICTOR HUGO.
Authorised Copyright English Translation.

"The merits of 'Les Miserables' do not merely consist in the conception of it as a whole; it abounds with details of unequalled beauty. M. Victor Hugo has stamped upon every page the hall-mark of genius."—*Quarterly Review.*

XXIX.—BARBARA'S HISTORY.
BY AMELIA B. EDWARDS.
"It is not often that we light upon a novel of so much merit and interest as 'Barbara's History.' It is a work conspicuous for taste and literary culture. It is a very graceful and charming book, with a well-managed story, clearly-cut characters, and sentiments expressed with an exquisite elocution. The dialogues especially sparkle with repartee. It is a book which the world will like. This is high praise of a work of art, and so we intend it."—*The Times.*

HURST & BLACKETT'S STANDARD LIBRARY

XXX.—LIFE OF THE REV. EDWARD IRVING.
BY MRS. OLIPHANT.

"A good book on a most interesting theme."—*Times.*
"A truly interesting and most affecting memoir. 'Irving's Life' ought to have a niche in every gallery of religious biography. There are few lives that will be fuller of instruction, interest, and consolation."—*Saturday Review.*

XXXI.—ST. OLAVE'S.
BY THE AUTHOR OF "JANITA'S CROSS."

"This novel is the work of one who possesses a great talent for writing, as well as experience and knowledge of the world. The whole book is worth reading."—*Athenæum.*
"'St. Olave's' belongs to a lofty order of fiction. It is a good novel, but it is something more. It is written with unflagging ability, and it is as even as it is clever. The author has determined to do nothing short of the best, and has succeeded."—*Morning Post.*

XXXII.—SAM SLICK'S TRAITS OF AMERICAN HUMOUR.

"Dip where you will into this lottery of fun, you are sure to draw out a prize. These 'Traits' exhibit most successfully the broad national features of American humour."—*Post.*

XXXIII.—CHRISTIAN'S MISTAKE.
BY THE AUTHOR OF "JOHN HALIFAX, GENTLEMAN."

"A more charming story has rarely been written. It is a choice gift to be able thus to render human nature so truly, to penetrate its depths with such a searching sagacity, and to illuminate them with a radiance so eminently the writer's own."—*Times.*

XXXIV.—ALEC FORBES OF HOWGLEN.
BY GEORGE MAC DONALD, LL.D.

"No account of this story would give any idea of the profound interest that pervades the work from the first page to the last."—*Athenæum.*
"A novel of uncommon merit. Sir Walter Scott said he would advise no man to try to read 'Clarissa Harlowe' out loud in company if he wished to keep his character for manly superiority to tears. We fancy a good many hardened old novel-readers will feel a rising in the throat as they follow the fortunes of Alec and Annie."—*Pall Mall Gazette.*

XXXV.—AGNES.
BY MRS. OLIPHANT.

"'Agnes' is a novel superior to any of Mrs. Oliphant's former works."—*Athenæum.*
"Mrs. Oliphant is one of the most admirable of our novelists. In her works there are always to be found high principle, good taste, sense, and refinement. 'Agnes' is a story whose pathetic beauty will appeal irresistibly to all readers."—*Morning Post.*

XXXVI.—A NOBLE LIFE.
BY THE AUTHOR OF "JOHN HALIFAX, GENTLEMAN."

"Few men and no women will read 'A Noble Life' without feeling themselves the better for the effort."—*Spectator.*
"A beautifully written and touching tale. It is a noble book."—*Morning Post.*
"'A Noble Life' is remarkable for the high types of character it presents, and the skill with which they are made to work out a story of powerful and pathetic interest."—*Daily News.*

XXXVII.—NEW AMERICA.
BY W. HEPWORTH DIXON.

"A very interesting book. Mr. Dixon has written thoughtfully and well."—*Times.*
"We recommend everyone who feels any interest in human nature to read Mr. Dixon's very interesting book."—*Saturday Review.*

HURST & BLACKETT'S STANDARD LIBRARY

XXXVIII.—ROBERT FALCONER.
BY GEORGE MAC DONALD, LL.D.
"'Robert Falconer' is a work brimful of life and humour and of the deepest human interest. It is a book to be returned to again and again for the deep and searching knowledge it evinces of human thoughts and feelings."—*Athenæum.*

XXXIX.—THE WOMAN'S KINGDOM.
BY THE AUTHOR OF "JOHN HALIFAX, GENTLEMAN."
"'The Woman's Kingdom' sustains the author's reputation as a writer of the purest and noblest kind of domestic stories."—*Athenæum.*
"'The Woman's Kingdom' is remarkable for its romantic interest. The characters are masterpieces. Edna is worthy of the hand that drew John Halifax."—*Morning Post.*

XL.—ANNALS OF AN EVENTFUL LIFE.
BY GEORGE WEBBE DASENT, D.C.L.
"A racy, well-written, and original novel. The interest never flags. The whole work sparkles with wit and humour."—*Quarterly Review.*

XLI.—DAVID ELGINBROD.
BY GEORGE MAC DONALD, LL.D.
"A novel which is the work of a man of genius. It will attract the highest class of readers."—*Times.*

XLII.—A BRAVE LADY.
BY THE AUTHOR OF "JOHN HALIFAX, GENTLEMAN."
"We earnestly recommend this novel. It is a special and worthy specimen of the author's remarkable powers. The reader's attention never flags for a moment flags."—*Post.*
"'A Brave Lady' thoroughly rivets the unmingled sympathy of the reader, and her history deserves to stand foremost among the author's works."—*Daily Telegraph.*

XLIII.—HANNAH.
BY THE AUTHOR OF "JOHN HALIFAX, GENTLEMAN."
"A very pleasant, healthy story, well and artistically told. The book is sure of a wide circle of readers. The character of Hannah is one of rare beauty."—*Standard.*
"A powerful novel of social and domestic life. One of the most successful efforts of a successful novelist."—*Daily News.*

XLIV.—SAM SLICK'S AMERICANS AT HOME.
"This is one of the most amusing books that we ever read."—*Standard.*
"'The Americans at Home' will not be less popular than any of Judge Halliburton's previous works."—*Morning Post.*

XLV.—THE UNKIND WORD.
BY THE AUTHOR OF "JOHN HALIFAX, GENTLEMAN."
"These stories are gems of narrative. Indeed, some of them, in their touching grace and simplicity, seem to us to possess a charm even beyond the authoress's most popular novels. Of none of them can this be said more emphatically than of that which opens the series, 'The Unkind Word.' It is wonderful to see the imaginative power displayed in the few delicate touches by which this successful love-story is sketched out."—*The Echo.*

HURST & BLACKETT'S STANDARD LIBRARY

XLVI.—A ROSE IN JUNE.
BY MRS. OLIPHANT.

"'A Rose in June' is as pretty as its title. The story is one of the best and most touching which we owe to the industry and talent of Mrs. Oliphant, and may hold its own with even 'The Chronicles of Carlingford.'"—*Times.*

XLVII.—MY LITTLE LADY.
BY E. FRANCES POYNTER.

"This story presents a number of vivid and very charming pictures. Indeed, the whole book is charming. It is interesting in both character and story, and thoroughly good of its kind."—*Saturday Review.*

XLVIII.—PHŒBE, JUNIOR.
BY MRS. OLIPHANT.

"This last 'Chronicle of Carlingford' not merely takes rank fairly beside the first which introduced us to 'Salem Chapel,' but surpasses all the intermediate records. Phœbe, Junior, herself is admirably drawn."—*Academy.*

XLIX.—LIFE OF MARIE ANTOINETTE.
BY PROFESSOR CHARLES DUKE YONGE.

"A work of remarkable merit and interest, which will, we doubt not, become the most popular English history of Marie Antoinette."—*Spectator.*

L.—SIR GIBBIE.
BY GEORGE MAC DONALD, LL.D.

"'Sir Gibbie' is a book of genius."—*Pall Mall Gazette.*
"This book has power, pathos, and humour."—*Athenæum.*

LI.—YOUNG MRS. JARDINE.
BY THE AUTHOR OF "JOHN HALIFAX, GENTLEMAN."

"'Young Mrs. Jardine' is a pretty story, written in pure English."—*The Times.*
"There is much good feeling in this book. It is pleasant and wholesome."—*Athenæum.*

LII.—LORD BRACKENBURY.
BY AMELIA B. EDWARDS.

"A very readable story. The author has well conceived the purpose of high-class novel-writing, and succeeded in no small measure in attaining it. There is plenty of variety, cheerful dialogue, and general 'verve' in the book."—*Athenæum.*

LIII.—IT WAS A LOVER AND HIS LASS.
BY MRS. OLIPHANT.

"In 'It was a Lover and his Lass,' we admire Mrs. Oliphant **exceedingly**. It would be worth reading a second time, were it only for the sake of one **ancient Scottish spinster**, who is nearly the counterpart of the admirable Mrs. Margaret **Maitland**."—*Times.*

LIV.—THE REAL LORD BYRON—THE STORY OF THE POET'S LIFE.
BY JOHN CORDY JEAFFRESON.

"Mr. Jeaffreson comes forward with a narrative which must take a very important place in Byronic literature; and it may reasonably be anticipated that this book will be regarded with deep interest by all who are concerned in the works and the fame of this great English poet."—*The Times.*

WORKS BY THE AUTHOR OF
'SAM SLICK, THE CLOCKMAKER.'
Each in One Volume, Frontispiece, and Uniformly Bound, **Price 5s.**

NATURE AND HUMAN NATURE.

"We enjoy our old friend's company with unabated relish. This work is a rattling miscellany of sharp sayings, stories, and hard hits. It is full of fun and fancy."—*Athenæum.*

"Since Sam's first work he has written nothing so fresh, racy, and genuinely humorous as this. Every line of it tells in some way or other—instructively, satirically, jocosely, or wittily. Admiration of Sam's mature talents, and laughter at his droll yarns, constantly alternate as with unhalting avidity we peruse the work. The Clockmaker proves himself the fastest time-killer a-going."—*Observer.*

WISE SAWS AND MODERN INSTANCES.

"This delightful book will be the most popular, as beyond doubt it is the best, of all the author's admirable works."—*Standard.*

"The book before us will be read and laughed over. Its quaint and racy dialect will please some readers—its abundance of yarns will amuse others. There is something to suit readers of every humour."—*Athenæum.*

"The humour of Sam Slick is inexhaustible. He is ever and everywhere a welcome visitor; smiles greet his approach, and wit and wisdom hang upon his tongue. We promise our readers a great treat from the perusal of these 'Wise Saws,' which contain a world of practical wisdom, and a treasury of the richest fun."—*Morning Post.*

THE OLD JUDGE; OR, LIFE IN A COLONY.

"By common consent this work is regarded as one of the raciest, truest to life, most humorous, and most interesting works which have proceeded from the prolific pen of its author. We all know what shrewdness of observation, what power of graphic description, what natural resources of drollery, and what a happy method of hitting off the broader characteristics of the life he reviews, belong to Judge Haliburton. We have all those qualities here; but they are balanced by a serious literary purpose, and are employed in the communication of information respecting certain phases of colonial experience which impart to the work an element of sober utility."—*Sunday Times.*

TRAITS OF AMERICAN HUMOUR.

"No man has done more than the facetious Judge Haliburton, through the mouth of the inimitable 'Sam,' to make the old parent country recognise and appreciate her queer transatlantic progeny. His present collection of comic stories and laughable traits is a budget of fun, full of rich specimens of American humour."—*Globe.*

"Yankeeism, portrayed in its raciest aspect, constitutes the contents of these superlatively entertaining sketches. The work embraces the most varied topics—political parties, religious eccentricities, the flights of literature, and the absurdities of pretenders to learning, all come in for their share of satire; while we have specimens of genuine American exaggerations and graphic pictures of social and domestic life as it is. The work will have a wide circulation."—*John Bull.*

THE AMERICANS AT HOME.

"In this highly entertaining work we are treated to another cargo of capital stories from the inexhaustible store of our Yankee friend. In the volume before us he dishes up, with his accustomed humour and terseness of style, a vast number of tales, none more entertaining than another, and all of them graphically illustrative of the ways and manners of brother Jonathan. The anomalies of American law, the extraordinary adventures incident to life in the backwoods, and, above all, the peculiarities of American society, are variously, powerfully, and, for the most part, amusingly exemplified."—*John Bull.*

"In the picturesque delineation of character, and the felicitous portraiture of national features, no writer equals Judge Haliburton, and the subjects embraced in the present delightful book call forth, in new and vigorous exercise, his peculiar powers. 'The Americans at Home' will not be less popular than any of his previous works."—*Post.*

LONDON: HURST AND BLACKETT, PUBLISHERS.

WORKS BY THE AUTHOR OF
JOHN HALIFAX, GENTLEMAN.
Each in One Volume, Frontispiece, and Uniformly Bound, price 5s.

JOHN HALIFAX, GENTLEMAN.

"This is a very good and a very interesting work. It is designed to trace the career from boyhood to age of a perfect man—a Christian gentleman, and it abounds in incident both well and highly wrought. Throughout it is conceived in a high spirit, and written with great ability. This cheap and handsome new edition is worthy to pass freely from hand to hand as a gift-book in many households."—*Examiner.*

"The story is very interesting The attachment between John Halifax and his wife is beautifully painted, as are the pictures of their domestic life, and the growing up of their children, and the conclusion of the book is beautiful and touching."—*Athenæum.*

"The new and cheaper edition of this interesting work will doubtless meet with great success. John Halifax, the hero of this most beautiful story, is no ordinary hero, and this his history is no ordinary book. It is a full-length portrait of a true gentleman, one of nature's own nobility. It is also the history of a home, and a thoroughly English one. The work abounds in incident, and is full of graphic power and true pathos. It is a book that few will read without becoming wiser and better."—*Scotsman.*

A WOMAN'S THOUGHTS ABOUT WOMEN.

"A book of sound counsel. It is one of the most sensible works of its kind, well written, true-hearted, and altogether practical. Whoever wishes to give advice to a young lady may thank the author for means of doing so."—*Examiner.*

"These thoughts are worthy of the earnest and enlightened mind, the all-embracing charity, and the well-earned reputation of the author of 'John Halifax.'"—*Standard.*

"This excellent book is characterised by good sense, good taste, and feeling, and is written in an earnest, philanthropic, as well as practical spirit."—*Post.*

A LIFE FOR A LIFE.

"We are always glad to welcome this author. She writes from her own convictions, and she has the power not only to conceive clearly what it is that she wishes to say, but to express it in language effective and vigorous. In 'A Life for a Life' she is fortunate in a good subject, and she has produced a work of strong effect. The reader, having read the book through for the story, will be apt (if he be of our persuasion) to return and read again many pages and passages with greater pleasure than on a first perusal. The whole book is replete with a graceful, tender delicacy; and, in addition to its other merits, it is written in good careful English."—*Athenæum.*

NOTHING NEW.

"'Nothing New' displays all those superior merits which have made 'John Halifax' one of the most popular works of the day."—*Post.*

"The reader will find these narratives calculated to remind him of that truth and energy of human portraiture, that spell over human affections and emotions, which have stamped this author as one of the first novelists of our day."—*John Bull.*

THE WOMAN'S KINGDOM.

"'The Woman's Kingdom' sustains the author's reputation as a writer of the purest and noblest kind of domestic stories. The novelist's lesson is given with admirable force and sweetness."—*Athenæum.*

"'The Woman's Kingdom' is remarkable for its romantic interest. The characters are masterpieces. Edna is worthy of the hand that drew John Halifax."—*Post.*

STUDIES FROM LIFE.

"These studies are truthful and vivid pictures of life, often earnest, always full of right feeling, and occasionally lightened by touches of quiet genial humour. The volume is remarkable for thought, sound sense, shrewd observation, and kind and sympathetic feeling for all things good and beautiful."—*Post.*

WORKS BY THE AUTHOR OF
JOHN HALIFAX, GENTLEMAN.
(CONTINUED.)

CHRISTIAN'S MISTAKE.

"A more charming story, to our taste, has rarely been written. Within the compass of a single volume the writer has hit off a circle of varied characters, all true to nature—some true to the highest nature—and she has entangled them in a story which keeps us in suspense till the knot is happily and gracefully resolved; while, at the same time, a pathetic interest is sustained by an art of which it would be difficult to analyse the secret. It is a choice gift to be able thus to render human nature so truly, to penetrate its depths with such a searching sagacity, and to illuminate them with a radiance so eminently the writer's own. Even if tried by the standard of the Archbishop of York, we should expect that even he would pronounce 'Christian's Mistake' a novel without a fault."—*The Times.*

"This is a story good to have from the circulating library, but better to have from one's bookseller, for it deserves a place in that little collection of clever and wholesome stories which forms one of the comforts of a well-appointed home."—*Examiner.*

MISTRESS AND MAID.

"A good, wholesome book, as pleasant to read as it is instructive."—*Athenæum.*

"This book is written with the same true-hearted earnestness as 'John Halifax.' The spirit of the whole work is excellent."—*Examiner.*

"A charming tale charmingly told."—*Standard.*

A NOBLE LIFE.

"This is one of those pleasant tales in which the author of 'John Halifax' speaks out of a generous heart the purest truths of life."—*Examiner.*

"Few men, and no women, will read 'A Noble Life' without finding themselves the better."—*Spectator.*

"A story of powerful and pathetic interest."—*Daily News.*

A BRAVE LADY.

"A very good novel, showing a tender sympathy with human nature, and permeated by a pure and noble spirit."—*Examiner.*

"A most charming story."—*Standard.*

"We earnestly recommend this novel. It is a special and worthy specimen of the author's remarkable powers. The reader's attention never for a moment flags."—*Post.*

HANNAH.

"A powerful novel of social and domestic life. One of the most successful efforts of a successful novelist."—*Daily News.*

"A very pleasant, healthy story, well and artistically told. The book is sure of a wide circle of readers. The character of Hannah is one of rare beauty."—*Standard.*

THE UNKIND WORD.

"The author of 'John Halifax' has written many fascinating stories, but we can call to mind nothing from her pen that has a more enduring charm than the graceful sketches in this work. Such a character as Jessie stands out from a crowd of heroines as the type of all that is truly noble, pure, and womanly."—*United Service Magazine.*

YOUNG MRS. JARDINE.

"'Young Mrs. Jardine' is a pretty story, written in pure English."—*The Times.*

"There is much good feeling in this book. It is pleasant and wholesome."—*Athenæum.*

"A book that all should read. Whilst it is quite the equal of any of its predecessors in elevation of thought and style, it is perhaps their superior in interest of plot and dramatic intensity. The characters are admirably delineated, and the dialogue is natural and clear."—*Morning Post.*

LONDON: HURST AND BLACKETT, PUBLISHERS.

WORKS BY
MRS. OLIPHANT.

Each in One Volume, Frontispiece, and Uniformly Bound, Price 5s.

ADAM GRAEME OF MOSSGRAY.

"'Adam Graeme' is a story awakening genuine emotions of interest and delight by its admirable pictures of Scottish life and scenery. The plot is cleverly complicated, and there is great vitality in the dialogue, and remarkable brilliancy in the descriptive passages, as who that has read 'Margaret Maitland' would not be prepared to expect? But the story has a 'mightier magnet still,' in the healthy tone which pervades it, in its feminine delicacy of thought and diction, and in the truly womanly tenderness of its sentiments. The eloquent author sets before us the essential attributes of Christian virtue, their deep and silent workings in the heart, and their beautiful manifestations in the life, with a delicacy, a power, and a truth which can hardly be surpassed."—*Morning Post.*

THE LAIRD OF NORLAW.

"We have had frequent opportunities of commending Messrs. Hurst and Blackett's Standard Library. For neatness, elegance, and distinctness the volumes in this series surpass anything with which we are familiar. 'The Laird of Norlaw' will fully sustain the author's high reputation. The reader is carried on from first to last with an energy of sympathy that never flags."—*Sunday Times.*

"'The Laird of Norlaw' is worthy of the author's reputation. It is one of the most exquisite of modern novels."—*Observer.*

IT WAS A LOVER AND HIS LASS.

"In 'It was a Lover and his Lass,' we admire Mrs. Oliphant exceedingly. Her story is a very pretty one. It would be worth reading a second time, were it only for the sake of one ancient Scottish spinster, who is nearly the counterpart of the admirable Mrs. Margaret Maitland."—*Times.*

AGNES.

"'Agnes' is a novel superior to any of Mrs. Oliphant's former works."—*Athenæum.*

"Mrs. Oliphant is one of the most admirable of our novelists. In her works there are always to be found high principle, good taste, sense, and refinement. 'Agnes' is a story whose pathetic beauty will appeal irresistibly to all readers."—*Morning Post.*

A ROSE IN JUNE.

"'A Rose in June' is as pretty as its title. The story is one of the best and most touching which we owe to the industry and talent of Mrs. Oliphant, and may hold its own with even 'The Chronicles of Carlingford.'"—*Times.*

PHŒBE, JUNIOR.

"This last 'Chronicle of Carlingford' not merely takes rank fairly beside the first which introduced us to 'Salem Chapel,' but surpasses all the intermediate records. Phœbe, Junior, herself is admirably drawn."—*Academy.*

LIFE OF THE REV. EDWARD IRVING.

"A good book on a most interesting theme."—*Times.*

"A truly interesting and most affecting memoir. 'Irving's Life' ought to have a niche in every gallery of religious biography. There are few lives that will be fuller of instruction, interest, and consolation."—*Saturday Review.*

LONDON: HURST AND BLACKETT, PUBLISHERS.

WORKS BY

GEORGE MAC DONALD, LL.D.

Each in One Volume, Frontispiece, and Uniformly Bound, Price 5s.

ALEC FORBES OF HOWGLEN.

"No account of this story would give any idea of the profound interest that pervades the work from the first page to the last."—*Athenæum.*

"A novel of uncommon merit. Sir Walter Scott said he would advise no man to try to read 'Clarissa Harlowe' out loud in company if he wished to keep his character for manly superiority to tears. We fancy a good many hardened old novel-readers will feel a rising in the throat as they follow the fortunes of Alec and Annie."—*Pall Mall Gazette.*

"The whole story is one of surpassing excellence and beauty."—*Daily News.*

"This book is full of good thought and good **writing**. Dr. Mac Donald looks in his stories more to the souls of men and women than **to their social outside**. He reads life and Nature like a true poet."—*Examiner.*

ROBERT FALCONER.

"'Robert Falconer' is a work brimful of life and humour and of **the deepest human interest**. It is a work to be returned to again and again for the **deep and searching** knowledge it evinces of human thoughts and feelings."—*Athenæum.*

"This story abounds in exquisite specimens of the word-painting in which Dr. Mac Donald excels, charming transcripts of Nature, full of light, air, and colour."—*Saturday Review.*

"This noble story displays to **the** best advantage **all the powers of Dr. Mac Donald's** genius."—*Illustrated London News.*

"'Robert Falconer' is the noblest work of **fiction that Dr.** Mac Donald has yet produced."—*British Quarterly Review.*

"The dialogues in 'Robert Falconer' are so finely blended with humour and pathos as to make them in themselves an intellectual treat to which the reader returns again and again."—*Spectator.*

DAVID ELGINBROD.

"A novel which **is the work of a man of genius**. It will **attract the highest class of** readers."—*Times.*

"There are many beautiful passages and descriptions in this book. **The characters are** extremely well drawn."—*Athenæum.*

"A clever novel. The incidents are exciting, and the **interest is maintained to the** close. It may be doubted if Sir Walter Scott himself ever **painted a Scotch fireside with** more truth than Dr. Mac Donald."—*Morning Post.*

"David Elginbrod is the finest character we have met in fiction for many a day. The descriptions of natural scenery are vivid, truthful, and artistic; the general reflections are those of a refined, thoughtful, and poetical philosopher, and the whole moral atmosphere of the book **is** lofty, pure, and invigorating."—*Globe.*

SIR GIBBIE.

"'Sir Gibbie' is a book of genius."—*Pall Mall Gazette.*

"This book has power, pathos, and humour. There **is not a character which is not** lifelike. There are many powerful scenes, and the **portraits will stay long in our** memory."—*Athenæum.*

"'Sir Gibbie' is unquestionably a book of genius. It abounds in humour, pathos, insight into character, and happy touches of description."—*Graphic.*

"'Sir Gibbie' contains some of the most charming writing the author has yet produced."—*Scotsman.*

"'Sir Gibbie' is one of the most touching and beautiful stories that has been written for many years. It is not a novel to be idly read and laid aside; it is a grand work, **to be** kept near at hand, and studied and thought over."—*Morning Post.*

LONDON : HURST AND BLACKETT, PUBLISHERS.

WORKS by the AUTHOR of 'JOHN HALIFAX.'

Each in a Single Volume, with Frontispiece, price 5s.

JOHN HALIFAX, GENTLEMAN.	CHRISTIAN'S MISTAKE.
A WOMAN'S THOUGHTS ABOUT WOMEN.	A NOBLE LIFE.
	HANNAH.
A LIFE FOR A LIFE.	THE UNKIND WORD.
NOTHING NEW.	A BRAVE LADY.
MISTRESS AND MAID.	STUDIES FROM LIFE.
THE WOMAN'S KINGDOM.	YOUNG MRS. JARDINE.

WORKS by GEORGE MAC DONALD, LL.D.

Each in a Single Volume, with Frontispiece, price 5s.

DAVID ELGINBROD.	ALEC FORBES.
ROBERT FALCONER.	SIR GIBBIE.

WORKS by MRS. OLIPHANT.

Each in a Single Volume, with Frontispiece, price 5s.

IT WAS A LOVER AND HIS LASS	ADAM GRAEME OF MOSSGRAY.
THE LAIRD OF NORLAW.	PHŒBE, JUNIOR.
A ROSE IN JUNE.	AGNES.

THE LIFE OF THE REV. EDWARD IRVING.

WORKS by the AUTHOR of 'SAM SLICK.'

Each in a Single Volume, with Frontispiece, price 5s.

NATURE AND HUMAN NATURE.	THE OLD JUDGE; OR, LIFE IN A COLONY.
WISE SAWS AND MODERN INSTANCES.	TRAITS OF AMERICAN HUMOUR.

THE AMERICANS AT HOME.

LONDON: HURST AND BLACKETT.

13, Great Marlborough Street, London.

MESSRS. HURST AND BLACKETT'S
LIST OF NEW WORKS.

EIGHTEENTH CENTURY WAIFS. By JOHN ASHTON, Author of 'Social Life in the Reign of Queen Anne,' &c. 1 vol. imperial 8vo. 12s.

CONTENTS: A Forgotten Fanatic—A Fashionable Lady's Life—George Barrington—Milton's Bones—The True Story of Eugene Aram—Redemptioners—A Trip to Richmond in Surrey—George Robert Fitzgerald—Eighteenth Century Amazons—'The Times' and its Founder—Imprisonment for Debt—Jonas Hanway—A Holy Voyage to Ramsgate One Hundred Years Ago—Quacks of the Century—Cagliostro in London.

SHIKAR SKETCHES: WITH NOTES ON INDIAN FIELD SPORTS. By J. MORAY BROWN, late 79th Cameron Highlanders. With Eight Illustrations, by J. C. DOLLMAN, R.I. 1 vol. imperial 8vo. 12s.

CHAPTERS FROM FAMILY CHESTS. By EDWARD WALFORD, M.A., Author of 'The County Families,' &c. 2 vols. crown 8vo. 21s.

"There is a mine of wealth in the 'Family Chests' which no one has yet brought to the surface, and from this Mr. Walford has contrived to excavate a mass of acceptable matter—a treasury of narrative curious and romantic."—*Globe.*

"The reader will find much curious information in Mr. Walford's chapters of agreeable narrative."—*Scotsman.*

REMINISCENCES OF THE COURT AND TIMES OF KING ERNEST OF HANOVER. By the Rev. C. A. WILKINSON, M.A., His Majesty's Resident Domestic Chaplain. 2 vols. With portrait of the King. 21s.

"An interesting book, entitled 'Reminiscences of the Court and Times of King Ernest of Hanover,' has just been published by Messrs. Hurst and Blackett. The two volumes in which these reminiscences of a septuagenarian are comprised abound in characteristic stories of the old king, in anecdotes of many celebrities English and foreign, of the early part of this century, and, indeed, of all kinds and conditions of men and women with whom the author was brought in contact by his courtly or pastorial office."—*St. James's Gazette.*

THE EGYPTIAN CAMPAIGNS, 1882 TO 1885, AND THE EVENTS WHICH LED TO THEM. By CHARLES ROYLE, Barrister-at-Law, of ALEXANDRIA. 2 vols. demy 8vo. Illustrated by Maps and Plans. 30s.

"Mr. Royle has done well in the interests of historical completeness to describe not only the entire military drama, but also the political events connected with it, and whoever reads the book with care has gone a considerable way towards mastering the difficult Egyptian question."—*Athenæum.*

"The Egyptian fiasco has found in Mr. Royle a most painstaking, accurate, and judicious historian. From a literary point of view his volumes may be thought to contain too many unimportant incidents, yet their presence was necessary perhaps, in a complete record, and the most fastidious reader will unhesitatingly acquit Mr. Royle of filling his pages with anything that can be called padding."—*St. James's Gazette.*

MESSRS. HURST AND BLACKETT'S NEW WORKS—*Continued.*

THE PALACE AND THE HOSPITAL; or, CHRONICLES OF GREENWICH. By the REV. A. G. L'ESTRANGE, Author of 'The Village of Palaces,' 'The Friendships of Mary Russell Mitford,' &c. 2 vols. crown 8vo. With Illustrations. 21s.

"Mr. L'Estrange has provided for those who have a taste for topography, or rather for the historical and biographical annals of a locality famous in history, two volumes which are rich in romantic interest, and his pages abound in curious and interesting glimpses of old manners."—*Daily News.*

THE REAL SHELLEY: NEW VIEWS OF THE POET'S LIFE. By JOHN CORDY JEAFFRESON, Author of "The Real Lord Byron," "A Book about Doctors," "A Book about Lawyers," &c. 2 vols. demy 8vo. 30s.

"Those who have read Mr. Jeaffreson's account of Byron will be prepared to find that impartiality is the distinguishing feature of his endeavour to clear away the fancies and misconceptions which have been given to the world in some of the biographies of Shelley, and they will not be disappointed. The author has striven to ascertain, fairly and fully, the truth concerning a poet whose influence, while it has been greatly exaggerated by his most enthusiastic admirers, is still a living factor in the life of many."—*Morning Post.*

THE FRIENDSHIPS OF MARY RUSSELL MITFORD: AS RECORDED IN LETTERS FROM HER LITERARY CORRESPONDENTS. Edited by the REV. A. G. L'ESTRANGE, Editor of "The Life of Mary Russell Mitford," &c. 2 vols. 21s.

"These letters are all written as to one whom the writers love and revere. Miss Barrett is one of Miss Mitford's correspondents, all of whom seem to be inspired with a sense of excellence in the mind they are invoking. Their letters are extremely interesting, and they strike out recollections, opinions, criticisms, which will hold the reader's delighted and serious attention."—*Daily Telegraph.*

THE BRONTË FAMILY, With Special Reference to PATRICK BRANWELL BRONTE. By FRANCIS A. LEYLAND. 2 vols. 21s.

"This book is so full of interesting information that as a contribution to literary biography it may be considered a real success."—*Academy.*

"Mr. Leyland's book is earnest and accurate, and he has spared no pains to master his subject and present it with clearness; the book is valuable, and should be read by all who are familiar with the previous works on the family."—*Graphic.*

MEMOIRS OF A CAMBRIDGE CHORISTER. By WILLIAM GLOVER. 2 vols. crown 8vo. 21s.

"In these amusing volumes Mr. Glover provides us with the means of spending a pleasant hour or two in his company."—*Times.*

"These volumes contain a miscellaneous set of reminiscences, comments, and anecdotes, written in a light and jocular style. Mr. Glover is always cheerful and never didactic."—*Athenæum.*

WITHOUT GOD: NEGATIVE SCIENCE AND NATURAL ETHICS. By PERCY GREG, Author of "The Devil's Advocate," "Across the Zodiac," &c. 1 vol. demy 8vo. 12s.

"Mr. Greg has condensed much profound thought into his book, and has fully succeeded in maintaining the interest of the discussion throughout."—*Morning Post.*

"This work is ably written; there are in it many passages of no ordinary power and brilliancy. It is eminently suggestive and stimulating."—*Scotsman.*

FOOTSTEPS OF JEANNE D'ARC. A Pilgrimage. By Mrs. FLORENCE CADDY. 1 vol. demy 8vo. With Map of Route. 15s.

"The reader, whatever his preconceived notions of the maid may have been, will soon find himself in sympathy with a writer who, by the charm of her descriptive style, at once arrests his attention and sustains the interest of her subject."—*Morning Post.*

MESSRS. HURST AND BLACKETT'S NEW WORKS—*Continued*.

THE LIFE AND ADVENTURES OF PEG WOFFINGTON: With Pictures of the Period in which She Lived. By J. Fitzgerald Molloy, Author of "Court Life Below Stairs," &c. *Second Edition.* 2 vols. crown 8vo. With Portrait. 21s.

"Peg Woffington makes a most interesting central figure, round which Mr. Molloy has made to revolve a varied and picturesque panorama of London life in the middle of the eighteenth century. He sees things in the past so clearly, grasps them so tenaciously, and reproduces them so vividly, that they come to us without any of the dust and rust of time."—G. A. S. *in Illustrated London News*.

WOMEN OF EUROPE IN THE FIFTEENTH AND SIXTEENTH CENTURIES. By Mrs. Napier Higgins. Vols. 1 and 2 demy 8vo. 30s.

"The work is likely to be of permanent value to the students of history."—*Morning Post*.

ON THE TRACK OF THE CRESCENT: Erratic Notes from the Piræus to Pesth. By Major E. C. Johnson, M.A.I., F. R. Hist. S., etc. With Map and Upwards of 50 Illustrations by the Author. 1 vol. demy 8vo. 15s.

"The author of this bright, pleasant volume possesses keen power of observation and vivid appreciation of animate and inanimate beauty. It will brighten hours for many readers who will only follow the track of the Crescent through its pages and its numerous illustrations."—*Morning Post*.

MEMOIRS OF MARSHAL BUGEAUD, From His Private Correspondence and Original Documents, 1784—1849. By the Count H. d'Ideville. Edited, from the French, by Charlotte M. Yonge. 2 vols. demy 8vo. 30s.

"This is a work of great value to the student of French history. A perusal of the book will convince any reader of Bugeaud's energy, his patriotism, his unselfishness, and his philanthropy and humanity."—*Athenæum*.

GLIMPSES OF GREEK LIFE AND SCENERY. By Agnes Smith, Author of "Eastern Pilgrims," &c. Demy 8vo. With Illustrations and Map of the Author's Route. 15s.

"A truthful picture of the country through which the author travelled. It is naturally and simply told, in an agreeable and animated style. Miss Smith displays an ample acquaintance and sympathy with all the scenes of historic interest."—*St. James's Gazette*.

MONSIEUR GUIZOT IN PRIVATE LIFE (1787-1874). By His Daughter, Madame de Witt. Translated by Mrs. Simpson. 1 vol. demy 8vo. 15s.

"Madame de Witt has done justice to her father's memory in an admirable record of his life. Mrs. Simpson's translation of this singularly interesting book is in accuracy and grace worthy of the original and of the subject."—*Saturday Review*.

PLAIN SPEAKING. By Author of "John Halifax, Gentleman." 1 vol. crown 8vo. 10s. 6d.

"We recommend 'Plain Speaking' to all who like amusing, wholesome, and instructive reading. The contents of Mrs. Craik's volume are of the most multifarious kind, but all the papers are good and readable, and one at least of them of real importance."—*St. James's Gazette*.

WORDS OF HOPE AND COMFORT TO THOSE IN SORROW. Dedicated by Permission to The Queen *Fourth Edition.* 1 vol. small 4to. 5s.

Under the Especial Patronage of Her Majesty.

Published annually, in One Vol., royal 8vo, with the Arms beautifully engraved, handsomely bound, with gilt edges, price 31s. 6d.

LODGE'S PEERAGE
AND BARONETAGE,
CORRECTED BY THE NOBILITY.

FIFTY-SIXTH EDITION FOR 1887.

LODGE'S PEERAGE AND BARONETAGE is acknowledged to be the most complete, as well as the most elegant, work of the kind. As an established and authentic authority on all questions respecting the family histories, honours, and connections of the titled aristocracy, no work has ever stood so high. It is published under the especial patronage of Her Majesty, and is annually corrected throughout, from the personal communications of the Nobility. It is the only work of its class in which, *the type being kept constantly standing*, every correction is made in its proper place to the date of publication, an advantage which gives it supremacy over all its competitors. Independently of its full and authentic information respecting the existing Peers and Baronets of the realm, the most sedulous attention is given in its pages to the collateral branches of the various noble families, and the names of many thousand individuals are introduced, which do not appear in other records of the titled classes. For its authority, correctness, and facility of arrangement, and the beauty of its typography and binding, the work is justly entitled to the place it occupies on the tables of Her Majesty and the Nobility.

LIST OF THE PRINCIPAL CONTENTS.

Historical View of the Peerage.
Parliamentary Roll of the House of Lords.
English, Scotch, and Irish Peers, in their orders of Precedence.
Alphabetical List of Peers of Great Britain and the United Kingdom, holding superior rank in the Scotch or Irish Peerage.
Alphabetical list of Scotch and Irish Peers, holding superior titles in the Peerage of Great Britain and the United Kingdom.
A Collective list of Peers, in their order of Precedence.
Table of Precedency among Men.
Table of Precedency among Women.
The Queen and the Royal Family.
Peers of the Blood Royal.
The Peerage, alphabetically arranged.
Families of such Extinct Peers as have left Widows or Issue.
Alphabetical List of the Surnames of all the Peers.

The Archbishops and Bishops of England and Ireland.
The Baronetage alphabetically arranged.
Alphabetical List of Surnames assumed by members of Noble Families.
Alphabetical List of the Second Titles of Peers, usually borne by their Eldest Sons.
Alphabetical Index to the Daughters of Dukes, Marquises, and Earls, who, having married Commoners, retain the title of Lady before their own Christian and their Husband's Surnames.
Alphabetical Index to the Daughters of Viscounts and Barons, who, having married Commoners, are styled Honourable Mrs.; and, in case of the husband being a Baronet or Knight, Hon. Lady.
A List of the Orders of Knighthood.
Mottoes alphabetically arranged and translated.

"This work is the most perfect and elaborate record of the living and recently deceased members of the Peerage of the Three Kingdoms as it stands at this day. It is a most useful publication. We are happy to bear testimony to the fact that scrupulous accuracy is a distinguishing feature of this book."—*Times.*

"Lodge's Peerage must supersede all other works of the kind, for two reasons: first, it is on a better plan; and secondly, it is better executed. We can safely pronounce it to be the readiest, the most useful, and exactest of modern works on the subject."—*Spectator*:

"A work of great value. It is the most faithful record we possess of the aristocracy of the day."—*Post.*

EDNA LYALL'S NOVELS

EACH IN ONE VOLUME CROWN 8vo, 6s.

DONOVAN:

A MODERN ENGLISHMAN.

"This is a very admirable work. The reader is from the first carried away by the gallant unconventionality of its author. 'Donovan' is a very excellent novel; but it is something more and better. It should do as much good as the best sermon ever written or delivered extempore. The story is told with a grand simplicity, an unconscious poetry of eloquence which stirs the very depths of the heart. One of the main excellencies of this novel is the delicacy of touch with which the author shows her most delightful characters to be after all human beings, and not angels before their time."—*Standard.*

"'Donovan' is told with the power of truth, experience, and moral insight. The tone of the novel is excellent and very high."—*Daily News.*

WE TWO.

"This book is well written and full of interest. The story abounds with a good many light touches, and is certainly far from lacking in incident."—*Times.*

"'We Two' contains many very exciting passages and a great deal of information. Miss Lyall is a capable writer and a clear-headed thinker."—*Athenæum.*

"A work of deep thought and much power. Serious as it is, it is now and then brightened by rays of genuine humour. Altogether this story is more and better than a novel."—*Morning Post.*

"There is artistic realism both in the conception and the delineation of the personages; the action and interest are unflaggingly sustained from first to last, and the book is pervaded by an atmosphere of elevated, earnest thought."—*Scotsman.*

IN THE GOLDEN DAYS.

"Miss Lyall has given us a vigorous study of such life and character as are really worth reading about. The central figure of her story is Algernon Sydney; and this figure she invests with a singular dignity and power. He always appears with effect, but no liberties are taken with the facts of his life. The plot is adapted with great felicity to them. His part in it, absolutely consistent as it is with historical truth, gives it reality as well as dignity. Some of the scenes are remarkably vivid. The escape is an admirable narrative, which almost makes one hold one's breath as one reads."—*Spectator.*

"'In the Golden Days' is an excellent novel of a kind we are always particularly glad to recommend. It has a good foundation of plot and incident, a thoroughly noble and wholesome motive, a hero who really acts and suffers heroically, and two very nice heroines. The historical background is very carefully indicated, but is never allowed to become more than background."—*Guardian.*

WON BY WAITING.

"The Dean's daughters are perfectly real characters—the learned Cornelia especially;—the little impulsive French heroine, who endures their cold hospitality and at last wins their affection, is thoroughly charming; while throughout the book there runs a golden thread of pure brotherly and sisterly love, which pleasantly reminds us that the making and marring of marriage is not, after all, the sum total of real life."—*Academy.*

"'Won by Waiting' is a very pleasing and well-written tale; full of graphic descriptions of French and English life, with incidents and characters well sustained. A book with such pleasant reading, and with such a healthy tone and influence, is a great boon to the young people in our families."—*Freeman.*

SIX-SHILLING NOVELS

EACH IN ONE VOLUME CROWN 8vo.

HIS LITTLE MOTHER.
By the Author of "John Halifax, Gentleman."

"'His Little Mother' is one of those pathetic stories which the author tells better than anybody else."—*John Bull.*

"This book is written with all Mrs. Craik's grace of style, the chief charm of which, after all, is its simplicity."—*Glasgow Herald.*

MY LORD AND MY LADY.
By Mrs. FORRESTER.

"A very capital novel. The great charm about it is that Mrs. Forrester is quite at home in the society which she describes. It is a book to read."—*Standard.*

"Mrs. Forrester's style is so fresh and graphic that the reader is kept under its spell from first to last."—*Morning Post.*

SOPHY.
By VIOLET FANE.

"'Sophy' is the clever and original work of a clever woman. Its merits are of a strikingly unusual kind. It is charged throughout with the strongest human interest. It is, in a word, a novel that will make its mark."—*World.*

A HOUSE PARTY.
By OUIDA.

"'A House Party' will be read, firstly, because it is Ouida's, and, secondly, because of the brightness of the conversations and descriptions. It is indeed more like a comedy than any other of the writer's books."—*Globe.*

OMNIA VANITAS.
By Mrs. FORRESTER.

"This book is pleasant and well meant. Here and there are some good touches. Sir Ralph is a man worth reading about."—*Academy.*

"This tale is well and cleverly written; the characters are drawn and sustained with considerable power, and the conversation is always bright and lively."—*Glasgow Herald.*

BETRAYAL OF REUBEN HOLT.
By BARBARA LAKE.

"This novel shows considerable power of writing. There are some striking scenes and incidents."—*Scotsman.*

"This tale displays elevation of thought and feeling, united to no little grace of expression."—*Post.*

THE BRANDRETHS.
By the Right Hon. A. J. B. BERESFORD HOPE, M.P.

"The great attraction of this novel is the easy, conversational, knowledgeable tone of it; the sketching from the life, and yet not so close to the life as to be malicious, men, women, periods, and events, to all of which intelligent readers can fit a name. The political and social sketches will naturally excite the chief interest among readers who will be attracted by the author's name and experience."—*Spectator.*

THE NEW AND POPULAR NOVELS.
PUBLISHED BY HURST & BLACKETT.

ST. BRIAVELS. By MARY DEANE, Author of
"Quatrefoil," &c. 3 vols.
"The authoress throughout writes with moderation and consistency, and her three ample volumes well repay perusal."—*Daily Telegraph.*
"'St. Briavels' is a story replete with variety, and in all developments of her plot the author skilfully maintains an unabated interest."—*Morning Post.*

A LILY MAID. By WILLIAM GEORGE WATERS.
3 vols.
"A story of the keenest interest. Mr. Waters' plot is neat, and his style is bright and pleasing."—*Daily Telegraph.*
"'A Lily Maid' is throughout exceedingly pleasant reading."—*Morning Post.*

LIKE LUCIFER. By DENZIL VANE. 3 vols.
"There is some pleasant writing in 'Like Lucifer,' and the plot is workmanlike."—*Academy.*
"Denzil Vane has a talent for lively, fluent writing, and a power of tracing character."—*Whitehall Review.*

A DAUGHTER OF THE GODS. By JANE STANLEY. 2 vols.
"'A Daughter of the Gods' is very pretty. That is a description which specially suits the easy-flowing, love-making story."—*Athenæum.*

LUCIA. By Mrs. AUGUSTUS CRAVEN, Author of
"A Sister's Story." Translated by LADY HERBERT OF LEA. 2 vols.
"This is a very pretty, touching, and consoling story. The tale is as much above the ordinary romance as the fresh air of the seaside is better than the stifling atmosphere of the fashionable quarter of the gayest city."—*St. James's Gazette.*
"'Lucia' is as good a novel as has been published for a long time."—*Academy.*

LOVE, THE PILGRIM. By MAY CROMMELIN,
Author of "Queenie," "A Jewel of a Girl," &c. 3 vols.
"'Love, the Pilgrim' is a pretty story, which, beginning quietly, develops into one of very sensational incident indeed."—*Graphic.*
"A tale of thrilling interest."—*Scotsman.*

THE KING CAN DO NO WRONG. By PAMELA SNEYD, Author of "Jack Urquhart's Daughter." 2 vols.
"This novel gives evidence of imagination, insight into character, and power of delineation."—*Athenæum.*
"Shows command of exceptional narrative and descriptive power—the story is told with cleverness and force."—*Scotsman.*

THE COURTING OF MARY SMITH. By F. W. ROBINSON, Author of "Grandmother's Money," "No Church," &c. 3 vols.
"One of the finest studies that any of our novelists has produced of late years. To read such a book is to strengthen the soul with a moral tonic."—*Athenæum.*
"The book is full of the truths and experiences of actual life, woven into a romance by an undoubtedly clever novelist."—*Morning Post.*

THRO' LOVE AND WAR. By VIOLET FANE,
Author of "Sophy: or the Adventures of a Savage," &c. 3 vols.
"'Thro' Love and War' has a succinct and intelligible plot, and is written with a quaint combination of acute perception, veiled sarcasm, and broad fun, which is certain to ensure for it a wide popularity."—*The World.*

THE NEW AND POPULAR NOVELS.
PUBLISHED BY HURST & BLACKETT.

PASSAGES IN THE LIFE OF A LADY in 1814, 1815, 1816. By HAMILTON AÏDÉ, Author of "Rita," "Penruddocke," "Poet and Peer," &c. 3 vols.

TILL MY WEDDING DAY. By a French Lady. 2 vols.

THE GREEN HILLS BY THE SEA: A MANX STORY. By HUGH COLEMAN DAVIDSON. 3 vols.

VICTIMS. By THEO GIFT, Author of "Pretty Miss Bellew," "Lil Lorimer," &c. 3 vols.

THE BROKEN SEAL. By DORA RUSSELL, Author of "Footprints in the Snow," &c. 3 vols.
"Miss Dora Russell writes easily and well, and she has the gift of making her characters describe themselves by their dialogue, which is bright and natural."—*Athenæum*.

MURIEL'S MARRIAGE. By ESME STUART, Author of "A Faire Damzell," &c. 3 vols.
"Much of the interest and charm of the story, and both are considerable, are due to the delineations, not merely of the two principal personages, but of the minor characters."—*Scotsman*.

ONCE AGAIN. By Mrs. FORRESTER, Author of "Viva," "Mignon," "My Lord and My Lady," &c. *(Second Edition)* 3 vols.
"A really fascinating story. Bright and often original as is Mrs. Forrester, her peculiar gifts have never been seen to better advantage than in 'Once Again.' An undercurrent of tragedy runs through this startling tale, and this, together with its graphically drawn characters, sets it completely apart from the ordinary society story."—*Morning Post*.

A WILFUL YOUNG WOMAN. By A. PRICE, Author of "A Rustic Maid," "Who is Sylvia?" &c. 3 vols.
"A very readable story. Mrs. Price has drawn her *dramatis personæ* with some power and vigour."—*Academy*.
"The story is throughout both sound and high-principled."—*Literary World*.

THE SURVIVORS. By HENRY CRESSWELL, Author of "A Modern Greek Heroine," "Incognita," &c. 3 vols.
"There is cleverness in this book, and occasional brilliancy and wit."—*Academy*.
"An amusing comedy of modern life; there are some good situations and striking episodes in the book."—*Athenæum*.

A WICKED GIRL. By MARY CECIL HAY, Author of "Old Myddelton's Money," &c. 3 vols.
"The author of 'Old Myddelton's Money' always manages to write interesting stories."—*Academy*.
"The story 'A Wicked Girl' has an ingeniously carried out plot. Miss Hay is a graceful writer, and her pathos is genuine."—*Post*.

THE WOOING OF CATHERINE. By E. FRANCES POYNTER, Author of "My Little Lady," &c. 2 vols.
"The figures are drawn with clear, bold strokes, each individual standing before us with marked personality, while the backgrounds are effective and striking."—*Literary World*.

www.ingramcontent.com/pod-product-compliance
Lightning Source LLC
Chambersburg PA
CBHW031415230426
43668CB00007B/312